WINLESS

My Year with Football's Ultimate Underdogs

Carl Jones

The moral right of Carl Jones to be identified as the author of this book has been asserted in accordance with the Copyright, Designs and Patents Act of 1988.

Winless: My Year with Football's Ultimate Underdogs

All rights reserved. No part of this book may be reproduced, or stored in a retrieval system, or transmitted in any form or by any means, electronic, mechanical, photocopying, recording, or otherwise, without express written permission of the author.

Every effort has been made to fulfil requirements with regard to reproducing copyright material. All interviewees give their consent to be included within this publication. The author will be glad to rectify any omissions at the earliest opportunity.

Copyright © 2020 Carl Jones

Cover design: Jared Shooter

Photography: James Lobley

All rights reserved.

ISBN: 9798508510947

For the many volunteers who dedicate their lives to the love of the beautiful game

"It's easy to have faith in yourself and have discipline when you're a winner, when you're number one. What you got to have is faith and discipline when you're not a winner."

VINCE LOMBARDI

CONTENTS

Introduction

1	Welcome to New Mills	1
2	New Beginnings	11
3	The Road to Wembley	20
4	Mr New Mills AFC	28
5	Opening Day	40
6	Managing Expectations	51
7	Fortress Church Lane	66
8	Transfer Deadline Day	75
9	Wake Me Up When September Ends?	85
10	Time for Change	91
11	Hands-Free	101
12	There's More than One Paul Williams	110
13	Autumn Leaves	119
14	A New Mills Family Holiday	127
15	A Six-Pointer	139
16	The Winter of our Discontent	144

17	New Year, New New Mills	158
18	The Road to Little Wembley	172
19	A Point to Prove	179
20	Feeling Sykesed	184
21	Putting the Bootle In	198
22	Home is Where the Heart Is	204
23	The League Table Doesn't Lie	214
24	A Tough Crowd	222
25	No Such Thing as an Easy Three Points	232
26	We've Got Hopper/There's Only One Ollie Martin	239
27	Don't Stop Believin'	250
28	Underdog Day Afternoon	262
29	The Future's Bright. The Future's Amber and Black	269
30	Time to Say Goodbye	279

Four Years Later

INTRODUCTION

High up in the north-west corner of the Peak District, just straddling the A6 Buxton Road, sits a small town called New Mills. It's a place I've driven through a hundred times as I've weaved my way out of Derbyshire towards Manchester; always a mental landmark on the way to a gig, a football match or a trip to the airport. Never a destination. Bob Hope used to live here, apparently. The actor who played him in Emmerdale, that is - not Bob Monkhouse's mate. Always one step away from the spotlight.

On September 25th 2015, I had reason to visit New Mills for the very first time. As a stand-up comedian, I've experienced a wide range of different venues and unusual gigs. Chalkers Snooker Club would be no different.

'We've got a local chap who wants to do a bit at the top if that's alright?' the bar manager semi-suggested, semi-announced on my arrival. It's not usually the best way to get a comedy gig up and running and, as host tonight, it's my job to ensure things run smoothly. My mind's telling me 'no' but my body appears to be smiling and nodding enthusiastically.

'He's not done it before but he's written some stuff. He's got an MBE for charity work, y'know.'

Against the odds, and possibly out of politeness, people laughed. In the function room of a snooker centre, with a DIY backdrop that collapsed onto the stage during one of the intervals, it was a nice place to be. A patient, friendly crowd gave encouragement where they could and muffled their groans when they couldn't. Meanwhile, I paced around the green room, which doubled up as tables seven and eight, and observed the local papers on a backstage table beside a rider of warm Carlsberg and Lidl own-brand Doritos.

I like to check how the local football team is doing when I gig in smaller towns. I rarely use it onstage but, for me at least, it provides as much context to the place as a wander through the market square or a trip to a nearby Co-op for chilled beer and actual Doritos. A football club is often right at the heart of a community even when the vast majority of the population never step foot in the ground.

Growing up just outside Chesterfield in Derbyshire, I could see the floodlights of the now demolished Saltergate from my back garden. Apart from the famous crooked spire, impossible to ignore on the horizon, it was the only landmark I was interested in. It was a small but significant part of 'home'. I'd only go and watch my hometown club every now and then, but their success and failure was a part of me. When the football team of a provincial town is doing well, I'm sure you can actually sense it. It's in the air as you walk down the street.

Visiting my grandmother in Barnsley on Saturday afternoons as a kid, I'd lay on the grass, focusing in on the noise of the crowd on the breeze. If you listened hard enough and the wind was blowing your way, you could work out which team had scored. Oakwell on matchday was part of the aural landscape of a visit.

'How did they get on?' she'd ask me every Saturday, her eyes too deteriorated to tap into teletext and check the full-time scores. I'm not sure she ever stepped foot inside the ground but she always felt more complete knowing the result.

It wasn't a question you'd hear much in New Mills on that early autumn evening. Most would already have had a decent idea of the answer as an extraordinary new season across the country bedded in. As the league tables began to take shape and the transitioning established order wondered when Leicester City would kindly remove themselves from the upper echelons, things weren't quite so rosy a mile or so down the road from Chalkers.

As I sat backstage in a snooker club listening to a man with slightly dodgy material, but who was so likeable he could get both laughs and an MBE, New Mills AFC sat bottom of the Evo-Stick Northern Premier Division One, a regional league in England's eighth tier. Losing 3-0 at home to Scarborough Athletic on the opening day wasn't the best of starts. The 2-0 defeat at Northwich Victoria was no disgrace, considering Vics would eventually just miss out on promotion. Two 4-1 defeats against Droylsden and Ossett Albion looked ominous, but at least the Millers had finally found the back of the net.

Things would get worse. Much, much worse. A 3-0 defeat to local rivals Glossop North End left New Mills pointless going into September, where the month at least began with a semi-encouraging 1-0 defeat to eventual champions Warrington Town. By the time October had begun, they'd lost their opening 11 league games, conceding 44 goals along the way.

National media attention started to gather as the Millers became a context piece for the dismal starts of Aston Villa and Jose Mourinho. The press were cruel and the coverage wasn't kind. 'New Mills: The Worst Team In England?' pondered one BBC article in early November. 19 games, 19 defeats, 68 conceded. The stats were slowly, horrifically building up. Move aside, Monkhouse. New Mills was reluctantly stepping into the spotlight.

Instability had perhaps played its part. With former Norwich City midfielder Keith Briggs installed as manager over the close season, he'd left after just 23 days to take up a role at Sheffield United's academy. Andy Fearn and Shaun Goater held the reins for nine games but resigned in early September as the rot began to set in following a humbling 7-1 defeat to Prescot Cables.

Garry Brown and his assistant, former Premier League defender Paul Williams, arrived to steady the ship. As part of Wythenshawe's management team the previous season, they'd seen the Manchester side win all 39 of their league games. At New Mills, they were still looking for a first point. By the time

December 31st arrived, it's perhaps fair to suggest they were reflecting on a year of two halves.

Things would get better as 2016 arrived; by comparison at least. A first point of the season came in January against Witton Albion. Leading twice, the Millers held on for a 2-2 draw to prompt an unwelcome renewal of interest from the media. A second draw against Brighouse Town in April was followed by a 9-0 thumping against Spennymoor that would seal their fate and confirm relegation. A third and final point came, again, against Witton Albion – in this season of seasons, they'd completed an unlikely 'double' over the Cheshire side.

It was all too easy to caricature New Mills. The stats don't lie, but the headlines did. Mocking the spoilt, disinterested millionaires of Aston Villa? Fine. Poking fun at the bloated ego of the self-appointed Special One? Knock yourself out. Honing in on a small community club relying on volunteers, 'mates' rates' and players reimbursed with petrol money? Maybe it was better to stay out of the spotlight after all.

But what impact does all the negative press have on a club and the wider community? How do you rebuild, improve and inspire a side that hasn't won a game for 15 months? What motivates the dedicated team of people working behind the scenes to keep the club afloat? And what would success look like this season? Could promotion be entertained or would a year of consolidation be a success? Surely another season like the one that preceded it couldn't even be contemplated as the Millers readjusted to life in the ninth tier of English football – could it?

Well. You're about to find out.

Winless: My Year with Football's Ultimate Underdogs

1

WELCOME TO NEW MILLS

'You're gonna tell me you're Carl, aren't you?' asks Club Secretary Sue Hyde. Wearing a paint-splattered polo shirt as she emerges from behind a selection of beer pumps, she extends her hand to greet me before she's just about to head home.

'We've had one of our groundwork parties this morning,' she says as I observe one solitary man sat at the bar who appears to have joined in. 'That's Chris,' she adds. 'This is practically your second home, isn't it love?'

Up and down the country, clubs at all levels are beginning their pre-season campaigns with friendlies as varied as Airbus vs Barrow, Didcot vs Slough and Waltham Abbey vs Concord. There'll be no game for New Mills, though, as a scheduled fixture at Manchester League side Atherton Town fell victim to heavy rain overnight. It's a fitting way to mark a weekend that so many had pencilled in for a fairytale final in France. A sweepstake sheet pinned to a cork board near the entrance suggests Sue's hopes ended when Spain departed Euro 2016.

Above the bar is a Redbridge Rovers F.C pennant – a memento from recent filming of Sky 1 sitcom *Rovers*. Based around a failing football team, it brought more positive coverage and welcome respite for New Mills in the months that followed April's inevitable relegation.

'You've never seen such a mess in here,' Sue laughs as she

recalls the production team setting up camp in the snug clubhouse. 'It was unbelievable. I wasn't that starstruck until Sue Johnston came in. I mean, she's a legend isn't she?

'At the end of filming, the Location Manager took us out for a meal. He joked it was the easiest job he'd ever been on. Every time he had to find a prop, he'd just go "Sue, where can I find one of these?"'

I first got in touch with Sue at the beginning of June about the prospect of tagging along with New Mills for the season. Still sore from the coverage garnered during the previous campaign, her response was guarded to say the least. She's warm and friendly as we chat, though, introducing me to Chairman Ray Coverley who appears from the door behind the bar. He's her long-term partner on both a professional and personal level, with the pair having been a couple for more than 20 years, and he's filling a bucket from one of the beer taps while hurrying Sue along.

'You don't mind if I leave you to it?' Sue asks me. 'We've got to pick my dad up and get across for the Development Team's match. Garry will be here with the lads in a minute,' she adds. After a morning of decorating, her afternoon will now be filled watching the newly created reserve team in the hope of finding the next First Team star. So much for a day off.

Manager Garry Brown has swiftly reshuffled his plans for Saturday afternoon to bring his side in for training on the tired astro pitch adjacent to the Church Lane turf. One by one, players arrive and greet Sue while she introduces me as 'the blog guy', in reference to my credentials for being here. The welcome from the playing contingent is universally warm as I clarify why I'm there, even if I do have to state my efforts aren't just intended for the blogosphere this time around.

Talk between the growing group is varied. Some gentle joshing over Sue's post-match meal begins as she explains she cooks the lads' meal after each home game, with curry being something of a speciality.

Local signings are also on the menu as the recent transfer to Spennymoor of Gareth Seddon, one of non-league's most colourful characters following his starring role in the BBC's documentary series on Salford City, is brought up.

'What's he on there do you reckon?' ponder the players aloud.

'Two fifty a week?' says another.

'Is he worth all that? He was on 400 there!' comes the reply.

It's light-hearted in nature, if perhaps tinged with a little jealousy, especially given New Mills can afford just £20 a week expenses for their own playing staff. By comparison, Seddon is the EvoStik Wayne Rooney.

'Pitch looks good, Sue,' remarks one of the lads as he stares out of the window at an increasingly bright afternoon following the overnight torrential downpour.

'We've been feeding it,' she says proudly, giving no indication on whether or not it might be with her Lamb Bhuna.

'Keep feeding it,' he says. New Mills has its own microclimate, it seems, making pitch quality a year-round challenge. It's just another handicap the team dealt with last season.

I sit in the clubhouse discreetly making notes and listening into the conversations, already feeling honoured to be at the centre of these pre-season exchanges. There's nothing downbeat or defeatist about their demeanour; there's an atmosphere of a side ready to approach the new campaign with confidence.

I think it was this intimacy that first enamoured me with non-league football. Becoming slowly bored with the inflated ticket prices and sanitised saturation of the Premier League as a long-distance Spurs fan, I started going to watch Matlock Town with friends in 2010. With one of our mates finally finding his footing as a seventh-tier left-back following a busy C.V of semi-pro teams and a couple of years at Sheffield United and Scunthorpe, there was added motivation to support my local side.

Matlock Town's Causeway Lane, which has also been known somewhat grandly as the Autoworld Arena, has made more than a few lists of grounds to visit before you die. While perhaps smaller in scale than the name might suggest, it sits beneath the landscape of Riber Castle high up behind the cricket pitch end. I'll take a beer from the refurbished clubhouse watching football in those surrounds for less than a tenner a ticket every time.

Another feature of non-league far removed from the modern stadia of top flight football is the frequent lack of any segregation. Not to be misconstrued for any lack of unbridled passion that you might find higher up the league ladder, it tends to be indicative of the distinct lack of dickheads who tend to watch football at this level. I apologise for my use of technical jargon so early.

At Matlock, for example, one such fan goes as far as dying his middle-aged fringe blue on matchdays in a ritual not entirely dissimilar to how he might look if he were to collide headfirst with one of the North East Derbyshire buses that regularly make their way down Causeway Lane. Despite having never actually spoken to him directly, I did once have to diffuse a situation in which he told an opposition fan to "fuck off" for having the audacity to claim a borderline offside. He also threatened to enter the field of play to take up his remonstrations in the dugout.

As the full-time whistle brought an end to his two hours of tribal goading in the direction of any opposition fan in shouting distance (and one or two players for good measure), I observed a man seemingly recovering from the effects of a trance as the teams trudged off the field of play.

'I don't know what comes over me,' he announced aloud to his embarrassed mate as the collective of enemies he'd assembled that were preparing a collision with a nearby bus to finish off the look observed him in bemusement. 'I just get so excited.'

Football, from the local playground to the national stadium, stirs something deep in even the most unassuming, it would appear. In the case of the Wealdstone Ranger, such characters have even gone viral.

With my interest in the lower rungs of English football's ladder peaked, I spent two seasons following non-league's underdogs in the FA Cup from the early qualifying rounds through to Wembley – an undertaking that has earned me the label of 'the blog guy' with Sue.

While my visits to The Emirates to see Watford knock out the holders or a packed Valley Parade on quarter final weekend were exciting, nothing could match the passion of the Extra Preliminary Round. Sitting with the chairman of Penistone Church FC as he tried to verbalise what the FA Cup debut of his boyhood team meant after decades associated with the club while fighting back tears of emotion takes some beating.

'We'll get Silsden if we beat Squires Gate in the League Cup,' says another one of the lads, interrupting my train of thought as he analyses the fixture list on his phone.

'Not 'if', 'when'!' corrects Sue light-heartedly, but barely masking the underlying subtext of establishing a much-needed winning mentality.

'Sorry Sue,' he replies. 'Force of habit. Glass half-empty.'

Manager Garry Brown arrives, greeting an ever-growing collection of players in the clubhouse. He's an instantly likeable and friendly character from the second he warmly shakes my hand.

'We're after all the coverage we can get,' he tells me as Sue explains who I am. 'Anything to raise the profile in the community is a bonus,' he beams.

I stand and chat with Garry for a few minutes. While I'm keen not to impact further on his reassembled plans for the afternoon, he puts me at ease by giving me an overview of the task ahead.

'The coverage we had last season wasn't great,' he begins. 'Comparing me to Mourinho – I mean, come on. People forget I'm here painting the changing rooms, digging the pitch. But, for me, it wasn't a terrible season because of how the lads pulled together. We're one big family here and we played for each other. With all the postponements last season, we were playing three games a week sometimes. This bunch of lads are still turning up and playing for each other on £20 a week expenses. It's brilliant.

'We're building the foundations of something here. We've launched the Development Squad and the Under-18s. But you won't catch me on Twitter shouting about who we've signed because they'll just come in and take them. I prefer to keep it close to my chest.'

'They' refers to pretty much any local side with a bigger budget than the Millers – most of them, then – and we discuss the inevitability of the magpie mentality of sides at this level, where there's every reason to keep the next big thing, or perhaps just the next half decent thing, under your belt.

'We needed 60 players to get through a season,' he continues. 'Teams come in and offer them more money so they go. But then one bad game and they're on the bench and then they're not seeing that money and it's not easy to get back in. That's where it's different here. They've got time to develop and make mistakes. That's why we've got a good base now as we've got the lads who want to be here. That makes a big difference. We're a family.'

It's a term Garry repeats a few times as we chat. It certainly feels like a family after the bonding experience of last season, albeit one that's experienced a shared trauma, and he takes his paternal persona outside to his gathering squad to commence training. Not before he's generously offered me his mobile number, though, just in case I think of any extra questions.

'You're welcome here any time,' he tells me as he departs. 'Give us a bell when you're coming up and we'll be here with a brew waiting for you.'

Currently on bar duty is Fixture Secretary Derek. A young boy orders a Diet Coke and a bag of crisps – he appears to be the young son of Assistant Manager Paul Williams – and Derek downs the large folder he's busying himself with to attend to his pint-sized customer as he decides between salt and vinegar or ready salted.

I sit outside on a picnic bench and survey the pitch from behind the goal. While the interior shots of *Rovers* were shot elsewhere in a dummy clubhouse, all outdoor filming took place here at Church Lane. Absorbing the view, it's easy to see why.

At the opposite end of the pitch, just over the six-foot fencing, a picturesque scene of rolling green hills dotted with terraced housing sits on the landscape. To the left, the church spire from which the ground gets its name is concealed by large trees with the cemetery in full bloom. To the right, a slightly more industrial scene borders the training pitch as a collection of double decker buses loom high over the fence, offering an unorthodox option for an upper tier of sorts, or perhaps a makeshift Executive Suite.

Since agreeing to filming, Church Lane has been added to a location library used by a wide variety of production companies. It's meant yet more unusual requests landing on Sue's desk.

'I received an email from Samsung asking if they could come down and film an advert,' she tells me later. 'It was just after the bad publicity and I told them we weren't interested. He left it an hour and emailed again saying "Can I just ask you to think this through? It could be quite lucrative for the club."

'I picked up the phone and said "Firstly, can I just ask you to disregard my email." It was then that we made a decision about the negative publicity. It can either grind you down or we can make some money from it.'

The advert, involving Harry Redknapp giving New Mills a team talk through a virtual reality headset and name-checking several players including captain Ryan Hopper, had more than 300,000 views at the time of writing, as well as giving a more welcome boost to the profile and finances of the club.

I head back inside as Garry's training session begins with a game of keep-ball between bibs and shirts in the tight confines of the caged astroturf surface. Fixture Secretary Derek is filling in a crossword in the empty clubhouse.

He lives some 10 miles east of here in Peak Forest, with the Sheffield twang in his accent suggesting he's originally from a little further afield than that. A long-time non-league enthusiast, he considers himself a Newport County fan alongside his commitment to New Mills and boyhood team Sheffield United.

He tells me how he came to support Newport during his childhood when his father used to ask after their results as a young Derek read The Green 'Un, a Saturday afternoon sister paper of the Sheffield Star. It ceased printing in 2013 to become online only. A sad relic of a simpler time, I tell him I once had a byline for a piece about Neil Warnock in there in a vain hope to impress upon him my pedigree.

'I probably only get to a game or two a season,' he continues, The Green 'Un byline swiftly dismissed. 'It's a long way to go so it's mainly the away games and relying on them not clashing with fixtures here. There's perhaps one or two I might be able to get to this season.'

We dissect England's recent failures for a while by way of small talk before he tells me he fell out with the national side decades ago when they failed to employ "the right man for the job". I'm confident we're talking about Brian Clough but I don't get chance to ask. It could be Ron Atkinson for all I know.

'I went to Burton away to watch Newport and saw him there watching his son,' he continues, confirming my suspicions/educating me on the little-known career of Big Ron Junior. 'He had a bunch of heavies around him so you couldn't get too close.'

He's a relaxed presence in the empty clubhouse given the unexpected afternoon off. As the Millers' chief contact with the League and its fellow members, he might be considered the man most responsible for replacing the hole in the pre-season prep.

'There's no game Monday now either. I think that was one Garry set up but they want us to share the cost of the pitch which isn't normally the way. We've had all sorts of teams down here and we'd never ask them to pay,' he tells me. 'Friendlies are generally done on invitation. I know Matlock were looking for a game today as well but we can't host them here yet,' he says, gesturing in the direction of the developing but sodden pitch outside.

I sense Derek is slightly guarded about my presence here – it's something I'd expected more of – but we bond ever-so-slightly discussing Derbyshire non-league sides where his knowledge is so extensive, he namechecks my local Indian restaurant. It's another shared passion that hopefully bodes well for the future.

I repeat my intention of getting behind the negative headlines as I head for the exit, realising I might be over-egging it a little in my determination to win his approval as the words leave my mouth, before making my way outside. Garry's training session has developed into a full match now as he watches on with his coaching team. They occasionally give words of encouragement and ripples of applause from the sidelines. It's compelling viewing before making my way on the forty-minute journey north-west to the leisure centre complex where New Mills' brand-new development side are playing their first ever game.

Tucked away in the Manchester suburbs, the new side face AFC Mostonians less than a mile away from the Etihad Stadium which stands like a palace in an otherwise under-developed area of the city. A rundown collection of small local businesses pave the way to my destination, most notably the shared and heavily graffitied shutters of a Home Clearance Centre neighbouring an Adult Superstore. Everything you need under one roof.

I make my way up to the touchline to stand with a showered and refreshed Sue and Ray. My chat with Derek meant I missed kick-off and Sue laughs knowingly at this. 'He likes a chat, does Derek,' she observes. Sue's dad, Geoff, a well-dressed octogenarian, has also joined them and is just as vociferous on the touchline as New Mills Reserves repeatedly advance against inferior opposition. We talk more about *Rovers* and how Craig Cash and co. aren't the only famous faces who've been seen at Church Lane while we watch.

'We had United down here a few years ago for a friendly,' Ray tells me proudly as we attempt to bond. 'They put a decent young side out including Jesse Lingard. It was great for me as I'm a United fan,' he continues.

'We've had City there as well. The one thing they've got in common is that there wasn't a word of complaint. You get lads at our level who come in and moan about the facilities and this and that. Those lads who are at the top of the game don't say a word and that's a big part of it for some of them, just having that professionalism.'

New Mills has also seen a few famous siblings pull on the amber jersey too. The shirts of Giggs, Butt and Brown, all members of the treble winning side of '99, have all rested in the home dressing room; all belonging to the slightly less successful brothers of some of Manchester's finest sons. Always one step from the spotlight. In Rhodri's case, he might otherwise have chosen to remain there.

Our attention turns back to the game as New Mills continue to dominate. Most noticeable in amber is a tall and graceful centre-half who looks comfortably untested and a waspish striker who makes up in boundless energy what he lacks in stature and height. Keen to impress newly appointed Development Team Manager James Kinsey, the eleven put in an impressive performance to comfortably win 4-1, with their diminutive striker scoring the pick of the bunch with a neat clip over the advancing 'keeper. It could have easily been seven or eight, though, as Ray and Sue congratulate each player as they leave the pitch.

'He's good, that lad,' says Ray to James, gesturing towards the number six who confidently stepped up out of defence on more than a few occasions to dictate play.

'He's a model,' replies James. 'Just as well 'cause he's thick as fuck!' he laughs. The centre-half, seemingly in earshot, doesn't flicker and leaves us doubting whether it's an impressive poker face or a confirmation of the assessment.

'Are you gonna go in and say a few words?' asks Sue of Ray as we head past the dressing rooms and out towards the car park.

'No need,' he says. 'I've already told 'em well done.' It's early days, but there's clearly a noticeable satisfaction between the two of them that this new experiment has got off to a positive start. As we bid farewell in the car park, Sue is hollered back.

'Can I give you these kits now?' comes the shout. 'Yeah. Bring 'em down!' she says, mock-resigned at the prospect. A new set of shirts and shorts to wash alongside the First Team? The ever-varied role of New Mills Club Secretary acquires a new responsibility.

2

NEW BEGINNINGS

I'm not a big fan of pre-season. I suppose it's a necessary evil, allowing us all a break from the beautiful game to pursue other interests, but I maintain it's only marginally less fun for the fans than it is for the players themselves.

These days, pre-season is treated as an exhibition exercise by many of the top Premier League sides. In the past week, Spurs have played in Australia, reigning champions Leicester City in L.A and Manchester United in Shanghai. For these international brands, it's just as much a great way of shifting merchandise in far flung destinations as a useful preparation exercise for the season ahead.

It's a little different moving down the leagues. After their first two pre-season fixtures were postponed, New Mills were starting a little later than their rivals. With an opening 3-0 win against Sheffield United's Academy proving to be an encouraging start, a goalless draw against much-fancied Ramsbottom from the division above gave further reason for optimism.

Against Hyde, the third game of a compressed pre-season, a positive performance in the first half sees the Millers reach the dressing room a goal down despite having the better of the game. Seven subs later, in an attempt to spread out the minutes and try other formulas with different players, the Millers find themselves trailing 5-0. A superb late consolation does little to appease the

Chairman.

'You can't do that,' protests a frustrated Ray. '200 people through the gates and that first half was encouraging. Then they see us collapse like that in the second half and say, "same old, same old". It's not on. I have told him,' he complains, in reference to manager Garry Brown. The pressure to win pre-season games, even this far down the ladder, is now a mainstay of the modern game.

I reach Church Lane via a different route from Derby for the fourth and final friendly against a Stockport County XI and get an ever more impressive view of its surroundings. Visible for miles as a settlement built into the hills, the only real indicator that this old town belongs in the modern age are the bird-like silhouettes of jetliners crossing the Pennines on their slow approach to Manchester Airport.

The side road is busy with cars at 7.15pm as I approach the double turnstiles. A chap who's presumably visiting from neighbouring County is scrolling through his phone suggesting he has an email that grants him free entry to the ground. The response he's getting isn't entirely positive, before a suggestion of whether he'd like to make a donation in lieu of a free ticket is mooted. I make a sidestep to avoid creating a freeloader bottleneck.

'Hello. I'm...' I begin, before I'm interrupted by a voice from the opposite turnstile.

'Don't let him in!' Sure enough, Sue's on gate duty. In the end, both the chap from Stockport with the smartphone and I make it into Church Lane.

Sue introduces me to James Lobley. He's an 18-year-old student with a decent camera and a keen interest in New Mills. Having joined the club last season, he looks after the social media accounts, takes photos and edits the match day programme. I probe him for what the season ahead might hold.

'Congleton – that'll be an interesting one,' he tells me as we discuss the opening competitive fixture in the FA Cup Extra Preliminary Round. 'It's a young team we've got though. We could be up there; we could be scraping to stay up. In the past, you've tried to compare the teams to other divisions but you just can't this season. The games come quick and fast and a month from now we could be first with 18pts, we could be last with no points! I just don't know.

'To win in the FA Cup would be great. I'd love it if we won, got through and played a side we played last season to show how far we've come. We've got that opportunity with Farsley (awaiting the victors in the next round). I think they beat us 4-1 last season. But I'll think about that after Saturday.'

His optimism is endearing, especially given the season that's just passed. James attended most games and took photographic evidence of many of the maulings.

'It's about half and half of who was here last season and who we've brought in,' he continues, observing the matchday squad warming up. 'We've kept the 'keeper, Ollie Martin, which is good because he won Player's Player of the Year, Manager's, Fan's…everything. Another one we've got is Hopper. He played for Accrington. It was only eight games but he's played in League Two and he's our captain this year. A lot of these players are fairly new and came in at the back end of the season. We've got different players with different experience.'

He points out another player in the warm-up who played for Stockport County a few times and joined recently.

'I had to write all the player profiles for the programme,' he continues. 'I was like "I don't know! I think they're a midfielder? I just don't know!" I've been involved (as Media Officer) with three or four clubs. The atmosphere here is second to none though. We had a night out in Lancaster with the squad and it's all anyone was talking about for two months. It kept the team together. I always go in the changing rooms because I like to hear the team talk and the dressing room is different class.'

He tells me he was involved at Wythenshawe Town with Garry before here, following the manager across to New Mills last season. 'It's nice to have a second season here but the main reason I joined was because Gaz said we needed better media exposure. It's a much better standard and, although it was an awful season, it was really enjoyable. I think a lot of people think I'm mad saying that. The only one I didn't enjoy was Spennymoor. Losing 9-0 on a three-hour trip...,' he tails off with a shake of the head.

'I remember reading the coverage at the time and people were commenting saying "How are they the worst team in England when there are divisions below them?"' It's a fair point that I'll hear repeated about the unfortunate moniker that New Mills were labelled with.

'If it wasn't for the photography then I'm not sure I'd be involved as that's the bit I enjoy most. It's a great backdrop. I remember doing a night game last season with all the lights coming on in the houses behind. It was fantastic. We lost 5-0 though, unfortunately,' he adds dejectedly. A familiar end to a match at Church Lane, then.

'I think I've missed three or four games out of 25 or so,' he continues. 'It's the midweek games that are the hardest. I live in Altrincham so it's an hour forty-five on the bus. I usually try and get a lift with one of the players from Cheadle. I wasn't sure at first that I'd enjoy the commute but it proves it's a nice place to come to.'

As the players head out of the tunnel, the referee and his assistant stand impatiently on the pitchside.

'Come on lads! We're waiting!' shouts the ref. 'Can you imagine if they all came out on time? Just once?' he quietly queries with his Assistant.

A healthy pre-season crowd of at least 100 have gathered as kick-off approaches. A significant number are assembled behind the goal in dark blue having made the short journey from Stockport. Sue's laugh can be heard from our vantage point as she finishes gate duty, banters with the regulars and immediately busies herself with another task that's gone undone while she's minded the gate.

It's a good start for my first match. New Mills take the lead in the 10th minute as a whipped cross from the left is turned in predatorily.

'It's a young side, this,' says the Stockport fan next to me to his mate as he observes his own team's line-up. It's just the start Sue was looking for, though, as she joins me to watch – but not before sorting out who is ironing the kits for Saturday's match at Congleton. It looks like it's her. Again.

'It's about £1500 for winning the Extra Preliminary Round,' she says, beginning to turn her attention to the weekend's FA Cup game as we watch the Millers dominate. 'I printed out the prize money breakdown earlier! It's huge to us to get that in the bank after pre-season. It'd be a great start. We're quite sound financially at the moment but if you get a few games called off in October and November, that's when it begins to count. You only have to look at our fixture list, see January with only one home game and think "well that's gonna be a tough month" and you shouldn't, but that's the reality.

'Ray and I and the Committee are honest. A lot of clubs spend a lot of money in the early months based on the FA Cup. As soon as they're out, they just drop all the wage bills. We've never been those sorts of people. We try and keep it low to spread it out over the season because it's not fair on the lads and it's not fair on the manager.'

The concept of signing players on year-long contracts is alien to the Millers these days. With players tied down based on loyalty to the manager and their weekly petrol expenses, the task becomes a difficult one against sides eyeing up an FA Cup run as a lucrative opportunity – and the chance to bring players in on longer contracts as a by-product.

'If we don't get through, we don't get through,' she continues. 'I said to Garry that if we go out then our first game is (the league game against) Maine Road away on Monday night. We're taking a few away on the bus and I think that'll boost a few of 'em.'

Despite being neighbours to a coach company, taking a bus to an away game is something of a new concept for New Mills. After making the initial enquiry, they asked Sue if she wanted to hire a double decker for the legions of fans expected to travel. She's settled for an oversized mini-bus.

She continues: 'Congleton have been in this league since we were in there before we went up and came back down again. I was sat next to their Secretary at the league meeting last week and they've got a couple of contract players so they're obviously putting a bit of dosh behind it but hey, it's as it is. We were at the first League meeting (following relegation) and everyone was saying "it's good to have you back" and we were thinking "it's not good to bloody be back!"'

Sue doesn't travel far from her day job to take on the ever-varied night job at Church Lane. She's worked in the transport office for confectionary company Swizzells, located just up the road, for many years. Unsurprisingly, peak time is just before Halloween. She's cut off mid-sentence as she tells me about how many sweets she ships around the country when the ball is hoofed high over the far stand and onto Church Lane itself. The gate attendant-cum-kit-woman has just been promoted to ball girl. I watch as she leaves the main gates and chases off down the road. Chairman Ray takes up the story as he watches his side and barks constant encouragement.

'It'll be difficult for us against Congleton. They've got a couple of contract players…well done! Decent, that!' he shouts, interrupting his own observation to yell encouragement in the direction of the pitch before continuing.

'They always pay money out early doors and if it doesn't pay off, they let them go. But if it does work and they win a few rounds then it was worth it. It's a bit early though, really, for the FA Cup. Normally you've got a couple of games under your belt but they've let a lot more enter it this season. PRESSURE! Well done!'

As we discuss the progress during pre-season, Ray tells me the 5-1 defeat to Hyde was disappointing given the 1-0 deficit at half-time where, he felt, the home team were the better side. It's clearly still something he has a bee in his bonnet over as he continues to relay his frustrations to me.

'We made seven changes at half-time and I think that was the manager's mistake. I did tell him. When you're playing a side from a higher level, you don't go and make wholesale changes. You've got to keep your spectators happy. We were one down to a bit of a fluke goal but we were playing well and then he brings lads on who are blatantly not good enough and we know they're not. He says "I had to bring 'em on"…well, no you don't! The fans go away saying we lost 5-1. They're not talking about us playing well in the first half.'

New Mills go in at the break in the lead. A decent and commanding performance is the main topic of conversation in the Portacabin that doubles up as a media room, matchday office, hosting area for the opposition's visiting party with a sandwich selection and is even home to a stretcher. Ray seems quietly pleased with the first half as he washes an egg mayo down with a cup of tea.

We're joined by a chap who is perhaps in his early 70s, Roy, who is busy drawing the raffle. A member of the committee, he's carrying out his duties with his grandson beside him. A younger man, dressed in a smart suit that appears to also be linked to the committee, is discussing ways of getting the fans engaged over the course of the season via the website. Sue keeps the hot drinks flowing for all concerned.

'They try and get in when the gates open at half-time,' says Sue, in reference to a couple of fans who regularly arrive at half-time when the turnstiles are officially left unmanned. 'It's annoying because there's one bloke who always slags us off online on the forum and he waits until it's free to get in. They won't today though cos my dad's guarding the gate!' she laughs, while pouring another cup of tea. If he's anything like his daughter, they certainly won't be challenging his authority.

'I reckon there'll be another twenty or thirty trying it after half-time,' says Ray. 'They'll be queuing up.'

As the sun disappears behind the hills, Roy suggests the floodlights are put on. It's in Ray's plans but, with one eye on the budget, the switch isn't flicked until the very end of half-time. They're still slowly warming up as the game restarts in the August dusk.

Stockport played a decent passing game in the first half and employ the same tactic after the break. They score around the hour mark and again with 15 minutes to go, carving the New Mills backline open to create chances that are practically one on one. A few spurned chances, including one where it looked easier to score but ends up in the car park, are all New Mills have in response. It's a disappointing end to pre-season in a game that showed considerable promise.

'We should have been 3-0 up at half-time if we'd put away our chances,' observes Sue. 'But it's coming. There are loads of positives around the ground from the fans. Let's just hope they are on Saturday at full-time! Do you know what I love? Away games. I don't have to do 'owt!'

It's not the only reason Sue has to be cheerful. She continues: 'I'm glad pre-season is over though – I hate it. All the extra kits to wash, all the extra shirts. They're all nagging about this kit and that. It's just a nightmare – but we're through it! No more meaningless games. It all matters now.' Manager Garry Brown is similarly upbeat.

'A really good performance,' is his summary post-match. 'I've got 20 players and I've got to try everybody,' he adds, with perhaps a hint of the defensive over his Chairman's recent feedback. 'We've had chances, we've hit the post but it's just the way it goes. I've just told them now I'm pleased with what I've seen. First half, I've tried a different shape and system and it worked. I'm happy with that and I know my XI. Everything's positive, the fans can see it. I've made eight subs tonight. It's like Browny at the back, he's a good player, but he's just come back from America on holiday. If I over-exert him, he's not gonna be right.'

A positive assessment from the gaffer, then, and he continues the charm offensive as he makes his way around the empty ground, chatting with the last remnants of fans and volunteers as the floodlights go out.

'We'll be giving it our best shot,' he says to Committee

member Roy as he wishes the team luck for Congleton. 'It's not gonna be like last season.'

'Oh I know you will,' replies Roy, warmly. He seems taken aback slightly by the manager's off-the-cuff reassurance but seems appreciative of the gesture.

'Positive' is definitely the word with Garry. He's an undeniably likeable bloke who exudes warmth and energy. Looking a little deeper, though, there's a glimpse of the understandable anxiety he's feeling in the search for that first win. With the hint of pressure on his pre-season selections already vocalised by the chairman following their disastrous season, I'm already firmly on his side.

'I'm chuffed to bits you've chosen us,' he tells me as I shake his hand and make my way out. 'You'll get the family feel. We've lifted the place, painted everything and it's positive.'

It's hard to do anything but root for him and there's no doubt his positivity has lifted team spirit higher than it perhaps has any right to be. With pre-season over, the first test comes at Congleton.

3

THE ROAD TO WEMBLEY

The first day of the English football season is special. Eagerly anticipated by fans across the country with nothing better to do of a weekend, the childlike optimism over new signings, local derbies and the pre-match pie keep so many going throughout the long summer months. I'm one of them.

Football-less months seemed endless growing up. The three-month chasm of tournament summers were at least replaced with an international binge and bittersweet misery. With the memory of defeat to Iceland still fresh following a turbulent June, though, anticipation for 2016/17 seemed genuinely palpable.

The prospect of Jeff and the boys back on TV and the preview pull-out in the 'paper were staples of my teenage memories of the regular season returning. Our family holiday would often straddle the two opening weekends of the Football League and Premier League season and would involve me and my dad finding a bar in France, Spain or wherever the family caravan had landed us and parking up in a local bar for the afternoon. If you were lucky, you might even pick up a live game with foreign commentary – the bigger the satellite dish outside, the better your chances.

When the season does get underway, non-league in the summer months is particularly special. Unreserved standing, affordable pricing and beer in the sunshine are just some of the benefits you can find at a ground near you. The same hopes, dreams and aspirations are there too, even if, perhaps, the new signing might be more of an unknown quantity than the nine-figure transfer target Sky Sports News have trailed since late May.

Another lesser-known highlight of the summer football calendar is the advent of the FA Cup. Just eleven weeks after Manchester United lifted the famous old trophy at Wembley, hundreds of sides from the ninth and tenth tiers lock horns in the Extra Preliminary Round. Long before the First Round fireworks around Bonfire Night or the depleted Premier League sides entering the Third Round after a busy festive period, New Mills find themselves a mere fourteen wins away from English football's showpiece event.

For all of the lustre it's supposedly lost over the years, the FA Cup remains big business for sides at this level. Prize money is around £1500 for a win – or roughly a month's playing staff expenditure on the Millers' tiny budget.

Driving through the pretty market town of Congleton towards the ground is surprisingly challenging with local roadworks causing the kind of build-up you might expect approaching the home of Stoke City, renamed as the somewhat vulgar Bet365 Stadium from this season. Ample time, at least, to appreciate local salon Curl Up and Dye or the intriguingly named Beartown Spices – an Indian restaurant that presumably doubles up as a Mexican-themed gay bar.

Congleton's ground is hidden in the middle of a rabbit warren of cul-de-sacs and side streets. Only a couple of road signs offer reassurance that Google Maps isn't dropping you off at a random doorstep. That, and the sight of the New Mills mini-bus parked immediately outside the turnstiles and squeezed up a tight driveway.

'An hour and a half it's taken us to get here,' complains Ray as I arrive in the clubhouse. 'It's forty minutes from New Mills and then we get stuck in that. Don't ask!' An ill-advised route across the High Peak towards Staffordshire inadvertently took in the festival traffic of a local 70s-themed concert that was further compounded by Congleton's traffic planning committee. It's not been a great start to the afternoon.

A well-equipped and modern clubhouse set back from the pitch offers a friendly atmosphere for pre-match drinks. Inside, a senior looking Labrador watches fans come and go. Above the bar there are a collection of motivational phrases and quotes for all who await a pint and a bag of pork scratchings.

Without you, we are nothing. With you, we are something. Together, we are everything.

A cricket team loudly sing Petula Clark's Downtown as kick-off approaches. Further inspection reveals the cricket outfits are merely fancy dress. Congleton's merry band of day drinkers have turned out in force for the first game of the season and always come dressed to the nines, the sixes and, sometimes, the fours.

For once, Sue is relaxed and enjoying a beer.

'I love away games,' she says. 'I can just watch the football!'

Sitting alongside Ray and Sue are a healthy number of the New Mills travelling contingent. A friendly bunch, all interested in my reasons for joining them, they're agreed on two things: it's too early in the season for an FA Cup game and the coach driver needs a different route on the way home.

While sides at this level are used to knockout football before the summer holidays are out, it's rarely ever been the first league game of the season. With prize money being so significant, it's made pre-season preparation even more vital. Taking into consideration the two early games postponed, followed by a shaky second half showing against Stockport, there's an unspoken feeling among our contingent that Garry's men might not quite be ready for the test ahead.

Congleton start on the front foot from the off and almost score within the opening minutes. It's a sign of things to come, as they set up camp in the New Mills half. Behind the goal, the cricket fans sing loud and proud. Over the fence behind them, the owner of a terraced house sits in her raised garden on a sun lounger watching the match in the warm August rays. There's no admission fee required from her comfortable vantage point, at least.

Ray himself is also getting a little hot under the collar. He's made no secret that he's opinionated about first team matters – as manager of the First Team himself once upon a time, it goes with the territory - but it becomes increasingly apparent early on.

'Get out! GET OUT! You're too deep!' he screams as he walks through the empty terrace behind the goal. Garry's dugout is at the opposite side of the field but it's almost impossible to ignore from both the bench and, most likely, the pitch. He's getting louder as he gets closer.

'Why are they dropping that deep?' asks an increasingly frustrated Ray to no-one in particular. 'They need to get out. GET FUCKING OUT! I dunno why I'm shouting it because nobody's taking a blind bit of notice.'

There can be no denying his passion but, at times, it makes for slightly uncomfortable viewing. Like the most vocal parent at the school football match, no player appears to want to make eye contact with their venting chairman behind the goal. Instead, they continue to invite pressure on with half-clearances coming straight back. Stringing passes together is also proving a challenge. It's not hard to see why the man at the top is getting so frustrated.

On the opposite side of the pitch, Sue stands with a couple of the travelling supporters. Whether this was in anticipation of Ray's frustration or not is unclear, but she seems to be making conversation to distract herself.

'He's telling 'em to relax and calm down!' continues Ray, gesturing towards Garry's fatherly advice as we reach Sue's vantage point. 'No! Don't calm down! Get excited!'

Ray's fears are realised inside the opening quarter of an hour. Congleton open the scoring with a well-worked goal that cuts New Mills apart. There's an inevitability about it that's all too obvious as the side trudge back to the centre circle.

'Well, we didn't see that one coming, did we?' asks Ray, again to nobody in particular. He'd appeared ready to combust before the goal. Now he quietens and disappears back around the pitch.

'I think he might have the sulk on with me,' Sue tells me soon after. 'I've told him that I understand why he's frustrated but it's not helping anyone shouting and screaming.' The calming effect of the Club Secretary on the Chairman in action? Or the reasonable and level-headed partner of a man in a high-pressure job encouraging him to calm down for his own sake if nobody else's? Either way, it's certainly effective.

It could be 2-0 minutes later but the ball goes high over the bar. It bounces along the roof tiles of the terraced houses and lands, helpfully, in the garden of a sunbathing woman who's continuing to enjoy a slightly obstructed view of the game from her sun lounger. The cricketers cheer as she returns the ball and retires back to her comfortable situ.

'I know he's frustrated because we're seeing all the same silly mistakes from last year,' Sue tells me softly with Ray out of earshot. 'I just say to him that what you're saying is right but it's not necessarily what they want to hear. He's the only voice you can hear sometimes.'

'Too quiet!' screams captain Ryan Hopper in the middle of the pitch. 'We're too fuckin' quiet!' He has a point. The side are devoid of confidence all over the pitch. Garry looks visibly deflated in the dugout. The monkey on the back of that long-awaited win already looks to be weighing heavy on the team just 15 minutes into the new season. The vim and vigour of his pre-season persona is already vanishing.

'We just need that win. For everybody…' Sue continues. 'There's a guy I work with who asks me every week "where were you playing? What was the result?" When we had the draw last season it was great to walk into work and say, "that was a great result!" When we beat Sheffield in the friendly, he said "is this the way it's gonna go now?" I said, "don't get too excited!"'

Getting a little more excited on the other side of the pitch is Ray, who is beginning to find his voice again. 'I think Ray's gonna have a heart attack,' Sue jokes. 'And it won't be me that causes it!'

Congleton continue to dominate, winning every 50/50 and

aerial challenge. It's threatening to become a hard lesson for the young Millers side on £20 expenses a week, with no contract guaranteeing their attachment from one month to the next. By contrast, the Congleton players brought in on fixed term deals in a bid to extend their FA Cup run look easier to pick out.

'I was at the league meeting with Ken from here the other week. He was telling me about his contracted players,' Sue says. 'I've known him for years from our North West Counties days. He was another one saying "Oh, it's lovely to have you back!"'

It's a bit like returning to work from a holiday, I suppose. You might *say* it's good to be back but you'd much rather be in the Mediterranean. The same applies to the Evo-Stik League. Sort of.

The Millers slowly start to give the travelling fans something to shout about but it's small crumbs against Congleton's dominance. Keeping the deficit down to one goal feels like a positive until they add another in the 41st minute. A third in first half added time puts the tie to bed. The Congleton cricketers sing the theme tune to Dambusters before chanting "Easy! Easy!" as New Mills trudge off towards the dressing room.

'Come on the Bears!' blares the announcement over the loudspeaker. 'He better shut up or I'll stick that microphone where it hurts,' is Sue's response. 'At least I'm getting a tan!' quips the Millers fan beside me in the warm August sun.

It's like a morgue in the portacabin that hosts the travelling party at half-time. The matchday announcer doubles up as catering manager, as he politely takes the drinks order of each of the New Mills travelling party and Sue considers the dimensions of his derriere versus the PA system. Ray is wearing a thousand-mile stare that suggests he needs something a little stronger.

'We could win 5-3!' says Sue, perkily.

'I can safely say we won't,' grumbles Ray.

'You never know. The magic of the FA Cup!' replies the Congleton announcer before gesturing towards more tea. Even the opposition, so embarrassed by the ease of their lead, is now offering patronising encouragement to the Millers. It's potentially a new low.

The second half is an improvement, even though it wouldn't have taken much. Congleton sit back and invite the fairly toothless pressure of their opponents on as regular fans grumble about the lack of a finisher. Sue congratulates Ray on his more positive tone in the second half and the cricketers become ever merrier before retiring for afternoon tea.

'Shall we get going so we miss the traffic?' a young lad in a Congleton shirt asks his mum beside me as the final whistle approaches. She laughs and gestures in the direction of the main stand. 'We're not at Stoke, love. I think we'll be alright!' she replies. He must have been worried about the roadworks outside Curl Up and Dye.

Sue maintains her jovial mood in the clubhouse post-match while I do my best to console Ray. We discuss the improved second half performance but, in truth, it's hard to take too many positives from the game.

'We lost it in the first 20 minutes. Do you remember me shouting and bawling?' enquires Ray, as I attempt to give the impression of casting my mind back at the recollection and try to look convincing. 'That's when they lost the game. We never got in the game. The only way you can get in the game is to get yourself into the game! If you can't beat 'em with skill, beat 'em with effort.

'But we'll see you on Monday night against Maine Road. They'll be better than these,' says Ray, already sounding resigned to a defeat. I leave him with his pint. There's not much anyone can say this afternoon.

'Safe journey,' I say to one of the travelling fans as I leave the ground and he boards the minibus.

'It'll be a fuckin' long journey home if he goes the same way!' comes the response. It's been another one of those days for New Mills. They've become all too familiar.

Winless: My Year with Football's Ultimate Underdogs

The Millers fans (bottom left) look on as pre-season optimism dissipates

4

MR NEW MILLS AFC

As we sit in the eerily quiet surrounds of Church Lane's clubhouse, Chairman Ray Coverley sips a cup of tea. There haven't been many opportunities to rest the legs that once marauded around the patch of grass he's so lovingly devoted to since he arrived at the ground at 7.40am and, on a match day, there won't be many more.

'I needed to let the groundsman in to prepare the pitch. Then there's the trip to the supermarket, the brewery…' he tells me with a wry smile. So much for relaxing into retirement. For 66-year-old Ray, though, there's no place he'd rather be. After almost 40 years of association with his local side, this truly is his second home.

'I played for a local amateur club,' he tells me as we settle into our chat. I've booked an hour out of his busy schedule to discover how he came to hold almost every role conceivable within a football club. It's a story he's more than willing to share.

'We played on a ground about a mile and a half away but it was a farmer's field and he wanted it back. Around this time in the late 70s and early 80s, New Mills were in trouble. They weren't getting any crowds and, eventually, they folded. Roy Crabtree, the owner and Chairman at the time who was a local businessman, had wanted rid of it and asked us how we'd feel about playing on here,' he says, gesturing outside at the backdrop of green beyond the window.

'We came and had a look and the grass was up to your waist. The financial situation then was that they owed about £3,000 but he told us we didn't need to worry about that and we could just start up again as New Mills 1981 or whatever it would have been at the time. I had a chat with a couple of the lads and we decided we didn't want to do that. So, instead, we guaranteed the bank £2,000 each to get the Club going. We wanted to get off on the right foot and paid off the local traders which (was a debt) we carried around with us for a while. Amateur clubs weren't making very much at that time so it was a big commitment.'

With ownership of the Club sealed, Ray was joined by his teammates at Church Lane and the New Mills revival was underway. First though, there was a bit of TLC required.

'We got the grass cut, got everything good to go and applied to join the Manchester League,' he continues. 'We won the Lancashire and Cheshire League in our first year up here which guaranteed us entry. At the time, I was a player. After a few years in the Manchester League, I took over as player/manager and then manager until about 1990 when my mother died and I stepped away a little bit. I was still involved, still on the committee. We then decided we wanted to join the North West Counties (currently the ninth and tenth tiers of the football league ladder respectively) and they came back to me to see what I thought.

'Joining the League is a big step from going amateur to a little bit semi-professional. We had the ground grading and had a grant for the all-weather pitch and floodlights. We put the proposal together and it took us a year or so to get the grants. We did the work and we got in – we were in the North West Counties,' he says proudly, before grabbing a framed photo from behind the bar.

A youthful-looking Sue and moustachioed Ray proudly pose on the pitch with a big cheque alongside many familiar faces of old. One young blonde girl in an unmistakably 90s football kit attracts particular attention – it's barmaid Ashley, now in her 30s, who freezes with terror at the sight of the old frame making an appearance.

'The team we had then, while some of them had played at semi-pro level, were very amateur and we were finishing really low down in the second division,' he says, referring to a rung below the unwelcome new standing New Mills find themselves on in the league ladder. 'We were playing with lads from round here and even when we brought in a new manager and seven or eight players, they still weren't good enough. At this stage, I was just on the committee and they asked me if I wanted to be Chairman.'

As player, player/manager, manager and now committee member, Ray's progression to Chairman seemed like a natural one. And the new man in charge had the ambition to drive the club's new direction.

'I did tell them (the committee) that the whole thing changes when you go into the North West Counties, you have to spend a little bit more. And, in those days, this place was heaving every night. We had darts, dominoes, two pool teams. The players drank in here. We had a bit of money so I said I'd go out and get a manager. At the time, Tony Hancock had just taken Woodley Sports into the Unibond League and was available,' he continues.

For the removal of doubt, the Tony Hancock in question is a former footballer turned non-league manager with a handful of professional appearances to his name rather than the noted comedian of BBC radio fame. Hancock's Half Hour would usually mean he'd been subbed off before half-time. Always one step from the spotlight.

'I went to meet him and his coach. They said they'd both come and watch us with a view to taking over. No promises, and they wouldn't reveal they were potentially the new management team. So we're playing at Blackpool. I don't know if you've ever met this bloke but there's no way he can make himself incognito. You can tell he's a manager just by looking at him.'

Despite the less than subtle undercover approach, Coverley had got his men. It would be the beginning of an exciting new era for New Mills AFC.

He goes on: 'They came to me and said "we'll do it" but there was only about three players he wanted to keep. I didn't interview him for the job, he interviewed me! He wanted £400 a week playing budget plus £50 for each of them to manage. We were making that (through the clubhouse and gates) and it was comfortable so we did it. And we were having a great time.'

Ray speaks fondly of his former manager and his forthright ways. He's also happy to admit that, while learning on the job as a fledgling Chairman himself, the professionalism of his new management team would help change his own outlook in how the football club should be run.

'I was the Chairman and Barry Land, whose lad played for us, was the Secretary. We'd take the kit on a matchday and I still remember his first game in charge away from home. We rock up, put the kit in the dressing room and head off to the clubhouse. Telly's on, we'll have a pint. I get a phone call and it's Hancock.'

Ray laughs at the memory of his new manager interrupting his pre-match drink to find out where the kit was. 'It's in the bag' would be a reply that didn't wash.

'No,' was the response. 'It doesn't work like that. The kit goes on the peg,' he'd said.

'And he was right!' says Ray, continuing the story. 'I said to Barry "he's right, that's totally amateur."' And with that, Ray and Barry drank up and headed for the dressing room to finish the job.

'Everything he did was professional,' continues Ray. 'From that day on, that was the standard he set. Everything we did had to be spot on and we learned along the way.' The new approach would see a side that had previously struggled become a more formidable force in the tenth tier.

'In his first season,' Ray recollects, a hint of nostalgia in his eyes, 'we finished about eighth in the league and won the Second Division Cup. So in his first season, we'd won a trophy. He said he would! I remember him saying to me "it's like a train ride, Ray," and I'm sat there thinking, "aye, alright then Tony". He told me that he'd win me something that year, the next year he'd win me the league and the year after that, when we're in the Unibond, he'd ask me again what I wanted to do.

'"You'll have to put money at it" was the message,' Ray continues. 'Otherwise I had to get off the train. I never knew what he was on about with that,' he laughs before taking a slurp of tea.

After winning the Cup, they beat an AFC Fylde side - already on an impressive upward trajectory towards the top of the non-league pyramid themselves - to the title the following season. At this point, the playing budget began to creep up. Ray had a decision to make – was he going to stay on the metaphorical train or were there leaves on the line?

'Hands up, we made a mistake. You get a little bit carried away and, I'm the first to admit it, we maybe let it go a bit too far. The next year, we were on for promotion into the Unibond (now the Evo-Stik, from which New Mills were relegated last season). We'd beaten Fylde once who were the only other team going for the title. They were paying a lot more than we were but, by this stage, our wage structure had almost doubled.'

The lure of successive promotions and bigger gate receipts proved an intoxicating mix for the Millers who were on the cusp of promotion into eighth tier football for the first time in their history.

'We've all got ambition, haven't we? I'm loving it! We were favourites everywhere we went. The League had organised it so that we played Fylde on the last day of the season. We only needed a draw…and we got beat.'

AFC Fylde's convincing 5-0 victory in front of more than 1,400 fans saw them lift the title on goal difference. Despite 104 points, a 17-point cushion to third placed Newcastle Town and a club record 21 consecutive league wins, New Mills were the bridesmaids.

'Tony was devastated. He felt we only needed a draw. I blame him a little bit because he didn't pick the right team,' he says, with the mix of manager and chairman that was visible at Congleton coming through. 'He had players on the bench who I felt were better.' There's a pregnant pause as he relives the moment in his mind's eye.

Despite another excellent season the following year, scoring more than 100 goals and picking up 90 points, the Millers were nearly men once more as they struggled to keep pace with runaway champions Newcastle Town. Tony Hancock resigned.

'He did change his mind and come back but it was never the same after that. We had to bring the budget down. He took some notice for a few weeks and then he brought more players in. In the end, we met at a pub one Sunday about the budget. He said, "if that's the budget, I'll have to resign then." I'm still good friends with him but that was that.'

After being inundated with applications for the vacant manager's position, Ray went with former Coventry and Stoke defender Ally Pickering on the recommendation of club legend Carlos Meakin. The heartbeat of Hancock's side, Meakin had scored 150 goals in 200 games from midfield and is described by Ray as the greatest player to ever pull on the New Mills jersey. His voice carried weight.

'Ally wasn't well-liked and had a bit of a bad reputation with clubs,' Ray continues as he remembers his next manager. 'I never saw it myself. Carlos had a word with him and he agreed to do it for nothing for the first season. We'd wanted to lower the budget but ended up keeping it at a similar level. Everyone on the committee had agreed to it and, because we were winning, it was great,' enthuses Ray, before trailing off as he hints at the outcome. It's like listening to someone recount an episode of *Casualty* where the protagonist begins the episode up a ladder; you don't need telling that it's unlikely to end well.

The good times would continue a little longer for the Millers, though. This time, 102 points would be enough to finally seal that long-awaited promotion into the eighth tier of English football in 2011 – a level they would remain at until last season's fateful relegation.

'The killer punch for us at first was the Evo-Stik putting us in the southern section. We had trips down to Stamford and Loughborough. It's not so much the distance from here – it's very similar to the distance going the other way – but Ally couldn't get the lads to travel that distance from the other side of Manchester. In the end, we gave them a bit more money.'

As the after effects of the recession continued to bite, and despite relatively healthy crowds, turnover through the clubhouse was reduced and money was slowly being lost. A respectable ninth in Evo-Stik Division One South following a brief push for the play-offs was a credible return for the Millers who were later transferred sideways into Division One North for the 2012/13 season alongside Goole FC.

'We were doing well but, by this time, Ally was becoming a bit of a loose cannon,' Ray continues. 'He'd go missing! His assistant Jim would take over and make excuses for him. On more than one occasion, we went to games with one sub. Even though we were doing ok, it was unprofessional and I had the committee on my back.

'We went to Carlton in the FA Cup, a couple of qualifying rounds away from the First Round proper, a real money spinner. We'd barely got a bench due to players who didn't want to travel and he'd say "it's quality Ray, not quantity" but I was struggling to defend him by this point. When we lost to them, it cost us a lot of money. Eventually they (the committee) were fed up with him and it was left with me.'

Coach Ray Soule took over and almost led the Millers to another promotion. While Goole would narrowly escape relegation, New Mills enjoyed another champagne season as they finished third, once again scoring more than a century of goals along the way. An extra time defeat to Trafford in front of almost 500 fans would see the Manchester side go on to beat Cammell Laird on penalties in the final to seal promotion despite squeezing into the top six by just a point. The cruelty of the play-offs knows no level.

'Ally had brought Roy in to help him and later accused him of nicking his job which was far from the truth. Roy had been

Assistant at FC United when they started up. We battered Trafford in that first half but they did us in extra time.

'I have to admit we were bleeding money at this point. We built a little bit of debt which we'd thought we might get back if we went up (to the seventh tier). We'd get the likes of FC United, Buxton and Matlock visiting here. All crowds of 500 or so,' he says a little mournfully. 'We could have kept the budget as it was, but that's how it goes.

'What bothers me a little bit is that it's sometimes suggested that this was the decision of me and Sue. It was a committee decision and I take that on board because I'm Chairman. I should have probably done more to keep the reins on it. But you get carried away.'

That play-off defeat in May 2013 would prove to be the peak of the wave. It would be a steep descent back down the other side. As disagreements over the reduced budget continued, the Millers finished 16th in 2013/14 with 46 points from 42 games. Worse was to come the following season with the Millers picking up just 25 points in a fiercely competitive division that would see big hitters Salford City and Darlington 1883 contest a title race captured by the BBC's documentary crew. There would be no celebrity appearances from the Class of '92, however, when Salford did come to town; Rhodri remains the only member of the Giggs family to have graced Church Lane.

This time, Millers fans would see more than a century of goals flood in the opposite end as the tide turned. Finishing just one point above basement side Padiham would prove fateful in the end as a reprieve from relegation would follow.

'The rest is history,' smiles Ray. 'That's how we got to where we were and where we are now!'

Looking back, it appears there's a hint of regret about the reprieve. With the Millers clearly struggling to maintain their weight in the eighth tier, perhaps the lucky escape from relegation hadn't been the blessing it had first appeared?

'It's difficult,' he begins, thoughtfully. 'Hindsight is great but you want to stay as high as you can. I don't think we'd have had the season we had last year, though, had we taken the relegation,' Ray concedes.

With the Millers' ascendancy ending abruptly, bringing with it collapsing gate receipts and clubhouse takings, hard work on the commercial side of the club combined with friends in high places had at least helped keep things moving forwards in their attempts to maintain their footing on the football pyramid.

'We did have a sponsor,' Ray adds. 'Peter Ratcliffe, a local lad, made good. He was born and bred here. First lad from here to make Cambridge University. He married his childhood sweetheart, moved all over the world and eventually became President of Princess Cruises. He bought a house in Los Angeles, then bought another one on the beach,' Ray continues. It's all a very long way from New Mills, literally and metaphorically.

'He kept an eye on us over the internet and saw we were doing ok. He loved it here. He knew me as I went to the same school as I'm also a local lad - maybe not done quite so good! He'd come back to visit his mother and loved the ground and the outlook over the back of the stands.'

Ray tells the story of how this millionaire fan sat in the clubhouse with a cup of tea next to his wife and revealed his desire to move back to the High Peak town after retirement.

'"You'll be coming on your own!" was her response,' laughs Ray. 'He loved being involved and he was giving us a little bit as well, with the company logo on our shirts for a while. It wasn't a coincidence that we were doing well but he made you work for everything you did. He didn't just shell it out but he was very good to us.'

Recalling the tale of how Peter and a group of L.A. golfing friends would take an annual trip around the globe for a spot of recuperation on the fairways, Ray tells of how Peter convinced his melee of millionaires to make the trip to New Mills. Naturally, he called on his friends at the football club to help arrange a traditional English experience.

'Sue organised a game of crown green bowls in a church down the road with soup and sandwiches before they did a tour of New

Mills on a full-size coach. He even knocked on the door of where he used to live and they all traipsed through the house he grew up in. I don't know how much he must have paid them but money was no object to him. "*Faaaantastic!*" he continues, mimicking the American West Coast accent of his guests. The group all bought replica shirts before heading off for golf in Scotland.

Ratcliffe's association with the Millers came to an unspoken end following a period of poor health. 'He wasn't too enthusiastic about the ground move either,' Ray adds, in reference to the long-mooted prospect of redeveloping a new stadium on land at the opposite end of the town. 'He felt we should be here. We spoke about the cost of installing an all-weather pitch but it never went anywhere. I haven't spoken to him for a while.

'It was a lot of money (he invested into the club). It wasn't as much as what people thought. But it was four or five grand a year which covered a lot of the players wages.'

As we fast forward to more recent history, there's a slight grimace at the mention of the pantomime coverage the club have received over the past 12 months or so.

Despite the headlines, one broadsheet piece did at least set the record straight on the club's plight. 'The period was bad because we were getting a lot of bad press. A lot of newspapers wanted to talk to me about being the worst team in England and all of this – I didn't want to as they wanted to put a hilarious slant on it which I wasn't happy with. The guy from The Telegraph rang me and it was a brilliant piece. It didn't glorify us and it didn't make us look stupid.

'On the back of that, we had a lad walk into the club one day. I said to Sue "he looks like Craig Cash" and she said, "he is, he wants a word with you!" So I'm stood there talking to Dave from the Royle Family – he's no different in real life, he's not acting!'

From there, filming was agreed for *Rovers* and Church Lane became the unlikely venue for a Sky One sitcom. Ray attended every day during the week of filming with Sue stepping in for any night time shifts. They only used the exterior of Church Lane, however, opting to film the scenes inside the clubhouse in studios at Salford Quays. The experience provided brief respite from the misery on the field.

'We went up to Spennymoor and one of their guys asked me what my expectations were,' Ray recalls as he recounts their 9-0 defeat – a low point in a season where a creditable draw might be considered an orgasmic high. 'I said we wanted to keep it below double figures. They had a centre forward who was on more than my team and the coach bill up there combined. I'm not making excuses, but that's the reason.'

We're interrupted as the phone in the clubhouse rings. It's High Peak Radio asking for ongoing match updates throughout the afternoon. 'We'll do our best but I always forget,' laughs Ray. 'I'm too busy watching the match!'

As we resume our conversation, the issue of finances and keeping the club afloat returns. Ray characteristically pulls no punches about how difficult it is to maintain a community club in what is a relatively deprived town.

'The recession hit hard here,' he continues. 'The town is dying. Other towns and places of this size have got together, but not round here. The upkeep of the ground is expensive. The astroturf is nearly 20 years old now.'

Ray smiles as he recalls the opening of the adjacent pitch. The firm that installed it had a habit of bringing in a big name to mark the occasion. Step forward former Scotland international striker Brian McClair. It was a real treat for Ray, being a lifelong Manchester United fan.

And so, after an affiliation across five decades with his local side, how does Ray look back on his time? And how do you put a season like last year into context?

'I don't get much time to really. Over the years, it's been brilliant. All those good times. I must admit that it's become a little bit of a task in the last couple of years with the finances. We got stung once but we're now back on a bit of an even keel. None of that's a secret, we've always been transparent and the accounts have always been there for people to abuse us with! That's why

I've stayed around.'

There's a mixture of regret, self-preservation and a rightful pride as he reflects on his achievements. Whatever happens on the pitch, you can be sure Ray Coverley, ably partnered by Sue, will be rolling up his sleeves to keep things going off it.

For Mr New Mills AFC, there's no other way.

5

OPENING DAY

You spend months dreaming about it. Formations. Selections. Strength in depth or a splurge on a super striker? It's an annual dilemma that you'll never truly solve; those opening day decisions that will shape the rest of your season. I plumped for Zlatan up front and Negredo as the bargain buy. Premier League Fantasy squad sorted, team name nailed. By the time you're reading this, Xhaka Khan FC will probably be national fantasy champions.

This year, opening day wasn't quite so co-ordinated for many of the teams up and down the English footballing league. Despite all the marketing, including a superimposed Thierry Henry 'jogging' down a street filmed near to New Mills' Church Lane to promote Sky Sports' ever-lucrative offering, a busy opening Football League weekend had been followed by the First Round of the rebranded EFL Cup.

Further down the ladder in the ninth tier, sides that hadn't required an FA Cup Extra Preliminary replay had unusually begun their league campaigns under the floodlights in midweek. For New Mills, though, having seen their scheduled game against Maine Road FC postponed, today marked their first game in a division that had also undergone a rebranding from being formerly known as the North West Counties Premier. Welcome back to the Hallmark Security League.

Bouncing back from the Congleton defeat would be tough. In

just 90 minutes, I'd witnessed so much of the early optimism drain away from a side that looked low on confidence, short of ideas and scared of making mistakes. A postponement of what would've been their second away game in three days at Maine Road looked like it might be a blessing in disguise and now, on a warm August weekend, they'd be back in competitive action at Church Lane for the first time since April's 2-0 defeat to Kendal Town.

There was a slightly downbeat atmosphere around a blustery Church Lane on arrival. While understandably lower on numbers than the Stockport friendly, with Cammell Laird 1907 FC bringing fewer supporters across from Birkenhead, the home fans, too, seemed sparse. With half an hour to kick-off, the season was already feeling somewhat drained of optimism.

As I watch the players warm up, observe manager Garry pacing across the field and spot photographer James readying his camera for the afternoon's action, it becomes clear Church Lane is missing another vital ingredient today; there's no sign of Sue.

'She's gone home ill,' Committee member Roy tells me, donning a fluorescent yellow jacket. 'We've been let down again for volunteers. She's been here since half past eight getting everything sorted. It's a wonder she managed to stay as long as she did.'

There's a frustration in his voice. This is the first of at least 21 home games this season. If you're short of volunteers in midsummer, what happens in January?

'There are ten of us on the Committee but who is here? The same old faces,' he continues. 'You wouldn't believe what needs doing behind the scenes. We've printed the programmes off this morning because the copy was late. It all needs doing on a Friday.'

Sue's absence is more than noticeable. Her laugh and constant buzz is missing. It only adds to the downbeat feeling around the place. One constant source of enthusiasm, though, is Garry.

'More of a help as it allows players to come in and injuries to recover,' is his assessment on the midweek postponement. 'It's like a full-time job at the minute on top of a full-time job. We've brought a couple of new players in as well, including one lad from the Development Squad,' he says, gesturing towards eighteen players warming up with various levels of enthusiasm on the field before us. I'd already noticed David Lewis, the diminutive winger-cum-striker, who'd looked impressive during my first visit to meet Ray and Sue.

'We'll bring 'em through and see how they do because that's all we can do,' says Garry pragmatically. 'We can't afford to bring them in. We've forged good links with FC United of Manchester though now so I'm gonna bring a right back in as well. Until the season is in motion though, you can't get going, because they need to understand who they want. I've got a few players who are at work today and can't make it which is why I've said to the lads not to be disheartened if they get left out because we need a big squad. It's gonna turn again and your chance will come. That's the nature of it though. We've just got to let the ball do the work because we've got the pace and the skill.'

As we stand behind the goal, a ball whistles by our heads as the players warm up.

'HEY! Enough!' shouts Garry, his warm persona momentarily melting away to reveal his authority behind the dressing room door. 'I thought we'd be safe stood near the top corner,' jokes one fan beside me.

Ryan Hopper leads the side out again and barks orders at his side to be vocal. It's clearly been recognised as one of the weaknesses against Congleton from a young side still looking to gel and is perhaps still a little short on experience and leaders.

'I wanna hear you out there! Nice and fuckin' loud. It starts here, eh? Come on! I want it all over the pitch. Don't let up!' he shouts, clapping his hands with each instruction. They look focussed and ready for battle as they march onto the pitch.

'Don't be getting any shit ones of me!' instructs Hopper to James who's already started taking photos.

'For once, mate,' adds goalkeeper Ollie Martin, wearing a fluorescent pink top that's visible from space, 'I don't want one!' It's not his usual attire and Fixture Secretary Derek lays the blame of the late kit change at the feet of the visitors.

'We're required to notify the opposition of shirt colours before the game,' he says, somewhat annoyed. I'm beginning to pick up it's something of a default characteristic. 'So we sent them our colours earlier this week. What do they do? Turn up with the same colour goalkeeper jersey!'

The atmosphere behind the goal is positive at kick-off. Warm and encouraging advice such as 'start well, lads' and 'get on top of 'em early boys' is the general chorus. It seems to have the desired effect.

The Millers are unrecognisable from the side that started against Congleton. They control the ball, keep it on the floor, pass and hold possession and look threatening going forward. Whatever happened between them reaching the dressing room last Saturday and kick-off this afternoon appears to have worked.

Until the 9th minute, that is.

Cammell Laird's first attack of the game results in the opening goal. To compound matters, it's an own goal.

'Ever get a feeling of deja-vu?' asks one fan of his mate beside me.

'We've been the best bleedin' side!' is his exasperated response.

Undeterred, the team go again. It's still positive and they still look the better side but the goal has deflated some of the goodwill in the stands already. Every little mistake draws the ire of the fans beside me. 15 minutes into the new season and the fans are already on their backs as each missed pass is bemoaned. It's not just the very top of the football pyramid where the pressure is unrelenting.

'Look at that!' screams one, as a rare attempt at a long ball over the top is cut out with ease. 'There's no building from the back! Just kick the fucker and hope for the best!'

I stand silent, wanting to chip in but knowing it's not my place. The performance is better than last week. There are a few positives. But then I didn't watch my side fail to win a game last season. After three months off from defeat after unrelenting defeat, it's hard to argue with the muscle memory of having a good moan if it doesn't feel like things have improved.

On 19 minutes, things get worse. Alex Martin fires the visitors into a two-goal lead with a superb solo run before opening his body and curling the ball into the far corner from the edge of the box. It's a touch of class that again comes against the run of play. A dumbfounded silence falls over Church Lane. What I'd give to hear Sue's laugh right now. There's not much to even smile about.

I glance over towards the bench where Garry stands, mouth agape. There's no shouting from the touchline or remonstrating with his players. From where I'm stood, they seem to be executing his game plan and have looked so much better than last weekend despite the scoreline. And yet still, the better side are two goals down. Welcome to a new season at Church Lane.

'The defence is non-existent!' is the silence breaker beside me as the mumbles of discontent begin again around the ground. It's a harsh assessment given the individual brilliance of what we've just witnessed from the opposition.

Haydn Foulds looks to be the home team's best chance at a way back into the game as he leads the line upfront and almost grabs a goal minutes later. Running with purpose into the box, he has the option to shoot, square the ball and even change his mind and shoot again before the goalkeeper dives at his feet to collect the ball. It's a golden opportunity that further frustrates everyone around me.

Undeterred, he steps up to take a 25-yard free-kick from just outside the box in the 21st minute. He sets his sights, curls it round the wall and into the top corner of the goal. It might have been helped on by the breeze gusting in the Millers' favour but it's 2-1, and the beginning of an unforgettable afternoon for him.

'Goal of the season in the first game!' is one summary.

'Woah! What a goal! I almost ducked then! Told you we were safe stood behind the top corner!' laugh the three Millers amigos beside me. Three minutes later, they're cheering again, as Foulds latches onto a ball over the top and slots it into the bottom corner beyond the advancing 'keeper to level matters. After fluffing his lines with all the time in the world earlier, he shows a more clinical side this time around.

'Bloody hell! We never score two! Never mind two in three minutes by the same player!' Those early season doubts are but a memory now. Church Lane hasn't bounced like this in a while.

More chances come their way without success before the half-time butties are served but the resilience and domination are the main topics of conversation in the portacabin after the players receive warm applause at the break for their response since falling two behind. Sue's dad pours the tea and offers out the sandwiches. When I suggest that I pour my own and he should take a seat, he announces that he's here to serve me. Sue's hospitality is extended through her father even in her absence.

'We should be winning really, shouldn't we?' is Chairman Ray's summary while halfway through an egg and cress on white sliced – no prawn sandwiches here. 'Shouldn't have conceded though. We scored two good goals, mind. I was shouting that he'd missed that one from a yard out so how did he expect to score one from thirty?' laughs Ray, recalling his own distinctive brand of motivation as Foulds had stepped up for the set piece. I'm beginning to tune into its rhythm in the same way the players hopefully have.

'Aston Villa are actually winning a game!' announces James as he catches up with the half-time scores. It really is a day for turn-ups to the form guide.

Joining us through half-time is the referee's assessor. A friendly man in his 50s, he offers observations on the game including the performance of Lewis on the left wing. It's been a lively debut against a right-back identified by all who witnessed his first half as a weak link in the Lairds side.

As the players emerge for the second half, he peers out at the blustery conditions and then down at his mug of tea.

'I wonder if I can assess the second half from in here?' he wonders aloud. The great British summer really is in full swing.

As well as tea bags, there's tension brewing. Committee member Roy has barely stopped for breath since I arrived and is counting cash in the adjoining office space. His grumbles suggest this is Fixture Secretary Derek's duty and he makes his feelings known as he comes out. Where is Sue's gentle arbitration when you need it?

'Have you got your coat?' enquires Roy as the second half kicks off.

'What coat is that?' asks Derek in reply.

'The one from the League. They were supposed to be arriving today.'

'I didn't know there was a coat. Where did you order that from?' enquires an increasingly intrigued Derek.

'Sue text me to ask me if I wanted one. They're forty quid,' replies Roy, with the tone of a favourite child cavorting a new toy in front of a jealous sibling.

'She didn't text me,' says a poker-faced Derek. I fix my stare on the game as the awkwardness ramps up a notch.

'We can't wear our Evo-Stik ones, you see. Sue says it looks like we think we're big time Charlies,' continues Roy.

'I think it says 'we wear what we've got because we can't afford anything else" counters Derek. I zip up my own jacket and pass comment on the weather. On the pitch, the Millers almost take the lead as they begin the second half much like the first.

'Need to be putting those away,' shouts Roy. 'Get him off!'

True to form, missing that gilt-edged chance is compounded by conceding against the run of play three minutes later. Roy is incredulous as the Laird lads celebrate in front of us. Derek stands agog. It's just as well he doesn't have his Evo-Stik coat on at the minute. At 3-2 down, New Mills look anything but big time Charlies. Somehow, the Millers have conspired to fall behind again.

Yet again, they come back. Minutes later, Will Wareing hits a shot from 20 yards that finds a deflection in a crowded box and sends the 'keeper the wrong way. The sides are level again but there's no time to dwell as Garry and his Assistant Paul "Willo" Williams scream from the sidelines to get back and into position.

What happens next will surely be talked about at Church Lane for years to come. In the 56th minute, the game's seventh goal arrives, via the boot of Haydn Foulds. The number 9 wheels away to be mobbed by the entire team in a mass pile-on that matches the explosion of relief, exasperation and general hysteria from the assembled fans. New Mills are actually winning a game, and the moment is captured by James in an image that would eventually grace the cover of this book.

As the mob withdraw and return to their positions, everyone attempts to compose themselves and calm down. Hat-trick hero Foulds retreats to the sidelines for treatment – somehow, in the melee, he appears to have picked up an injury.

'Took us all season to score three goals and now we've got three from one player,' says Sue's dad as he appears from the portacabin.

'Get back in there you,' says Roy, only half-joking. 'Every time you say summat, something goes wrong!'

Haydn Foulds rejoins the game after several minutes spent being patched up. A clash of heads following a teammate's over enthusiastic leap onto his shoulders has led to a half-inch wide and two-inch long gash on his forehead that probably requires stitches. It seems that a scar might accompany the memory of what could become one of the most memorable afternoons of his career.

The game is far from won, though, as the see-saw nature of the opening hour has demonstrated. New Mills have more than half an hour to go and produce a performance of grit and determination. It's not easy, as Lairds push forward and look threatening. At the other end, a couple of half-chances exasperate Willo on the touchline as the Millers fail to put the game out of sight.

On 85 minutes, Garry Brown leaves the dugout. Walking down the touchline, he heads in our direction. The stress and worry is etched over his face as he forces a smile on approaching us.

'You need a strong heart for this, don't you?' he asks, as he lingers for a moment.

'Congratulations,' says Sue's dad. 'I think you've done it today!' Garry and I look at each other and burst into nervous laughter. Thankfully Roy isn't in earshot at this fairly gigantic temptation of fate. There's at least eight minutes to go, the manager is so nervous he can't maintain his position in the dugout and he's being congratulated for a game that hasn't finished yet. I begin to chew my own nails on his behalf.

He continues pacing, up and down behind the goal, amongst the fans and back down the touchline. The pressure on this result is clear. A new season, maybe, but the chance to shake the monkey from their backs on the opening day is clearly massive. Willo holds fort on the bench and shouts instructions to help keep focus and shape.

The sound of the referee's final whistle is greeted with the biggest roar Church Lane has heard for a while. As the lads congratulate each other, Chairman Ray shakes his manager's hand and congratulates him. It's a lovely moment between two men who've had to trust each other and have finally got their reward.

Another chap with a southern accent approaches Garry to congratulate him, telling him he's travelled up from Essex on a groundhopping mission with his wife to watch the game. There's every chance the Millers might cover his travel expenses next time given the lucky omen he's proved to be.

The players receive a warm reception as they head back in. Garry disappears in the direction of the car park. On his return, he's holding a tabletop speaker and a microphone. He heads straight for the dressing room and closes the door behind him. It won't soundproof the celebrations that take place.

'ALTOGETHER NOW! ALTOGETHER NOW! ALTOGETHER NOW! IN NO MAN'S LAND! TOGETHER!'

The words of The Farm's 1990 classic are screamed with force by the manager as the soundwaves emanate through the walls to the delight of everyone outside. Inside, a mixture of players join in the impromptu anthem from the gaffer while others laugh uncontrollably at the passionate rendition of a song older than half of the dressing room. This uncensored and unrestrained release from the manager seems to hit just the right note - even if Garry's singing might not.

I linger outside for a while, as do more than a few fans seemingly unhurried in pursuing their endeavours for the evening. Everyone is soaking up that unfamiliar winning feeling. Haydn Foulds is one of the first to emerge from the dressing room with a large blue plaster on his forehead and he tries to make a quick getaway.

'Get back here,' shouts Garry, hot on his heels and gesturing towards James' camera. 'You're Man of the Match!'

'Come on then. Let's make it quick,' he replies.

'He needs stitches in that,' says James as he walks away. 'He says he's not going though 'cos he's got work tomorrow.'

I get chatting to a tanned chap in his 40s smoking a cigarette and we sit overlooking the houses high on hills behind the far goal of the emptying Church Lane. It turns out he was more invested in the win than most – his son, Ollie Martin, was in goal.

'Good game, wasn't it?' he says. 'I think he'll be disappointed with that one on his near post. He'll get sharper after a few games and he'll be back in it again. The first two goals, he didn't have a chance but he will be disappointed with that one. He did well enough though, but I know what his standards are,' he says, every inch the supportive dad. 'I'm not gonna say nowt to him.

'Seven goals, a low admission price and a really entertaining game – why go anywhere else?' he continues. 'I look at all my mates going to City and United and tell 'em they don't know what they're missing out on. Sitting here, having a beer and a cig...' he says before tailing off as Ollie emerges with club captain Ryan Hopper.

'GET IN!' says Hopper, greeting us. 'Nice feeling! I've missed it! Quality!' he says, in broad Mancunian tones.

'Well done, Oll,' says his dad, greeting the big goalkeeper. 'Deserved that mate. Takes the pressure off now for the next five or six games as well, especially if you can get a couple of wins and a few points under your belt. Was it an own goal the first one?' he says, before leaving a big pause. Despite his pledge to remain tight lipped, I can feel the words emerging from his mouth before he's even said them. 'And I know you got beat on the near post for this one here…'

I head for the gates, not wanting to intrude on a nice moment between father and son.

'You need to come every week,' says Ollie as I depart. As I reach the turnstiles, a pale and unwell looking Sue arrives. Unwilling to get too close to me for a hug in case she passes on the lurgy, she's been glued to social media all afternoon.

'It is a rollercoaster watching New Mills,' she laughs. 'I had to turn it off in the end as I couldn't bear it! And that was on Twitter! Imagine if I'd actually been here!'

Having missed the beginning of Radio 5 Live's Sports Report, it takes most of my journey home to catch up on the afternoon's results. New Mills, it seems, aren't the only side recently mocked and derided who have gone on to grab all three points this afternoon. Aston Villa have also registered a win in their new surroundings of the Championship. Maybe 2016/17 is all change after all?

The Millers mob goalscoring hero Haydn Foulds - injuring him in the process!

6

MANAGING EXPECTATIONS

I've never had reason to visit Droylsden before; it's not generally known for its tourist traffic. Situated in the Metropolitan borough of Tameside in Greater Manchester, it's the home of the first machine woven towel in the world – the terry towel – produced in 1851. It's the hometown of 2008 X Factor finalist and former Pontins Bluecoat Scott Bruton, eliminated in week three after his performance of That's Life left mentor Simon Cowell with no choice but to send him home. Thanks Wikipedia.

It's also the home of Droylsden Academy, a building so modern it looks positively space age in its humble surroundings. As I pull up in the car park at half past five on a warm August Thursday afternoon, Garry Brown is pulling a large sports bag from the boot of his 4x4 with Assistant Paul 'Willo' Williams offering a helping hand. Dressed in a smart navy blue suit minus the jacket, he's clearly just knocking off from the day shift and is about to start the evening one. Willo has found time to slip into his New Mills tracksuit. They give me a friendly wave as they finish unloading the car before heading into the cavernous empty sports hall that will be the meeting place for the First Team's weekly training session in just under an hour.

Garry couldn't have been more welcoming to me since we first met; having said that, I still feel a little nervous sitting down with him armed with a page of questions covering the previous season. With the adrenalin of Saturday still pumping, and perhaps combined with taking some encouragement of a narrow defeat against a much-fancied 1874 Northwich that followed in midweek in their second league fixture of the new campaign, it feels cruel to reopen the gaping wound that was the Millers' 2015/16 season. As I fumble around with audio recorders, he and Willo sit patiently.

To begin, we start with how Garry became the manager of New Mills. As a youngster, he was part of Oldham Athletic's youth system. With no Apprenticeship available, Garry would continue his football career abroad.

'I joined the Royal Air Force where I spent four and a half years in Cyprus and played for RAF Cyprus,' he begins. 'All my background was in the Forces which was great training. I learnt a lot off Joe Royle and Willie Donachie at Oldham Athletic but your likes of Joe Jordan who was managing Bristol Rovers at the time used to come to Cyprus for their summer training and we'd get trained by him as well. So it was just picking up a little bit of their skills and their approach.'

After several years of picking up wisdom from some of the top names in English football, injury would sadly end any hope of Garry's playing career at a young age.

'I ruptured my cruciate ligaments playing for the RAF,' he continues, 'so that was when I decided to take badges and get into coaching. I came back and it was a new life for me outside of the Forces, moving to an area where there was no football at all, nothing for the kids to do. So we set up a grassroots football club at Moorside in Oldham that's still going now. From there, I spent a bit of time at Boundary Park, I've done a bit with Bolton Wanderers and then Evo-Stik level with Paul,' he says, referring to his long-time friend and colleague beside him.

'We've got a bit of a reputation of being at clubs when the going gets tough. Rossendale United didn't have any budget. The budget was cut, to the point where we were going until the water was cut off. And when the water was cut off, the lights went out,' he says, as Willo laughs at the memory. 'We turned up one night, you can't have showers and so the match has to be abandoned.

The bills weren't being paid or anything. So we've been there!' he laughs, remembering times that make a winless streak at a comparatively well-run football club pale by comparison.

By virtue of there only being so many jobs in one area, the clash of loyalties that might come with representing rival clubs is less intense at this level. Garry and Willo arrived having previously managed the Millers' fierce adversaries Glossop North End. To make things worse, Glossop have undergone something of a rise into the Evo-Stik League recently and narrowly missed out on a further promotion last season – by contrast, New Mills were enduring one of the worst seasons on record. Garry's words add a little more heat to the two sides' healthy rivalry.

He says: 'We had a successful spell at Glossop. I think they finished second in the first season, we put plans in place to get them into the Evo-Stik but unfortunately they didn't think we could get the calibre of players in. The players that they did get in I'd been in touch with already,' he adds pointedly, 'but there's no sour grapes there, we left on good terms. We do it for no payment whatsoever so…fine!' he laughs. 'I'll shake your hand and go.'

From there, it was a drop a little further down the ladder into the Manchester Leagues to take on Wythenshawe. As was becoming their trademark, it was another club in peril that would eventually go on to experience a record-breaking spell under the leadership of Garry and Willo. Seeds of promise, perhaps, for a brighter future at Church Lane?

'One of the ex-players had taken over at Wythenshawe who hadn't won a game all season,' Garry continues. 'I think they'd drew one and lost the rest which is a worse record than what we came into here! So we weren't the worst team in Great Britain,' he says, his voice trailing off slightly as he says it. It's a label that clearly still rankles.

'I'd hung my managerial boots up then (after Glossop) and said "that's me done. I've given a lot to football." But Paul enticed me back and convinced me to come down. So we went down, brought new players in, had a spell where we didn't even draw a game, we just won every game. We've had the highs of being 'The Incredibles' in The Sun newspaper and The Mirror. Okay, it was in the lower leagues, but still.

'We were told they had the ambition to get to North West Counties League but we couldn't see that happening. The infrastructure wasn't there. When you're doing it for nothing, you have to see progression. If you've given the progression on the pitch, there has to be something to back it up to say they're doing their bit. And they still haven't put the floodlights up even now!' says Garry turning to Willo who laughs and shakes his head in agreement.

That spell brought national attention – for the right reasons – including at Church Lane, where the Millers were looking to recover from a difficult 2014/15 season in which they'd narrowly avoided relegation via a reprieve.

'Then we heard New Mills were looking and had advertised. They hadn't just had a poor run last year, they've had a poor run for the last few seasons. They did have a major backer but they pulled out and, with football at grassroots, there's no money. It's all up at the top as you know. If they just gave a percentage of what they earn we'd be in a much better place. But I put my name in the hat. I didn't get the job and they went through another three managers.'

This new information adds extra context to their appointment. While New Mills toiled and went through one manager after another, Willo and Garry were flying high in the Manchester League.

'They gave it to Keith Briggs who did a pre-season with 'em,' continues Garry. 'But he was offered an Academy job at Sheffield United which he took. Then they offered the job to his Assistant, Fearney, a nice lad but you need local knowledge and local players. They were in a position where they were losing heavily every week and the lad's done the best he can but he lives in Tamworth so he's managing a team but not able to bring additional quality in. Shaun Goater arrived but he didn't stay long. I think he was going through his coaching badges and using it to help with that.

'I got the bat signal then to ask if I could come and help 'em out. So we went watching against Ashton United and we knew then. We said to Ray "we're not miracle workers here, if you finish second bottom, third bottom, you're lucky but we'll come in and we'll do the best we can,"' he recalls, before Willo chips in.

'I did the opposite then because I dropped out of football and he dragged me back in!' he says with his familiar warm laugh.

As we chat, captain Ryan Hopper is the first to arrive for training.

'Alright Gaffer,' he says as he sits on a neighbouring table and sorts loose change. 'I'm not interrupting am I?' he asks as he picks up on his manager's candid tone about his side's shortcomings. Garry's happy for him to listen in.

He continues: 'They'd already lost 16 games when we came in and were losing them heavily. Players were just on expenses. When the local media asked, we'd say "yeah, we'll finish midtable" but behind the scenes we were saying it was a tough task and if we finish third from bottom here, we've done well. We didn't expect not to win a game but that's the difference in the leagues.

'The first thing I did, and Hopper'll back me up on this, is that I told everyone that I didn't care what they'd been on. You're all on twenty quid a week now. I lost a few players through that, but that allowed me to see who had the guts to continue and that was our base to start from.

'The players we'd used at lower levels, we'd built their trust so they came and we see that as a good thing to do really because they get to play at a higher level. They couldn't get up to speed quick enough, fitness wise, and couldn't cope with the mental stress when you have to perform week in, week out – or when you're losing week in, week out.'

That difficulty in finding the quality of player on a shoestring who had the mental strength to come into a side losing every week was Garry and Willo's biggest challenge – and a big reason for massive player attrition as the season went on.

'We just took a week at a time,' he says. 'We got the margin of losses down. We got spanked at Spennymoor but they were on three hundred quid a man full-time. We're on three hundred quid for everybody! And on a Tuesday night, they only get paid once a week, and because of the backlog of games we were playing three times a week. We were travelling to Spennymoor, which is Middlesbrough, and we're taking 16-year-olds with us just to get us through.'

The Spennymoor result Garry refers to was the particularly devastating 9-0 defeat they received when relegation was already all but confirmed. With negative national press becoming all too regular, a revolving door of players coming in and out and the margin of defeats occasionally creeping up to embarrassing, it had felt like the very future of the football club could be in jeopardy.

'My own mindset, and I don't know if it's true or not, was that if we didn't fulfil a fixture then we would struggle with the fines,' confesses Garry. 'As soon as you cancel a fixture, you're paying for their expenses, the other side's expenses. So it was just about getting a squad out, getting through the fixtures and through the season. Harrogate Railway Athletic got relegated and they were on £800 a week budget and we're on nothing. We managed to fulfil the fixtures every single week,' he says with a frisson of pride.

Willo adds: 'The difference as well is that a lot of sides were tapping into the league clubs and bringing young pros in. Virtually every side we came up against had four or five players who came from that level whereas we couldn't even pay expenses, like fifty quid. We just didn't have it and that was the biggest problem we had. So we begged, borrowed and stole players to get through.'

Garry continues: 'Those are the positives. There's always a negative. It took a lot out of me. The BBC…' he says, stumbling slightly over his words as he composes himself while going back over the memories of that period. 'I've blocked them on my phone because they were still trying to ring. I'll never speak to them again. I thought it was cheap journalism. They don't understand what we're trying to do, and for *nothing*! And to benchmark us against Mourinho? And the worst team in Britain? How can you be the worst team in Britain when you're in the seventh or eighth tier? It was just cheap. That was gut-wrenching and it was hard to pick the lads up again. If they'd have got on the other side of us, maybe it'd have improved things.

'But we've gained a lot of friends,' he goes on, brightening a little. As always with Garry, it comes naturally to focus on the positive. 'We've earned respect, especially within the Evo-Stik leagues, because we didn't go out to kick people. We went out to play football in the right way. We adopted the football approach and allowed players to come in, make their mistakes and develop, because at that level, if you make mistakes then you were out. We were telling players to come in and make their mistakes and we'll develop them and they're better players for it.'

It's a remarkably positive outlook from a proud man who took on an impossible job and is clearly beginning to feel like it's now slowly turning around.

He adds: 'The inevitable happened (relegation from the Evo-Stik League) and it allowed us then to take stock. I think it was a good thing. They got a reprieve the year before, maybe they should've taken the relegation then and bit the bullet but that's all hindsight. It gave us chance to regroup, plan a pre-season and get the right structure in place.

'I'm a great believer in using science to develop players. It's alright saying "I've seen this, you need to x, y and z" but I invested in some GPS trackers which the players wear in vests. It gives them heat maps so you can see if you're a left-sided player on the right side, there's obviously something going wrong. It tells us how many impact runs they've done, how many kilometres they've run in a game and it's just to feedback to them – "you're doing well, you're a central midfielder but you're over to the left more."'

I can't be certain, but heat maps and impact runs at the ninth tier feels revolutionary. And, on a shoestring budget, Garry has bought the kit from his own back pocket to ensure his players get the best possible chance to fulfil their potential. And there's more.

'We've brought a Data Analyst into the club in Dan. He brings individual data analysis as well as team analysis on pass completion, possession, shots on target, shots off target. So again, we're giving the players the tools to improve themselves. It really has paid dividends, I feel, because now we have a team here with a winning mentality. We're going into every game saying "we're gonna win this" and we went from devastation to ecstasy on Saturday because within 10 minutes we go two down. We were the better team and we were absolutely peppering them. You have to get some leadership over onto the pitch.

'I've done all that. I've done my Stuart Pearce impersonations on the sidelines last year,' he jokes, referring to his own blood vessel busting style at times. 'I'm not doing that this year.

'The lads battled, though,' he continues. 'They showed leadership qualities on the pitch. Two-all at half-time. Went in at half-time, used the science, used the data and just said "keep doing what you're doing, let's just keep the possession, keep position" and it paid off. So then Tuesday came, we're in top spirits. Northwich 1874 have spent a lot of money close season bringing players in from the Evo-Stik while we're still growing players from Academies.

'They're tipped for winning the league or being up there and we matched them all over the park. They've had two opportunities from our mistakes gifting them a ball into the box, the other is a set piece. One of 'em has come off a ricochet from a defender, he's cleared and it's hit him…' says Garry, hesitating for a second, as he ponders whether to give me the full details.

'It hit him in the nuts!' chips in Ryan Hopper, chuckling like a schoolboy. 'But we matched 'em,' he adds, backing up his Gaffer's claims.

'We matched 'em,' continues Garry, 'and we should have had a penalty at the end. Deven has run into the box, we're going for it, he's about to strike it and he just gets taken out. Everybody in the ground, even their bench, said it was a penalty. So that was a bitter pill to swallow, but we take the positives.'

As always, for Garry, it comes back to the positives. It's hard not to feel motivated when surrounded by his optimistic approach.

'For however long I'm at the club for, the club is in a better place for us being here,' he adds. It's slightly out of the blue given the direction of the conversation and I can't help but read into it as he continues.

'It's difficult with a full-time job and a family while you're developing players. I get more out of developing players and seeing them aspire to better things. We've seen Jake Williams go to FC United and get first team football. Even just to get a text off 'em, which I do, saying "Thank for everything you've done, Gaz", that's what I do it for.

'We've brought in a new Development Squad, new Development management and they're playing tonight. We're also utilising their players into the First Team. They were struggling for players and bringing lads out of the 16s and 18s and you're leaving them short.

'I've bridged gaps with the Junior team now and I've said I'll hold a training session as long as they do the ball boys. So that's there now. However long we're here, we've done good for the club and we've given it stability to go again when they're ready to go. Last year we brought in 65 players just to get us through and this year we've gone through 40 players to get 25. On the ones going back out the door, it's a mixture of everything. One is the quality, they've had their opportunity and it hasn't worked out. Another one is we've found the rough diamonds from the lower leagues.'

Garry's model of bringing in so-called rough diamonds to polish has its flaws, though, as he's more than happy to admit.

'A great example is a lad we brought in, he was a winger. We've moulded him into a striker. He went to a team, scored two goals against Witton. After the game, they offer him £120 to go and play for them. That's exactly what we're up against all the time. It's happened again this year with people taking them, but what I do demand is commitment. Don't come in thinking you're gonna get an easy game at New Mills anymore because you're not. We expect 'em to run 10k in a midfield or forward position. You get away with 8k in defence, 6 or 7k in the centre of defence. Expectations are there, so if you're not at that level then you need to get to that level quickly because we're not here to make the numbers up anymore. There's a great expectation here now and it's healthy.'

Garry is fired up now and talking passionately about his side. There'll be no more easy pickings at Church Lane.

'Everyone knows what they have to do,' adds Ryan Hopper, now engrossed in the discussion.

'We've got bungees here and belts,' continues Garry, on a roll now. 'They'll be wearing those tonight to keep the shape, moving together while playing football. I mean Ryan, he's played for Accrington, he's played at Football League level. And the League levels, the Academies, it's a completely different level. You get more time in those leagues, but you get punished for your mistakes. We knew that from our experience, so we were having to coach Ryan in the right way and…we had to drop ya. Didn't we?'

'Yeah,' nods Ryan, somewhat sheepishly. He's possibly wishing he'd continued quietly counting the loose change on the table before him now, or at least missed the bus for training.

'He wasn't happy about it but we wouldn't expect him to be,' says Garry, retaining his fatherly tone as he looks at his captain. 'We just needed to bring him to one side and say "we need this, we need that. We need you to do this, we need you to do that," and now he's ten times the player. And hopefully that will stand him in good stead to go again because we won't stand in anyone's way. But we didn't see it at its worst. It was sticking plasters at first but we've made it better.' It's a point Hopper is keen to jump in on.

Ryan adds: 'The difference between this year and last year is massive. If you'd have watched that game (the opening league match against Cammell Laird) with the side we had last season, we'd have been all over the place. Me and Gaz always say the light was flickering and now it's going and shining bright again. To go behind three times in a game, when you shouldn't really be going behind, to come back and win is some character. Last year, if we'd have conceded three it'd have been heads down. Now we're saying "hang on a minute, we shouldn't be losing this game of football. Get your head up, keep doing what we're doing" and it could've been seven.

'Even for lads like meself, they make you better players. I'm still learning, we're all still learning and they're giving us advice to say, "do this and they can't get near ya" and I'm thinking "yeah, I need to do that because I'm struggling here". Speaking for myself, I was taking too long on the ball, turning, and Gaz and Willo were saying I needed to move it quicker and they won't be able to get near ya.'

Garry chips back in now.

'What it is with Ryan's game, you need him to look at the space to get into rather than getting hold of the ball and keeping it on the blind side. There's a space, move the ball into the space and then play. To be honest, we could have had five against the league favourites on Tuesday night. But that's what I always do in the dressing room. What did we do well, what can we improve on? It's always positive. It's been tough.'

Garry's passion for the game and his willingness to learn from his YTS days through to the RAF and beyond combined with his positive and relatable approach to man management are his most obvious strengths. Even now, after more than a quarter of a century in football, he's still a student of the game, as he recalls how he and ex-Pro Paul Williams came to form a partnership.

'When I was coaching at Oldham I used to go and see Pro License coaches and always take a pad and a pen in case there were things I could take back to Boundary Park,' says Garry. 'And then I just got a call asking if I fancied coming and coaching up here with Willo at Rossendale…not realising they were just about to cut the water off! We became good friends and we're still together. Everything happens for a reason,' he says, of what is clearly a close working relationship based on mutual respect that also borders on a bit of a bromance.

Football isn't Garry's only consideration, of course. A career managing in the lower reaches of non-league football doesn't pay the bills. Judging by his suit and car, though, it's not just the dugout where he's experienced success. Juggling the day job with the night one is far from easy.

'It was tough last year. It's even tougher this year. I work for Warburton's which is a major blue-chip company. I'm a Utensils Manager which basically means we've got ten bakeries, thirteen depots and we deliver close to thirteen million products a week in 1.3 million baskets. I'm in charge of those baskets,' he says. Suddenly, managing New Mills doesn't sound quite so difficult.

'From Aberdeen down to Basingstoke and plants in Glasgow down to London, I have to make sure those plants keep running. When it's weather like this and you're on buns, a pallet only holds half as many buns so you need twice as many baskets. It can be stressful at times. It's like today, I've got up at half past six and I've not been home yet. There are people who work hard at the club. Sue and Ray are trojans. And on top of that you've got a family to fit in, a daughter going to university, so it can be stretching. At times you wonder how long you can carry it on for because, you know, work pays my mortgage.

'At the end of the day, if I'm being totally honest, this is a hobby,' he confesses. 'I don't know what it is but I've always wanted to do well by people because I've always had that done to me. I've always felt I can improve players and when you're playing in stadia in front of a good crowd, it's a good buzz. I had that in the Forces, obviously Willo's had that. But Willo's history, the lad's played at every single level,' he adds, with respect to his colleague's 300+ Football League appearances that included a handful in the early days of the Premier League.

Garry's passion for football isn't just about the addiction to that winning feeling, however. His passion is player rehabilitation. It's something he believes there's a big market for as the millionaire conveyor belt discards tonnes of fresh meat each season.

He continues: 'I think there's a market out there, I really do, because there's a lot of broken players who've been let down. Who've probably been at Academies for many years and I do feel the Academies are like a conveyor belt. They're all treated the same and they either fall off the end or start the same process for another year and I think football needs to be individualised. You can do the same training as the team but you need to tap into what that individual requires, what are his skills and weaknesses. If you can tap into that, you can fulfil their dreams still. That's what drives me, not managing football. Managing football is…is…' he says, tailing off.

'Hard work!' chips in Willo.

'It's hard at grassroots level for no financial reward whatsoever,' continues Garry. 'It's a lot of time away from your family, it's a lot of effort, you make decisions and you stand by your decisions. You take the flak and people don't realise how hard you're working for it. The media…' he adds, again tailing off when he ventures near the memory of those hurtful headlines. 'That took a lot to get through. But when you look at Sue and Ray and how much they put in. They were my inspiration for getting them through last year.

'Whoever my long-term successor may be,' continues Garry, again voluntarily beginning to ponder on his own future, 'I hope they take a grasp of what we've done and build on it because I'm not in it long-term for the managing. But I believe in it, I don't do anything I don't believe in, and I believe we've put a structure and a philosophy into this club. No matter how long it lasts, we've done good and we can walk away with our heads held high.'

It feels odd listening to Garry talk about the future in this way. I ask about the pressure of results versus the transient nature of both players and managers at this level – not least because, by his own admission, he's effectively a volunteer.

'I'm under no pressure in terms of people taking my role,' he says with confidence. 'I've said to Sue and Ray, if you think anyone can do a better job then please get them in because I'm not here for any other reason than the club. I'm just trying to help good people and I have, so whether that's a week, a month or a year then I've done my bit.

'It's like at Wythenshawe. We've built winning teams wherever we've been. It's the philosophy you set, it has to be hard graft. We train hard and we play like we train. When he asked me to dust my boots off and join him there,' he says, referring to Willo, 'I went watching them with him from the sidelines and it was absolutely terrible. At that level though, half of it is fitness. We had games where we were losing 2-1 and ended up winning 3-2 because we knew we could keep running. I think that's the difference now (at New Mills) because they've got it in the tank. It's the pre-season, it's prior preparation. Everything is planned.

'I don't believe in running players around an athletics track. We're not long jumpers or hurdle runners. And it's a mental state because if you're telling a player to run around a track, they're thinking "it's cheap coaching, this". If you can do something where they're kicking a ball but still doing the same, they think they're playing football but they're not, they're still getting their sprints in. So we adapt our training to doing something with the ball so they are doing their 5ks etc,' he says, dropping his voice slightly as more players begin to arrive and seat themselves nearby. I feel like I'm getting an inside scoop on the tricks of the trade within earshot of the unknowing subjects.

'We've got links with gyms but, this year, we've got links with a gym in New Mills,' says Garry. 'I went down and told them we can't afford to pay them but we can give advertising and they give them sessions and I told them to really go to town on them. It's the community link though and local people doing good for the club.'

And, alongside the new links forged with the community during the tougher times, it's also no surprise to learn that Garry has developed a new outlook to dealing with adversity that's beginning to translate to his young side on the field.

'The trigger is not to deflate when something bad happens,' he says defiantly. 'It's to inflate. And that's what happened on

Saturday. That's how we play now. And now I think they're at a decent level to progress.'

With an early season win under their belts and positivity emanating from the dugout from a duo with a track record of turning things around, things were starting to look a little brighter for New Mills AFC.

7

FORTRESS CHURCH LANE

Think of mid-August in the football calendar. For me, it represents goalkeepers in caps peering out into the bright sunshine, more beer than Bovril and topless fans conga-ing down the front of the main stand, still drunk on early season optimism. Saturday 20th August 2016 wasn't quite like that.

As one large, dark cloud after another rolled in over the Derbyshire hills, it was an afternoon to pack your coat for the football. For Stoke City's Giannelli Imbula, still perhaps acclimatising to the UK climate after his winter window move from Porto, there seemed ample reason to also wear gloves. While they didn't help to prevent a 4-1 drubbing in the day's early televised game, they did at least keep his delicate digits toasty. Not quite enough to protect him from the ire of the old guard on Match of the Day, however.

On my arrival at Church Lane, it looked like the unpredictable weather might also have had an impact on the crowd. The visit of Barnton, a Cheshire village with a population of little more than 5,000, wasn't perhaps the biggest draw but there was still a little disappointment that the win just a week earlier had seemingly failed to encourage a few more locals out to join the revolution.

'Tricky conditions,' says Ollie's dad as dark clouds gather and gusting winds pick up. 'August Saturdays, eh?'

Conversations centre on the unfortunate midweek defeat and the consensus from those that witnessed it first hand is consistent with Garry and Willo's assessment that the side played well against strong opposition and deserved more.

'We were robbed in midweek!' says Sue. 'I wasn't there but apparently we should have had a penalty in the last minute. But hey ho, that's how it goes. Congleton got somebody lower in the next round of the FA Cup as well,' she says, musing over what might have been. 'I can't remember who it was but it was a bloody good draw.' With that she disappears, seemingly busier than usual today.

Warming up is David Lewis, the diminutive winger who'd played an impressive cameo the previous Saturday. He's starting today but has taken a knock to the ankle in warm-up and heads back to the dressing room for strapping.

James, meanwhile, has cracked the lens on his camera earlier in the week and managed to inflict £1500 of damage as a result. It's not great news for an 18-year-old about to head off to university.

'I threw my bag down and didn't realise it was open and it cracked against a wall,' he recalls mournfully. He perks up slightly when I introduce the possibility of his parents' home insurance.

The familiar sound of studs on concrete is met with applause as Ryan Hopper leads the lads out. As the game kicks off, the heavens begin to open and the small gathering behind the goal either head inside or for the makeshift shelter of the scaffolding outside the clubhouse. Barnton emerge in a deep claret red shirt that resembles a retro AS Roma kit I've kept from my teenage years that still just about fits. Alongside me is Chairman Ray and a bloke in his mid to late twenties holding a pint glass in a tracksuit who I haven't seen before.

As the game kicks off, I begin to tune into the conversation between Ray and the tracksuited guy. He's at least 6ft tall and well-built with a shaven head. His initial line of questioning and commentary suggests he's a footballer without a club. He's worked out who the Chairman is and begins a charm offensive in the Derbyshire downpour.

'Anyone want a go on me raffle?' asks Sue as she braves the

sideways rain.

'Aye, I will,' says Ray.

'What do you win, a brolley?' quips a quick-witted fan. There's no shelter for Sue as she continues her duties down the main stand.

'Get your coat on, it's wet outside,' she shouts to her grandson who is running around in a t-shirt with a ball at his feet.

'I'm not blind!' he retorts before ignoring her request.

'He won't live to be nine…' says Sue, with the determination of a disobeyed grandmother.

The game kicks off at two minutes to three. It might seem an unusual thing to notice, perhaps, but it becomes pertinent when Haydn Foulds finishes sharply in the second minute to open the scoring. As the majority of games are getting underway up and down the country, the Millers are already one-nil up.

'What position do you play then?' enquires a fan, standing with us for shelter, of the prospective new signing as the ball makes its way back to the centre circle.

'Centre forward mate,' comes the reply from the tracksuited bloke. 'I won this league last year,' he adds after a pregnant pause.

'Did ya?' enquires Ray, with a tone that's difficult to ascertain between genuine interest or slight sarcasm. 'GREAT TOUCH, DOUGIE!' shouts Ray as Daniel Douglas-Pringle, the experienced striker alongside Foulds who can hold the ball up to a standard that looks several tiers above the Hallmark Security League, takes the ball on and retains possession.

'His quality of passing and holding the ball up is brilliant,' says Ray with some admiration. 'It's a pity he doesn't get a few more goals but he's such a good player. He brings so many players into the game.'

'Does he not score many?' chips in Super Striker, seizing on the one slight criticism in Ray's appraisal.

'He could get more but he's a superb player, giving other players options. But sometimes he'd rather pass than shoot,' replies Ray.

'He can pass it to me then, can't he?' is the confident response.

'Then I can score!'

I feel myself grimace slightly. He's laying it on thicker than the margarine on the half-time ham sandwiches but it's either going unnoticed or everyone around me has a better poker face than I have.

'How many goals did you get last season?' asks the fan as he begins to do a bit of groundwork on behalf of his seemingly oblivious Chairman.

'I was injured half the season,' he replies, 'but I got eighteen in the second half of the season. I played for Glossop the season before and won the League with them as well. They tried to sign me again last week,' he goes on, as his idle chat sounds ever more like a job interview. 'But Garry rang me so I've come here today.'

'Is that Paul Williams?' asks the striker as the New Mills bench give instruction from the sidelines.

'It is, yeah. Him and Garry. Do you know Garry? Everyone gets on with Garry, he's a cracking lad. He really is a nice bloke,' says Ray proudly.

As this conversation takes place, New Mills launch a free-kick into the box, and the Millers' specialist hold-up centre-forward connects to send the ball beyond the visiting 'keeper and make it 2-0. As he wheels away to celebrate, I bury my chin low into my coat to disguise a wry smile. It's Dougie's goal and New Mills are two-nil up at 3.04pm. It's not a great day to be interviewing for the position of centre forward.

'It's gonna be about six nil!' exclaims the striker.

'I'll be happy with the win,' retorts Ray. 'They just need confidence at the minute. We still need a big centre midfielder and…well, someone like yourself who can score goals. You can always do with that, can't you?' says Ray. I'm not sure if it's the summer downpour, the striker's hard sell or he's drunk on the euphoria of the best start to a game at Church Lane for as long as anyone cares to remember but he appears to be coming round to the idea.

'Did you see that?' Ray asks, referring to Dougie's goal, as Sue returns with her raffle tickets.

'No!' she says.

'It's a long season, but we'll build it up and we'll get there,' continues Ray as Sue wanders off with a pocketful of change and half a book of raffle tickets to tear up.

'You'll be top five, I reckon,' predicts the striker, gushingly, and based on just eight minutes of football.

'Yeah, definitely,' replies Ray. 'I expect to be. No pressure with Garry. But it's top or nothing, no play-offs in this division. When we came in, we were busy in the clubhouse in those days and we had a half-decent budget. We won the Second Division pretty easily, but to get out of this division? Two years running we finished with over one hundred points and came second. You win it with 93, 95pts normally.'

'107 points, we got,' says the striker. '108 points, we got,' tops Ray. 'Lost it on goal difference.'

'He's a good player, that seven,' says the striker referring to Lewis. 'I always look for a good, quick winger who can get the ball into the box. And he's alright, him,' he says, nestling his size twelves a little more comfortably under the table. 'What are the centre halves like, are they any good?' To his eternal credit, Ray ignores this completely. He seems slightly bored of being interviewed himself.

'Go on, Dougie! His touch is great,' says Ray.

'My touch is great!' comes the increasingly familiar reply.

'Touch and in the net, that's the touch you want, isn't it?' says Ray. And then, as if by some kind of magic, New Mills score again. Dan Johnson's mishit shot somehow finds its way into the net and the Millers are 3-0 up inside 12 minutes.

'Don't even ask if I saw it!' says Sue as she comes out of the clubhouse a minute or two after the third has gone in and Ray begins a familiar line of enquiry. 'Fella in there said "three in the first half? We didn't score three all season,"' she chuckles as she heads in the direction of the half-time buffet that's been prepared for the visitors.

'It's dropping now. Come on, keep up the tempo Millers!' shouts Ray. Even at 3-0 up, old nerves die hard. 'Nowt wrong with that! NOWT WRONG WITH THAT!' he shouts as the referee gives a decision against the Millers. 'I'd have been unhappy with it, mind,' he adds as a cheeky aside.

As the sun emerges, we all step forward to watch the game from behind Ollie Martin's goal. A long ball over the top finds the run of Dougie who effortlessly takes the ball in his stride and finishes coolly. The need for a new super striker seems to be diminishing by the minute.

'Hey!' shouts Ollie, turning around to us. 'I told you. You should come every week!' It seems like I've inadvertently become a lucky mascot.

'For the sake of your health, DO NOT ask!' says Sue. 'That's four I've missed now.'

'A result like this'll put another twenty on the gate for Wednesday now,' observes Ray as he scans the stands. There's fewer than a hundred people here and around a third of their average gate a few years back when the club began to sow the seeds that would eventually see them reach the Evo-Stik. 'They're a good bunch of young lads and they've dropped a division so it's nice to see it coming to fruition.'

'Hey, he's a big bugger stood with you isn't he?' says Sue as she hands me a half-time cup of tea. I try to play my poker face as I'm keen to see what the Chairman actually thinks out of earshot of the hardest sell in football. He remains tight lipped.

'Ray are you gonna announce the raffle?' adds Sue. Nearly everyone in the ground has a ticket in their hand, thanks to a sodden Sue – maybe that's the second hardest sell.

'Yeah. What number is it?'

'Two seven six to two eighty.'

'Two seven six to two eighty?'

'Yeah.'

Ray heads for the microphone: 'Winning raffle number, two six eight…'

'NO! Two seven six!'

'Two seven six,' he says, laughing slightly into the microphone.

'Are you gonna do it again?'

'Yeah. Two seven six?'

'Yeah!' He announces it again. 'Dunno how I got that wrong,' he says to me. 'Fluffed me lines.'

Within a few minutes, a man appears at the door. 'Ayup!' says Sue as she greets him. 'Have you won the raffle? There's a selection of prizes here. Did you hear him? Ray, it's Christian who has won it. He says you're not allowed on it again. We're gonna have to ban ya!'

'I didn't introduce you,' Sue says to one of the chaps tucking into the sandwich selection. 'This is Carl who is writing about us. Carl, this is John Hackney, one of our founding members. Him and Ray and Clive. They were here a long time before me because I'm a lot younger! So we've seen the highs and lows.

'When Kopparberg first came out,' says Sue, in something of an unlikely segway as she heads on a diversion down memory lane, 'we used to go to Ikea and bring back all of these fruit ciders. We used to make a fortune because we were buying 'em for about 79p and selling 'em for two quid! We had to go back every week!'

I opt to watch the game from the main stand in the second half, away from the Hallmark League's answer to Alan Shearer. New Mills struggle to match the level of the first half and are punished in the 61st minute when Barnton pull one back. Willo and Garry are up in the dugout straight away, barking instructions at their team. There's clearly no room for standards to drop and it's great to see.

'You have to work for it!' screams Garry. There's no resting on their laurels, no sitting back on the lead. A four-goal advantage is now three, they're absolutely furious and several subs are immediately sent down the touchline to warm up. It's the kind of habits New Mills need to fall back into.

Haydn Foulds rounds the 'keeper and hits the post when it might have been easier to score on 75 minutes. Willo almost hits the roof as he walks past us up the touchline.

'You've got to finish 'em off!' he screams in the direction of the pitch. 'How many chances do they want?'

The Millers answer those questions with a couple more in the final ten minutes through Haydn Foulds' second and a Ryan Hopper penalty that the captain insists on taking despite his striker being on for a consecutive Church Lane hat-trick. It seals a 6-1 win that doesn't flatter them and two wins out of two at Church Lane. The lads receive warm applause as they leave the field.

'He should've let Haydn take the pen,' says James as he wanders back round with his camera. 'I think they did rock, paper, scissors to decide.'

Ollie's dad joins us too and we discuss talk of a title push that's been mentioned by a couple of fans today.

'Why not?' he ponders aloud. 'They're growing in confidence and playing some lovely stuff. I said to some mates I know at Congleton that if we play like we have in pre-season then it'll be a good game. We started off hoofing it and I couldn't believe it. But now they're passing again.'

Next up, Garry appears from the dressing room.

'What about that?' is his assessment. 'That sends out a statement. That's the real us. You'll never see a performance like that again out of me,' he says as James mentions Congleton have lost 6-0 in the next round of the FA Cup against a side from lower down the ladder. 'It's turning though, I told ya. Everything we did there, we did in training. I'm made up!'

As everyone heads to the clubhouse for a celebratory drink, Willo and Garry sit at the bar and soak up the atmosphere. Hopper and Ollie, two mature figures in a young side, still pick the bones out of the negative spell at the start of the second half and where they need to improve. As I prepare to leave the buzz of the home crowd lapping up the post-match celebrations, I go to congratulate Garry and Willo.

'Thanks for your backing,' says Garry as I shake his hand. 'It means a lot for someone to be putting a positive spin on what we're doing here. Everything we did on training after you left on Thursday, we put into practise this afternoon. I'll dream about that tonight,' he says.

'You'll dream about it?' laughs Willo to his best mate. 'I

wouldn't go that far! I mean, it was good but...'

Laughter, a full clubhouse and whispers of a title tilt? It's all change at Fortress Church Lane.

Daniel Douglas-Pringle celebrates

Tunde Owolabi with what would be one of his final goals for the Millers

8

TRANSFER DEADLINE DAY

Football is sometimes likened to soap opera for blokes. It's a lazy and all too gender-specific stereotype, really, but the truth within it is that football probably is soap opera for people who don't generally like soap operas.

With that in mind, Transfer Deadline Day is the twice annual extravaganza that's plastered all over the Radio Times. It's a plane crashing into the Woolpack. It's a tram landing on Coronation Street. It's Jim White trying to get you excited about Peter Odemwingie's rumoured whereabouts.

Like all good TV formats, there's a golden age where a good idea executed well becomes unmissable. It's open to debate, I guess, but mainstream shows like The Apprentice, Big Brother and The X Factor were actually pretty good for a short while when they bedded into a format and just had fun. But familiarity breeds contempt. Like the kitchen appliances of the future, the danger arrives when they become self-aware.

There was once a time when the excitement of Deadline Day was in the realms of unmissable telly. Fans of Premier League clubs wouldn't dare wander from the screen in case the roving reporter pitched up outside their team's gates spotted the shadowy figure of a star striker behind the boardroom curtain. Nobody questioned why they'd waited until half past eleven on a Thursday night to put pen to paper. It's just how it was.

Back in the studio, presenters would speak with fervour as the whoosh of breaking news tracked across the screen. Harry Redknapp would hang out of a car window and someone would inexplicably ask Alan Curbishley and Niall Quinn for insight on a League One player going out on loan to League Two.

Then, over time, everyone sort of cottoned on. Agents realised they could manipulate the system to generate interest in long-forgotten clients. Clubs could drive up valuations or pick at the leftovers of collapsed moves. Fans brought purple dildos along and poked them into the ears of roving reporters, live to the nation. We've all been there.

For every last-minute Fernando Torres deal, there were a hundred false stories, fuelled by the gossip of desperate agents. While Odemwingie's top level career would never fully recover from driving half the length of the country for a move that was, at best, only ever a reality in his own mind, the majority of rumoured moves just melted away into the background like the plotline of a much-loved soap star going out to pasture on a three-month loan deal to pantomime in Mansfield.

Listening to transfer deadline day via the radio over rolling TV coverage is marginally preferable. While still quite frantic, it's no more so than your average phone-in about the best position to play Wayne Rooney or why Jordan Henderson is definitely the new Steven Gerrard. It's the option I go for with my seven-year-old son on August 31st 2016.

Jacob's interest in football has been on the rise since around his fifth birthday. Keen not to push things too hard, too early, he's attended a few glamour games with me including an England game at Wembley. Disappointed to see his hero Harry Kane starting on the bench, the Tottenham striker came on and scored 45 seconds into his debut to keep up his side of the bargain in making football fantasy a perfectly plausible reality for schoolboys up and down the land. It was all he'd talk about for the week that followed.

As well as a growing interest watching football, he's also a more than dedicated member of our village side. A difficult start not entirely unlike the one endured by New Mills last year was forgotten when, with five minutes to go in the final game of his maiden season, he scored his first ever goal to grab a 4-4 draw. As a striker in a struggling side that didn't score many, never mind register anything other than defeats, it was a family moment we'll always cherish. The shocked expression on his face is one that my wife and I will never forget; he'd later admit that he forgot to celebrate in the way he'd practised in his head a hundred times, as the impact of the occasion had caused his eyes to fill with tears of delight. It hadn't started quite so well nine months earlier, when tears of a different sort had seemed more likely.

'Come on, lads! Keep going!' we'd shouted on that first rainy Saturday on the sidelines. The Falcons were 12-0 down at halftime. My then six-year-old son's U7s side had, unfortunately, been pitted against a team of talented Matlock Town youngsters for their first ever match. While the opposition coach ran his side of pint-sized Pele's through warm-up drills and talked tactics pre-match, our manager was pointing out which one was the halfway line. We watched and grimaced as half a dozen sub four-footers trampled our young lads' spirits into the mud. I think they ended up scoring 25.

Since then, we'd watched a squad of nine lads bond, work together and improve beyond recognition. More importantly, they'd left the field with a smile on their face after every match - barring one brutally cold Peak District morning with an icy crosswind that saw the ref abandon proceedings just after half-time, that is. Win, draw or invariably lose, the packet of Haribo and access to Pokémon that accompanied full-time always seemed to sweeten the deal.

There's a sneaking suspicion that Jacob's attendance with me tonight at Church Lane is out of opportunism to enjoy a late night rather than a lifelong ambition to see Hanley Town in action, but it's a chance I'm willing to risk. Stopping for fish and chips in the Peak District only adds to the nostalgia I'm already experiencing remembering trips to the North West with my own father to watch my boyhood team Tottenham in action.

'Dad,' he whispers, as we await a Fish Special and a child's fish cake, chips and curry sauce. 'Is that a New Mills shirt?' He nods at a chap in an unrecognisable fluorescent yellow Admiral-style home kit that looks older than me.

'No mate. We're not quite that close just yet.'

As we sit in the lay-by slurping Dandelion and Burdock, he tells me all about the latest additions to his Premier League Match Attax card collection. After almost completing his set last year, helped in no small part by spending the entirety of his first ever £5 goal bonus on packs, he's now abandoned hope of finishing off the Euro 2016 sticker album and has launched headlong into the 2016/17 season.

'I got a Jamie Vardy 101 Club!' he says as I manage to generate the requisite amount of excitement. I imagine this is just as good as when I managed to lay my hands on a Wimbledon shiny back in 1995/96.

Alongside the glamour of the Premier League and trips to Wembley, I've also introduced him to his local sides. We've seen Chesterfield once or twice and even shared a trip to Matlock Town where he asked his mum if he could bring along his pocket money to buy himself a pie and me a pint. It's hard to recall a moment when it felt like parenting could be going much better.

Sue is predictably excited to meet Jacob as we arrive at Church Lane a little later than anticipated. The rush home from work and the wait for food leaves just ten minutes to kick off. We invest in a Pools-style prediction game Sue has launched to raise funds and scan the fixtures before making our predictions which I somehow manage to fill out incorrectly. Whether it's the harum-scarum turnaround from leaving work via home and the chippy or the frenetic tone of TalkSport on the drive up, I feel slightly off-kilter somehow. This would become apparent moments later.

The teams come out from the dressing room in familiar fashion, fired up and shouting instructions back down the line. At this stage, two large metal gates are pulled out to create a tunnel to the pitch entrance. This duty generally falls to Sue and committee member Roy, who both guard the area to prevent fans crossing the entrance to the pitch for these few minutes at the beginning and end of each half.

Tonight, as Sue walks the gate out, she beckons me over.

'Carl, love, will you just stand here with the gate? I've got Shaun Goater at the back turnstile trying to get in!'

As sentences go, it's a surreal one. I can only assume it adds to my slightly dreamlike state as I replace her at her vantage point and she heads off to retrieve a Manchester City legend. It's here where the details become important.

As the opposition head out, their subs make their way onto the pitch. All but one, that is, who walks towards me and gestures to get past. The space between me and the edge of the pitch is just one person wide – the idea being that my vantage point blocks any spectator trying to get beyond until the players are on the field of play, as is my duty – and I step to one side to make way.

What happens next occurs in something resembling slow motion. As I let go of the gate and step to one side, its eight-foot square frame wobbles, the rusty metal hinges holding it buckle and it begins to fall. Spotting this, I make a grab for it and pull it back in my direction, causing the bottom half to jerk back towards me and the heavier top half to fall ever more quickly. It smashes onto the concrete floor merely centimetres from the Hanley Town starting eleven. Their sub, the architect of both the gate's downfall and my own, glances over his shoulder guiltily and quickens his pace to wherever the hell he needed to go that couldn't wait for one more sodding minute. All twenty-two players, previously hyped up and barking instructions to one another in the heat of pre-match, fall silent and look at me. The ref looks me up and down and gives a gentle shake of the head.

When I was five years old, I went on a school trip. One exercise involved making a small plasticine boat and racing it down a stream. Fiercely independent, I insisted on extending my small frame over the grassy bank to place my boat in the water myself rather than accepting the help of the teacher. The feeling of sitting alone on the coach home because nobody wanted to sit beside the kid who stunk of river water momentarily came flooding back as I stood over that stricken gate and the players begin a much quieter descent that usual down the steps and onto the pitch. Shock and embarrassment course through me.

'Don't worry, I've got it!' says a panic-stricken Sue as the players quietly jog onto the pitch and The Goat looks on. Jacob, meanwhile, looks up at me with a stare that begins to search my face for answers as to why he's been brought to a football match at which Daddy has just tried to maim a semi-professional football team.

I seat myself under the scaffolding for a moment as I attempt to work out what just happened. With the gate merely balancing on the base of a pole, it was capable of holding its own weight but only with the assistance of a gate monitor. My assumption that said monitor was merely guarding the space to prevent fans walking across was misguided at best and, at worst, had very nearly just caused the most sudden injury crisis in Hanley Town FC's history. It would be difficult to bring in quite so many new recruits this late on Deadline Day.

'Every time I look at you tonight, I'm gonna chuckle,' says Sue as she comes back and forth with her regular duties and I slowly stop shaking.

The Millers come into the game on the back of two defeats that had included a heavy 4-1 drubbing at Church Lane to West Didsbury and Chorlton. A further 4-2 defeat at Barnoldswick Town had quelled some of the early promotion talk almost as quickly as it had begun.

'Was that their goal?' asks Jacob as Hanley Town take the lead in the 13th minute. He's cottoned on to which team is which by the time Ryan Hibbert equalises for the Millers later on in the first half.

Tunde Owolabi, an athletic, skilful and speedy winger, causes mayhem with his direct runs down the left-hand side but comes in for some unwelcome attention when his physical but fair aerial challenge on the visiting 'keeper leads to half their team and fans behind the goal calling for the referee to take action. I ready myself near the massive gate in case he needs back-up.

'Aye! Expect it back next time, lad! Expect one,' says the Hanley defender to Owolabi threateningly as he lifts his own goalkeeper back to his feet.

'It's alright, that, Tunde lad,' reassures one of his teammates as he makes his way back down the touchline. Tunde reacts to neither and gets himself back into position.

'Watch the striker and how he moves,' I tell Jacob, perhaps optimistically attempting to coach my young son in the art of tracking back. A diminutive figure even at Under 8s level and with no offside rule to worry about just yet, he tends to position himself as far up the field as possible in the hope that the ball will reach him rather than the other way round.

As half-time arrives, a large Hanley Town contingency head for the half-time portacabin. It doesn't seem appropriate to take a child in so we sit on the pub bench.

'Aren't you coming in for a cuppa?' asks Sue, presumably feeling nervous upon realising I'm unattended and within 100 yards of a gate. Jacob immediately perks up – his interest in this entire project has been predicated by the promise of half-time cakes and a sneak preview of where Dad has begun spending every other weekend – and we make our way in.

There's one seat available in the crowded cabin and it shares a table with none other than Shaun Goater. I keep a low profile in case anyone recognises me from kick-off and we sit ourselves down across from him. He introduces himself immediately with his accent a familiar mix of Bermudian crossed with Mancunian that's recognisable from his occasional stints as a TV and radio pundit.

'It's not every day you meet someone who used to play in the Premier League,' I impress on Jacob as he shakes hands. His eyes widen slightly and I can tell he's keen to flick through his Match Attax cards to see if he can do a facial recognition match on the bloke in front of him.

Keen not to dwell on whether or not he realises I was responsible for 'Gate-gate', we discuss 'The Goat's' reasons for being here. He tells me he's been trying to get to a game for a while to say "hi" to some of the lads and happened to be passing through. He's currently scouting for Doncaster, which I suggest sounds like the name of a terrible tribute boy band and then immediately regret it. He laughs generously all the same.

'What's your celebration like?' he asks, upon hearing that Jacob is also a member of the strikers' union. He shrugs his little shoulders and suggests that he doesn't really know. I recall the familiar tale of his one goal to date with a bloke who once scored a winner at Old Trafford.

'You have to have a celebration,' he says forcefully. 'Alan Shearer? It was one arm up in the air. Everybody remembers that. Give it some thought. Why not run the length of the pitch with your hands up in the air?' Jacob nods thoughtfully.

We get on to Transfer Deadline Day and the latest rumours currently abound on Twitter. Tottenham and Everton appear to be attempting to gazump one another for Moussa Sissoko to the tune of £30m. It seems an inflated sum for a player who did little in a relegated side last season before a few impressive cameos in the European Championships.

'I only watch it right at the end,' confides Shaun. I'm keen to find out if he ever had any close shaves with the window closing and he recalls a simply brilliant story.

'When I was at Bristol City,' he begins, 'we heard Man City were coming in. I was trying to get the papers through with ten minutes to go before the deadline and struggling. The Mrs was cracking open the champagne to celebrate and I'm saying, "I can't get the fax machine working here!" It could all have been very different.' It's ironic to think a Brother fax machine, synonymous with City shirts in the nineties, could have stood in the way of Manchester City folklore. That's Deadline Day.

As the second half gets underway, Jacob engineers a toilet trip to catch the final moments of the Great British Bake Off – another excellent format slowly on the wane – from inside the comfort of the clubhouse. Keen not to miss the match while keeping an eye on him, I find myself watching non-league football through a glass window to the soundtrack of Mary Berry, like a budget hospitality lounge.

The visitors are reduced to ten men with quarter of an hour to play and it feels like opportunity might be knocking for the Millers. It's a chance they're unable to take as the game finishes all square. Tunde Owolabi is named Man of the Match after a blistering performance on the wing that continued to open up the Hanley defence.

'Have a great holiday,' I say to Sue as she finishes her final chores before a well-earned rest in the Canary Isles. 'I promise not to go anywhere near the gates while you're gone.'

The following Saturday morning, on the rain-soaked pitches at the bottom of our village, Jacob scores his second ever goal in the first game of the new season to put his side two-nil up. Following an instinctive finish, he wheels away before being mobbed by his teammates.

As he jogs off later to be replaced by a rolling sub, he's wearing a massive smile. The dad of a teammate congratulates him on his finish and asks a question which surely elicits the greatest response any goalscorer in North East Derbyshire U7s League has ever given.

'Where did you get your celebration from?' asks my mate, genuinely inquisitive as to where the focused sprint back down the pitch had come from. Jacob doesn't miss a beat, unaware of how ridiculous his answer might sound to the outside observer.

'Shaun Goater told me to do it,' he beams.

LEAGUE TABLE

		PLD	GS	GC	GD	PTS
1st	Irlam	7	14	12	+2	14
2nd	Bootle	6	19	9	+10	12
3rd	Barnoldswick Town	6	17	9	+8	12
4th	Runcorn Town	6	15	9	+6	12
5th	1874 Northwich	5	12	7	+5	12
6th	Atherton Collieries	5	14	6	+8	10
7th	Hanley Town	6	13	9	+4	10
8th	West Didsbury & Chorlton	5	10	7	+3	10
9th	Congleton Town	6	12	13	-1	10
10th	Squires Gate	5	13	11	+2	7
11th	New Mills	6	15	15	0	7
12th	AFC Liverpool	5	12	12	0	7
13th	Ashton Athletic	5	9	10	-1	7
14th	Padiham	6	7	8	-1	7
15th	Barnton	7	7	18	-11	7
16th	Runcorn Linnets	6	10	11	-1	6
17th	Abbey Hey	6	7	13	-6	6
18th	Maine Road	4	6	6	0	5
19th	Winsford United	4	5	9	-4	4
20th	Cammell Laird	5	7	9	-2	3
21st	AFC Darwen	5	4	19	-15	3
22nd	Nelson	6	2	8	-6	1

9

WAKE ME UP WHEN SEPTEMBER ENDS?

With August under their belts, the league table beginning to take shape and the Millers more than doubling their points total of the previous season after just six games, things were beginning to look a little brighter at Church Lane.

September would begin without Ray and Sue – sunning themselves in the Canary Isles but keeping a close eye on results via Twitter. A narrow 1-0 home defeat against Runcorn Town would start the month in all too familiar fashion, even if a creditable performance against one of the division's more fancied sides was no disgrace.

A midweek return to Congleton Town would follow as Garry Brown's men would seek to avenge their FA Cup defeat and show the progress made since that dreadful opening Saturday. With comedy commitments meaning I can't make the trip across to Staffordshire, I'm also glued to social media where I accidentally find myself involved in what the cool kids might call a 'Twitter spat' in the 13th minute with the main Congleton account.

> *GOAL! You won't believe this but new mills lead. 9 holds the ball until 10 supports him and finds the bottom right corner, 0-1.*

It's a naughty sentiment that suggests Congleton have turned up expecting to coast towards another victory. James calls them out on it via the New Mills account and there are several follow-ups. It's a reminder that, with the recovery from the previous season well underway, New Mills will no longer accept being the punchline.

Congleton equalise six minutes later but Tunde Owolabi's goal gives Millers the lead at the break. Captain Ryan Hopper adds a third shortly after half-time but, as ever, New Mills keep things interesting by conceding again two minutes later. The remainder of the match becomes one tense update after another as Ollie Martin repeatedly shows his quality as the last line of defence between the sticks. It's a performance that will earn him Man of the Match and, more importantly, three points. Discovering my inner keyboard warrior, I take to Twitter:

You won't believe this but @NewMillsAFC went on to score their 17th and 18th league goals in their opening 8 games to claim 3pts.

After a little back-pedalling, Congleton congratulate their visitors. To add insult to injury for the home side, New Mills also announce the signing of Congleton danger man Sam Marshall after the match, a quick and skilful winger with an eye for a cross. As I can't be there, I try to imagine the cricket team slumped at the bar, the PA system announcing the result following its painful removal from a delicate orifice by Sue and the woman on the sun lounger going in early to catch the second half of Holby City. It's another ghost laid to rest for Garry's men.

Two consecutive home games follow and offer the chance to continue the momentum. A 3-1 home defeat against AFC Liverpool in which New Mills never get going is followed by them quickly falling two behind to Ashton Athletic on a busy Wednesday night under the floodlights at Church Lane. Owolabi's 63rd minute goal to halve the deficit gives hope before Ryan Hopper steps up in the final minute to convert from the spot and secure a 2-2 draw. When Haydn Foulds opens the scoring at Winsford United the following Saturday, only to see the lead overturned in the second half to a 3-1 defeat, it feels like September's busy schedule has New Mills well and truly set for a season of consolidation back in the Hallmark Security League.

As I navigate the Manchester suburbs a few days later for yet another midweek match – their sixth in the opening eight weeks of the season during a hectic September schedule - something is missing on my arrival at Abbey Hey FC. It's not the obvious sight of floodlights stretching up into the early autumn dusk, although they do take some finding through a rabbit warren of housing estates. It's not the car park; while not immediately visible, I'm waved through gates by a man in a turnstile where I pay my ticket through the car window before driving alongside the pitch like a drive-in movie.

There's an appropriate soundtrack, as Oasis classic *Some Might Say* blares out through the PA system, and a 78-strong contingent braving the Tuesday night chill are present, even if many have taken refuge in the clubhouse bar overlooking the pitch from a first-floor vantage point; a great example of a non-league 'hospitality lounge' at just a fraction of the cost.

What is missing, however, is manager Garry Brown.

'Alright Craig!' says Ollie's dad as I arrive. It's at this moment that I panic. There is a small window of opportunity when someone calls you by the wrong name. It exists between the moment someone calls you by the wrong name and the moment you open your mouth to reply.

I've seen an embarrassing long-term problem quashed in a split second by the recipient of an incorrect name. That moment of awkwardness is merely a fraction of the medium to long-term pain of repeatedly accepting an incorrect name until, one way or another, the giver of the incorrect name realises their mistake.

'Hiya mate,' I reply, somewhat ironically really, because I'm also awful with names and have also forgotten his, beyond 'Ollie's dad' of course. 'Actually it's Carl...,' I should say, but it's in my head rather than out loud.

Blown it. The moment's gone. I'm Craig now. Is it too late to change the byline on the book?

He's with his youngest son, Ollie's little brother, who is a bundle of energy on the sidelines, singing songs and shouting light-hearted abuse at the opposition from time to time.

As the Millers emerge from the dressing room, Inspiral Carpets classic *This Is What It Feels* blasts out from the tannoy. I'm enjoying the playlist more than the prospect of the match.

'No Garry tonight?' I innocently enquire with Sue, as his assistant Paul Williams takes his place in the dugout.

'No, he's working,' she says as I try to read if there's anything more to it from her voice. 'Either that or it's all got a bit much. I haven't got over Saturday myself,' she adds, in reference to that painful defeat at Winsford. 'We didn't speak on the coach home. All the fans and players went together. Not a word. We should have been three or four up by half-time but they didn't bother in the second half. There was nothing to say.'

With a modest showing in the stands, every word on the pitch seems even more audible tonight as captain Ryan Hopper's repeated calls for his side to be more vocal on the pitch appear to have been heeded.

'Kick their butts, New Mills!' shouts Ollie's little brother Alfie. His dad tells a nice story of when Ollie was a similar age supporting Stockport County, and staring open-mouthed at the crowd around him singing a less than complimentary song about the referee.

'Can I join in, Dad?' he'd asked.

'Go for it, son,' came the response.

Alfie has embraced the spirit of his older brother as he continues to be a one-man band of vocal support for the Millers from the side of the pitch.

'What are you looking at me for mate?' the small-framed nine-year-old asks of an opposition player who enters our area of the pitch to take a throw-in. 'Do you want some? I'll give it to ya?' he says, mimicking the viral clip of the Wealdstone Ranger that has clearly made it to the primary school playground. He bursts out laughing at himself and raises a smile from the player retrieving the ball too.

The half-time buffet consists of ham sandwiches with more margarine than ham in a private bar and function area. An impressive number of committee members, mostly gentlemen in their 70s and 80s, sit in silence watching us devour the snacks on offer. A series of framed pictures in the style of dogs playing pool and, impressively, an image of Ron Atkinson during his Manchester United days and paying a visit to the room we're stood in, decorate the walls. As we finish our brew in the bowels of the clubhouse and hear the players head out for the start of the second half, I hear my phone ping on a quick trip to the gents. It's a Twitter update from New Mills AFC; they're 1-0 down, apparently.

Taking my place back on the sidelines, I'm exasperated that we managed to lose track of time to the point that the second half kicked off without us. Worse still, I've missed the goal that sees the Millers behind again.

Sue brightens the mood with a tale from her duties with the under-18 squad as they registered for the season.

'I couldn't believe it,' she says, of the difficulty some of the talented teens had in completing the requisite admin to sign up. 'They were struggling to fill in the most basic of information. Some of them were getting their name and surname mixed up. I don't think I could be a teacher because I actually had to say to them "I've had enough" at one point. I had to give one lad four forms – he couldn't even fill his details in.'

Dylan Stringer-Moth brightens things a little further with an equaliser in the 67th minute. That's how it stays as New Mills pick up a 12th point from 12 games. Hardly promotion form but enough to nestle comfortably in midtable.

'I think the next bus home is in about 45 minutes...' says James, somewhat leadingly. He's been quietly snapping photos for much of the game.

'Want a lift home?' I ask.

'Oh yeah! Do you mind?' While it's no doubt safer than it might appear to the outside observer, I feel the 40-minute detour out of my way to drop James off at his central Manchester student accommodation is a better option than leaving an 18-year-old with a couple of grand's worth of camera to navigate the public transport by himself.

'See you at the weekend, Craig!' shouts Ollie's dad as I grimace a smile and wave back. James doesn't mention it. I can't work out if it's because he's been calling me 'Carl' for the past couple of months and is now beginning to question if my name might be Craig after all.

'What do you make of all this with Garry?' I ask as we set our sights on the high rises of Salford on the long, straight trip down the A57. A confidante of Garry after following him over from Wythenshawe, if anyone has the inside scoop it will be James.

'I'm not sure,' he replies. 'I think he was considering packing it in but I don't really know. He hasn't said anything.'

We wouldn't have to wait long to find out.

We didn't know it at the time, but a new chapter was beginning at Abbey Hey FC

10

TIME FOR CHANGE

In the early afternoon of Thursday 22 September 2016, New Mills AFC release the following statement:

'*Manager Garry Brown has stepped down as manager of the 1st team.*

Garry Brown has stepped down as First Team Manager. The club would like to thank Garry for all the hard work he has put into New Mills AFC. Whilst Garry steps back and takes a well-deserved break Paul Williams, Daniel Douglas-Pringle and James Kinsey will take over the First Team. James will oversee the Development Squad team until we find a replacement. The club has a tough week with a home fixture on Saturday in the FA Vase, then two away cup games, at Shirebrook on Tuesday in the Derbyshire Senior Cup followed by an away fixture at Squires Gate next Saturday in the Macron Cup.

New Mills AFC Committee would like to thank Garry for everything he has done at the club in managing through a difficult year last season and leading this squad into the Hallmark Security League for this season's campaign. The hard work and time he has dedicated to the club both on and off the field has left Garry exhausted and he wants to take a step back and spend some much-deserved time with his family. Garry has been juggling work and family commitments with his role at New Mills AFC and needs to relax. He remains part of New Mills AFC Committee and after some time out we hope you will see Garry back at Church Lane supporting the club off the pitch.

The squad of players at New Mills AFC is strong and recent games prove we have the strength in depth to compete in this League and we hope all the players will remain at the club with the continuity of Paul, Daniel and James taking over leadership. The Development Squad have their next home game next Friday against Riasa South so please come along and support them.

Sue Hyde, Secretary New Mills AFC

It's headed with an image of Garry on the touchline in profile, pointing out instructions to his young side. My first instinct is to contact him and express my regret that he's stepping down. I hold back from doing this immediately, mindful that his phone might already be busy with many of his players perhaps having the same idea.

The first thing that comes to mind after absorbing the statement is our interview just a few weeks ago. Looking back, there were pointers to Garry struggling with the strain of the job. His candid words on this season being even tougher than the one that preceded it seemed strange given the difference in form, but now, with more pressure to win at the level below, and with a team of players he'd assembled, the strain was clearly mounting up. In simple human terms, though, the build-up of stress combining a busy day job with the all-consuming night career had probably just become too much.

The statement reflected well on Garry and his reasons for leaving. It also pointed towards continuity for the players in the short-term, at least, with Willo taking charge alongside Dougie, a mature and respected figure in the dressing room. James Kinsey stepping up from the Development Team offered further signs of progression opportunities within the club that Garry himself had worked hard to create.

I email Sue to express my disappointment and ask if the interim management team are intended for the long-term. She replies to say 'it's early days' and that 'the timing could've been better' with reference to the next three Cup games. Given her own juggling of commitments, it wouldn't be entirely surprising if she'd had to draft a statement on her lunch hour.

Garry's Twitter account, which is quiet at the best of times, has been deactivated. Anticipating the noise around his departure, he's gone for the switch-off approach. Now seems like the best time to text him and he quickly replies:

'I have been nothing but professional in my decision and have ensured the smoothest transition as possible, arranging the team for the last game and supporting Willo and the new managers. The recent run of up and down form has no bearing on my decision at all. It is a young team and needs time to get confident and consistent. Was always a marathon and not a sprint. The club has a great squad with only two players left from when I came in 12 months ago. I just had to take the emotion away and think with my head. I was going above the role of manager and had to redress the balance. No bridges burned, the club has been stabilised and can now push on. The philosophy of developing players individually and as a team will reap rewards, I am sure of that.'

The reaction online is less vocal than I'd expected. Garry was popular around the place and endlessly positive. For fans demanding results, of which there were undoubtedly some, it was always going to be an impossible job to win them over fully with anything less than a tilt at promotion. The players largely didn't react publicly as the dust settled but more than a few ex-colleagues, including several with a Glossop connection, commented on the quality of both the man and the manager.

On a personal level, I felt gutted. The man who'd welcomed me so openly into the Club from minute one was no longer in the hotseat. While he'd referenced the indifferent form not being a part of his decision, it's hard to argue that the job wouldn't have felt a whole lot more enjoyable with a few more wins under their belts and without the frustration of losing games they'd dominated.

'You are the only one who respected what was being done and that was saving a club from extinction and stabilising it to ensure football can be played within the community,' Garry goes on to text. It's a lovely sentiment to receive and another nod at Garry's lingering bitterness against the local and national media that had made a difficult job even harder during his tenure.

48 hours is a long time in football, at any level. When Saturday comes, and New Mills publish their match preview, Garry doesn't get much of a mention. Instead, the focus is on the new management trio in what is billed as their first game in charge. There's nothing too different about the mood around Church Lane on arrival other than the absence of Garry, who is usually overseeing the warm-up and chatting to fans behind the goal in the half-hour before kick-off.

Sue is her usual cheerful self in the clubhouse, busy behind the bar serving a respectable away following from Nottinghamshire side Radford FC and handing out the score prediction game she's recently introduced to drum up extra cash. She tells fans enquiring after Ray that he's got a heavy cold and might not show but, no sooner has she relayed this, the man himself arrives looking a little worse for wear. Initial signs his croaky voice is faltering would perhaps be tested later.

Derek, meanwhile, is once again unhappy at the shirt colour of the opposition 'keeper. He tells me at length that an email exchange confirming their salmon shirts will clash with Ollie's has been ignored and now the Millers custodian between the post is lining up with an Evo-Stik logo on his shirt. It's a recurring theme that's enough to send any fixture secretary over the edge.

Photographer James is more concerned by the departure of Garry, if not entirely unsurprised. As a friend of the former manager, who was brought to New Mills to provide media support having offered the same at Wythenshawe, he suggests that he'd suspected things were getting on top of him a few weeks back and that his decision seemed to be only a matter of time.

As the teams come out, Ray closes the fenced gates to create a tunnel and then steps aside, leaving them unaided to stand by themselves. Internally, I feel a mixture of justification as they stand without assistance combined with blind panic that they're going to wipe out half the squad at any second. At least somebody has fixed the dodgy hinge.

On paper, at least, today's game looks to be the kind of match a new manager might appreciate as his first ever opponents. East Midlands Counties Premier League side Radford FC are one rung down from New Mills on the league ladder and midtable in their respective division further south east in the regional set up. With a game of knockout football to come at home without the concern of league points, Willo and his team name a strong, attack-minded selection. Daniel Douglas-Pringle is back in the side and leads the line upfront.

First introduced in 1974, the FA Vase has long been the best opportunity for a semi-professional player to experience the thrill of Wembley's hallowed turf. Aside from a few years when it toured to stadiums as varied as White Hart Lane, Villa Park and the Boleyn Ground, non-league sides have run out beneath either the old twin towers or the arch that can be seen from across London and beyond, in a bid to join a storied list of local cult heroes who've reached the summit of amateur football wearing the colours of football's lesser lights.

For the Millers' closest rivals, Glossop North End, it's been the scene of two heartbreaking defeats in the final. For the likes of Whitley Bay, one of several sides from the North East of England who've excelled in this competition, it's made legends of local lads who might once have otherwise given up on their boyhood dreams of lifting a trophy at the National Stadium.

Last season, in an experiment that was largely considered a success by the non-league community, the FA combined the FA Vase Final with its slightly more senior sibling, the FA Trophy, to create the inaugural Non-League Finals Day. Consisting of Halifax Town vs Grimsby Town for the Trophy and a shock 4-1 defeat for Hereford against Morpeth Town, ensuring the Vase returned to the North East for the seventh time in the last eight seasons, 46,781 came out to support the day. While Hereford brought 20,000 fans and an actual bull called Ronaldo, Morpeth's trip was part-funded by a donation from Newcastle United. It was an example of how David vs Goliath ties aren't just limited to the FA Cup.

It was hard not to dream of Wembley a little at kick-off. Back in the Vase following relegation for the first time in three years, New Mills hadn't enjoyed the best of times during their short stint in the FA Trophy. Now they were back as one of the bigger fish in the FA Vase pond and could at least dream of a money-spinning run to boost confidence and maybe fuel hopes of a walk down Wembley Way. Sue would hopefully need to lay on more than a minibus from Derbyshire should that dream be realised.

Most noticeable for Radford was their dugout. With limitations in place as to how many playing and coaching staff could be named on the bench, they crammed no fewer than ten (and at times more like twelve or thirteen) individuals into the small space on the touchline. With the Millers' newly expanded coaching team a little further up the field, the technical areas of both sides combined was in danger of looking busier than the main stand.

The cumulative effect of having around a dozen representatives on the bench becomes evident early on. Radford hassle and harangue the refereeing team for every decision, taking it in turns to voice disapproval at each free-kick, offside and even throw-in that goes against their team. In truth, it becomes a little tiresome, not least the protestations of one member of the coaching team who bears a striking resemblance to Family Guy's Peter Griffin. If you're not familiar with the programme, rest assured that it's not an *entirely* complimentary comparison.

Radford take the lead on the half hour mark in an otherwise fairly even game in which Tunde Owolabi looks the stand out player down the wing. The visitors are a battle-hardened side, however, full of the kind of journeyman stereotype that's much less prevalent these days than those unfamiliar with non-league might imagine. Radford are certainly packing more than their fair share of slightly immobile bald-headed players who are no strangers to the physical approach; or a buffet, for that matter.

Willo is in the dugout awaiting the restart at least five minutes early – an ominous sign for his team, having clearly got his message across concisely. It doesn't work, though, as Radford score a second goal around the hour mark.

'These are the worst team I've seen here and we're losing 2-0,' observes a downbeat James. It's about to get worse. Radford get a third in the 65th minute. In the dugout, Willo shouts instruction but it's looking hopeless. Radford begin to shut up shop, even if their bench refuses to shut up. At that very moment, the best chance the lads in amber had of playing at Wembley appeared to be the discovery of a Maltese bloodline and a subsequent call-up for England's upcoming World Cup qualifier.

In the 78th minute, Dan Johnson rose highest to powerfully head home a corner and get what looked to be a consolation goal. That was until a free-kick on the edge of the Radford box just 30 seconds after the restart saw Ryan Hibbert curl a shot over the wall and into the top right postage stamp. A huge roar that's more than the sum of its parts goes up as the Church Lane faithful rally behind the team. The Millers continue to swarm over Radford, forcing several more chances before a through ball slices the defence apart and Tunde times his run to perfection to beat the 'keeper one on one in the 85th minute.

The entire New Mills team mob him in the corner that James and I are stood in as we explode with delight. I'm not proud to say that I direct an entirely unprofessional "GET IN THERE!" in the general direction of the Radford bench who are completely dumbstruck. Pete Griffin kicks a concrete post with the kind of force he'll probably regret in the morning.

'I can't believe it,' says James as we all calm down slightly. 'I really need them to win this now. I've booked a train for ten past. I don't want us to go out but I really need that six quid,' he says, in reference to the extra he'll need to pay for a new rail ticket. The life of a student, eh?

The Millers almost do just that, with Dougie hitting the bar and Tunde attempting to lob the goalkeeper and coming very close. As the final whistle blows, Radford are well and truly on the ropes and confusion reigns. Several players shake hands and

I spot more than a few fans leaving via the main gate. Due to an agreement between the two sides, however, the game will go to extra-time. To further add to the confusion, if it's level after an additional half hour then we go to a replay rather than penalties. The Vase allows sides to pre-arrange this before the game.

'Who'd be a fucking manager?' laughs Willo as we walk past the dugout. 'What have I got myself into here?' Meanwhile, the Radford bench relieve themselves behind their own dugout as the trip up the touchline to the toilets proves too much for some. It's a classy sight from a classy side.

There's no fun way of summarising the extra half hour. Rather than continue in the style that had seen them draw their visitors level, it instead consisted of New Mills regressing back to the performance that had made such a comeback necessary, allowing Radford to dominate in the process. With the midweek Derbyshire Cup game against Shirebrook now looking set for postponement to incorporate a trip to Nottinghamshire and a replay, the inevitable happens. Radford score with just three minutes of extra time remaining.

The visiting bench explode out of the dugout. At one point, Radford have twenty individuals on the pitch. As the Millers get ready to forlornly restart play, there remains twelve.

'Get off the pitch! Get off the pitch you fat bastard!' scream what seems like half the crowd. The tracksuited Peter Griffin, the most grotesque member of a likely line-up of Radford coaching staff, isn't just still on the field of play – he's stood in the centre circle awaiting kick-off.

Slowly – oh, so very slowly – he begins to retreat back to the dugout. A small band of kids behind the goal direct abuse at him as he goes. He flicks them two fingers and will resume exchanging expletive-filled insults with children at the full-time whistle a few minutes later when Radford have safely sealed their passage into the next round. A weak display from the refereeing team, who allow his deliberate time wasting to pass without comment, only adds to frustrations around the ground. Had he sent him to the stands, wherever that might be, Radford would still be exceeding touchline rules by at least half a dozen.

'Why didn't you send me off, ref?' he enquires later outside the changing rooms.

'Where am I going to send you?' asks the ref.

'They never settled after any of the goals,' he goes on to boast, explaining the reasoning behind his on-pitch protest. 'When that winner went in, I wasn't going to let their concentration go again. I'd have stood there all day if I could have.'

Good gamesmanship or an unfair advantage from having a minibus full in the dugout? I suppose it doesn't really matter now.

'The less said about the opposition the better,' tweets James from the main account at full-time. It's perhaps not the most sporting response and he retracts it later, opting to wish Radford all the best in the next round.

As we stand outside the changing rooms mourning the defeat, James and I get into conversation with the referee and his assistant, two approachable young men who've had a reasonable game and are presumably awaiting their modest expenses payment for the afternoon. We jokingly enquire if they get to file for half an hour's overtime.

'Eh! You can't go in yet, can you? Ya perverts!' shouts an ever-charming member of the Radford set-up. I realise they're referring to their female assistant ref who, in truth, did struggle to keep up with play during the game and was abused accordingly by the Radford minibus in the dugout.

'If she's as quick getting ready as she was on the line, you'll be here a while!' he adds. The walls of the changing room don't strike me as being particularly sound proofed. Poor performance aside, it's depressing to think that she's probably listening to every word and, as a woman making her way in the unchecked lower rungs of the league ladder, has probably heard much worse.

I feel for Willo. More softly-spoken than even the ever-amiable Garry, he cuts a disconsolate figure in the clubhouse afterwards. He drinks slightly separately from the group before leaving, presumably having not quite believed what he'd witnessed. An otherwise upbeat clubhouse full of Radford players and coaches tuck into Sue's bhuna regardless.

'I don't know how we went three down. When it gets to three all, we must be favourites. I thought we'd go on and win it in normal time. Frustrating!' is Ray's summary as he also stares into his pint.

The road to Wembley is closed. Diversions towards the Derbyshire Senior Cup in midweek will offer something resembling redemption for Paul Williams' men in midweek - which they take with a 1-0 victory over tenth tier Shirebrook Town — but it already feels like the early season optimism is beginning to ebb away without the driving force of Garry Brown.

The New Mills Ultras celebrate as the Millers peg back Radford. It would be in vain.

11

HANDS-FREE

'I'm on hands-free,' says the warm Lancastrian voice at the other end of the phone. 'I'm on my way to work. Can you hear me alright?'

A week has passed since Garry Brown left New Mills. Apart from a brief exchange of texts on the afternoon of the announcement, we haven't been in contact. It felt right to let the dust settle and the emotion drain away from the decision before quizzing him about it, but he's keen to chat all the same. And now, ahead of an evening of Europa League football from the stands of Old Trafford with his son, it seems like the best time to reflect on a remarkable 12 months in charge of the Millers.

'I'm fine,' he says in response to the simple opener of how he's getting on. 'Starting to relax away from the game and enjoying time away from football really if I'm being quite honest.'

It's the answer I expected; Garry tends not to dwell on the negative. But, one week on, I'm still in the dark as to why he did decide to leave.

'It was always a marathon and not a sprint at New Mills,' he begins. 'For me, the catchment area – people have to travel to get there – makes it a difficult area to bring players in but they've got a good squad. Being honest, I'd have liked to have a better start than we actually got. Having looked at it though, it was more than a management role and I didn't sign up for that. Personal circumstances have changed where my daughter's started university; my wife is at home on her own more. It was starting to affect my work time as well and I just couldn't do that,' he confesses.

'I still believe in the philosophy we've set, I still believe New Mills is in a better place as it is now. I've left with no bridge burnt, amicably and professionally. Kept the people in place. I didn't tell the players because I wanted 100% professionalism put into the midweek game,' he says, confirming my suspicion that he had set the team up for the game against Abbey Hey.

'Knowing they had a couple of weeks of Cup games and not League games where points matter was a good time to put in a transition really,' he adds. It's a sentiment that wasn't necessarily shared by Sue but, then again, when is a good time to resign as manager of a football club? Despite this, the relationship between Garry and the club remains intact.

'It's a great club,' Garry continues. 'Ray and Sue, they do a lot and work tirelessly. There's not enough people like that (within the club) if I'm being totally honest. I wanted to help save the club and get it back on an even keel. I've done that. Just too much is being asked away from management.'

As Garry speaks, I begin to reflect back on his words when we spoke before training in Droylsden. With each echo from that conversation, it occurs to me this has perhaps been at the back of his mind for a while.

'I set myself up at the start of the season to have a spine of players,' he continues. 'Don't forget the amount of players you need to try and be successful in keeping them afloat. The season before, 60-odd players just to keep them going. This season, there must be twenty-plus players brought in. We had a new side and they're a very, very capable side. And I set my stall out to build a team around a spine of players which I thought would be there week in, week out. And if I'm being quite honest, I've felt a bit let down. Players circumstances change, I'm not blaming them, but it just changes the whole picture. Then I'm on the road again, trying to sign new players who are interested. It just became a cycle.

'Maybe someone now,' he begins, considering his words

carefully. 'Now is a good time for me to step aside and someone come in with their nucleus of players,' he goes on. With his own Assistant Paul Williams looking most likely to step in for the short to medium term at least, it's perhaps an ominous omen with regards to the limited pool of players within their combined networks.

'I said to Sue and Ray: "Look. I've run out of players to ask, I've gone through that many players. Do you feel the Club would benefit (from a change)?" Not from a complete change of things because I do think the structure is now right. But a fresh look at things and someone who has got their own networks to add to what we've got. I think it's one or two additions away from a promotion side. They're in a good position, ten or eleven games on the board, twelve points, they're midtable. It's a good time to go for me in my own mindset.'

The simple mathematics of Garry running out of players to approach who might improve the side made sense. With reinforcements required, there was nobody left to contact. But it wasn't just the arranging of the team and tactics each Saturday that he'd taken on.

'I was trying to help out wherever I could, organising wages, sorting out training venues,' he explains. 'I was liaising with the Development Team and seeing if they needed training venues, all as well as trying to juggle a full-time job. It got to the point that I had to make a decision for the good of the Club, really, and that's what I did. It got to the stage where I was spending less and less time at home. Even when I was at home, I was spending time getting new talent in and making sure the current talent is fine. Sorting lifts out. Managers do that, but as well as focusing the team, I was trying to do other things to assist the Club like getting the players to join the 100 Club (a fundraising lottery-style game run by the club to raise funds) where I'd analyse whether the player – because they're only on expenses really – I'd analyse that, if they'd played more than three games then I'd take £10 off 'em for the chance of winning the £100 but that then needed managing. It got to the point where I thought enough was enough.'

With a week away from Church Lane to compose his thoughts, it sounds like there have been times when Garry reconsidered his decision. Despite some emotion audible in his voice, though, he seems set on the outcome he came to.

'I've wrestled with it,' he says after a long pause. 'I've gone through the feelings of letting the team down. But then I think about what I have done and soon got past that one! I spoke to all the players – I have had some fantastic texts off the players. Those players have been given opportunities and they're a good set of lads. It's been a good pre-season, they've got some good young players in there and they are set up to push on. That's what is needed at New Mills; a really good learning environment where, ok, they can't continually keep making mistakes. But they need to keep working on that.

'It was difficult on Saturday,' he says, reflecting on a rare afternoon off as the Millers toiled against Radford. 'I didn't know what to do with myself. I was like a bear with a sore head so I wasn't much company at home anyway. I got invited to another football match, I've been invited to plenty of those, but I didn't go. I've got better as the week has gone on. It was a massive bugbear because I wanted to go to training and face the lads,' he says, somewhat wistfully. 'But no, I've made my decision and I always said if I'd have gone with my heart then I'd still be there now. But I had to go with my head this time. It was a massive task but I've no regrets whatsoever and hopefully I've put some good into the Club and they can kick on, which I'm sure they will.'

A week on from his departure, the Millers have played two Cup games, with a third to come in the Macron League Cup on Saturday. In a period where fixtures come thick and fast, Garry acknowledged the importance of continuity. I'm intrigued as to how he feels about his long-term management partner Paul Williams taking the reins.

'I'm still talking to Willo, finding out how they're getting on and offering advice and so on,' he says, seeming a little guarded on the subject. 'I've been down and had a cup of tea with the captain Ryan Hopper and given him advice. Me and Willo go back years and there's very limited people you can trust in football. I've got his back and he's got mine. The players asked him to stay and I'm quite glad they did. It's something we've done together and he's taking over the baton and that's a good thing. He realises my situation has changed and he knows I've no remorse, no regret and no ill-feeling towards the Club and I will support them, but I just had to support them from afar while I deal with this different chapter of my life.

'There was no feeling of wondering why he's taken over now I've left,' Garry confirms a little more forcefully this time. 'I offered him my support and he rang me up on the way home from the match on Tuesday. I'll always offer him advice; whether he takes that is up to him. But we're good friends. I spoke to Dougie, gave him contacts to speak to. It's like I'm still involved but I'm not.'

Following their successful partnership of several years, I expect that chat with Paul must have been a tricky one. Only matched, perhaps, by the difficult conversation with Sue and Ray, after a year of working so hard to arrest the Millers' slide on and off the pitch.

'I spoke to Willo about my intentions,' Garry continues. 'I spoke to Sue and Ray about my intentions and was asked to sleep on it. I did take time out and I didn't sleep very well. And it is with a heavy heart, it really was, and I know they're all clichés but I put a lot into that club. I'm not one of these managers who walks away and takes all the players or offers them to other clubs. Quite the opposite.

'I'm not rushing back to be a committee member. I need to do it for myself. I've put a lot in and some of it has been from the kindness and goodness of my heart. I wasn't after sympathy but I've had some really nice texts and knowing you've had a positive impact on people's lives. That's reward enough for me. I've done my job.'

Reflecting on last season, we go back over a few of the points he'd made in our previous chat. Most pertinently, he mentions again that he felt the future of New Mills was potentially in doubt had things spiralled any further out of control last season.

'Last year, how we got through that? As soon as you fail to put a team out and the fines come in, that'd be it. We got a team out every week and that was blood, sweat and tears. You see these managers on three million a year doing silly things,' he says, in an unsubtle reference to the scandal that rocked the FA just a few days earlier with Sam Allardyce. 'We're on nothing.'

'This year, we said "this is what we're gonna do", the plan for pre-season. Individual development for team development as a whole, improve players individually and help them realise their dreams. I purchased GPS technology out of my own pocket which did heat maps. Dan Greaves, great asset, did individual stats. Spending four hours each weekend how many passes, forward passes, shots on. That team is still in place and there's no better place to develop than New Mills.'

I'm speaking to Garry in the week that the biggest football bust in years has taken place. Since the beginning of the week, The Times have released footage and transcripts of several big names being 'stung' by undercover reporters posing as business associates. Several names are tarnished, none bigger than recently installed England manager Sam Allardyce. While Big Sam might have a decade and more on Garry, their footballing paths might have once been more parallel, as the promising Oldham Youth player tried to break through the ranks while journeyman Allardyce was plying his trade up the road at Preston in the old Fourth Division.

I'm wary of how Garry feels about the direct comparisons – I know only too well how ludicrous he found the talk of Mourinho last season – but as he brought it up, and as a man who has dedicated much of his life to football, I'm intrigued to discover his opinion on the perceived greed culture at the very top of football that's helped to create the self-made sword that would be the now former England manager's downfall after just one game in charge. What does it say about the state of the game?

'People at grassroots level, volunteers, are just relying on local investment and local business,' he says, his voice finding a new strength and passion. 'And if they don't get that, they're on a hiding to nothing. There's not even the facilities to go and train on. I go on a pitch near my house and it's always waterlogged or there's massive divots or there's no grass seed down or it's not been cut properly. I'm having a go at the investment in football with that. You go abroad and these 3G pitches, they're free! It's like going to the park. Over here, the cheapest we could get was £25 an hour. That's five people through the gate just to get the lads to training.

'I think football has got to be separated between the haves and have nots. The Premier League will be a Super League eventually within Europe. I worry for football, I really do, because it just relies on people like us to do it for free. There's only so much you can take - the volunteers at grassroots level are the champions but we just don't get the recognition. I know the FA have invested in Academies but Academies are for the professional clubs where they go round picking individuals. We're on about Joe Public where, when I was a lad, I'd put my coat down and play football. There needs to be more investment in getting kids to play football without it costing them. For instance, look at cycling. Free classes and whatever. Look at the difference it's made. I feel for it, I really do.'

We talk about the fees I pay for my son. For £160 a year we get six to eight weeks of games either side of a ten-week period over winter where mud-soaked pitches and flooded car parks render games unplayable.

'Exactly,' continues Garry, all too aware of the similar issues faced by junior sides in New Mills who travel outside of the town to train and play. 'So then they say, "we've got so many 3G facilities" and that's an income for them. We've got an obesity problem in this country and we need to entice them back into sport. People can't afford £160. £5 a week when people are on benefits is quite a lot of money. So it's getting to a state where those who have, get, and there's a lot of talent being wasted.

That's why I've always done it. Maybe once I've had time out, I've got this burning desire to use my philosophy to make individuals feel they can improve. Individuals though, not groups, Academies are one size fits all. Making individuals improve, "you can do this, you can do that", that's what I'm interested in. But I won't manage again,' he says, with some conviction. 'That's me done for management.'

It's a surprise to hear him say this with such certainty. And, having seen the impact he's had on his young team and New Mills as a football club alongside knowing how much of his life has been devoted to football, it's more than a little sad.

'When you're doing it for petrol money now and again? It's impossible,' he continues. 'I purchased all the balls, I purchased a mat for the physio so she could come for training. It comes to a point when you can only give so much and I'm not saying people abused my good nature but, the sport, there's only so much you can put into it before it's taking over your life. Enough's enough. I sincerely hope they do well, I hope their plans for better facilities come off. I said to Ray and Sue when I came in, the light was going out. Now it's a lot brighter. I just hope local people get behind it, not to be looking for some multi-million business. Just to keep it running as a community club.'

And what about the expectations of the Club? Are they realistic?

'They had this bit of success in the past few years and I think they're just chasing that success a bit too quickly and that added to the pressure for me. I couldn't do it as quick as everyone wanted it. I always knew it was a marathon and this season was about maintaining, keeping the team together, getting the team together, galvanising. Consistency. After a rest, I've got an appetite for development and that's where my interest lies. That's what enlightens me and gets my juices flowing. I won't do management again and I think people just need to realise how much managers do.

'But overall, how do I reflect?' he says, before a long pause. 'Sense of achievement…definitely a sense of achievement.

Learned a lot about football, met some fantastic people and will always be friends. Learnt a lot about myself as well. I don't look back with any regrets whatsoever. I feel like I've had a positive impact on football and a positive impact on the club,' he says emphatically. 'And I'm happy with that.'

And will there be a few more trips to Old Trafford?

'I hope so,' he laughs. 'I've not done it for years. We've got a lad that's progressed to First Team football at FC United now so I'll go watch him. My lad has just started a PHD in Ormskirk so I'll be going to Man United with him. That makes me feel good. Like I've made the right decision. I went to see my daughter at University yesterday. I've put a lot of time into football and now I'll put more time into them. You'll see me at New Mills in time. I'll support them but it'll be as a spectator and a supporter. That's it for me with football for a bit.'

And with that, we bid farewell. He asks me to stay in touch. His car sounds like it's reached its destination and the engine has been switched off. There's a metaphor in there somewhere. I recommend a couple of good football books for his more leisurely upcoming weekends and we hang up.

I try to picture Garry arriving at Church Lane in the future to watch a game. It feels hard to imagine it'll be something he's willing to do this season, at least. The battle-scars seem too raw; there's a fire missing from his belly that was there before. There's also a calmness when speaking of the family time he has to look forward to that feels like it could keep the conflict of stepping away from football at bay – for a little while, at least.

Only one man truly knows. Garry Brown – former manager of New Mills AFC.

12

THERE'S MORE THAN ONE PAUL WILLIAMS

'You wanna go way back!' laughs Paul Williams. 'Where have I not played? Jesus Christ. Shall we get it up on Wikipedia?'

Paul Richard Curtis Williams was born in Leicester in 1967. With more than 350 appearances under his belt as a defender for Stockport County, West Bromwich Albion and Plymouth Argyle, he carved out a solid career across more than a decade in the professional game which included Premier League appearances in the sky blue of Coventry City.

For clarity, however, it should be noted that he's not the Paul Williams who also represented Derby County, Southampton and Stoke, nor is he the Paul Williams who scored goals for Sheffield Wednesday, Crystal Palace and the England Under-21s. He's most certainly not the Paul Williams who wrote the Academy Award-nominated Evergreen for Barbra Streisand, which was actually released around the time of his ninth birthday. Glad we cleared that up.

We begin our conversation slightly out of step with the chronology of this book. The opening half of our conversation takes place alongside my initial chat with Garry Brown in September. Still very much a management partnership at the time, Garry speaks warmly of his friend and colleague and invites him to share his experiences as a player. It's where this chapter begins.

'I started as an Apprentice at Leicester but even before that I went to the School of Excellence at Lilleshall. We did our schooling and then we went to training straight after that,' he says, referring to the now defunct FA scheme that ran for a decade and a half until its closure in 1999. 'That was run by The FA and we were the first intake of kids from school. Bobby Robson, Dave Sexton...' he says, pulling out his phone to proudly show me an Instagram image of the Class of '84. 'We had all the top coaches coming in, top players like Bryan Robson and Peter Shilton used to come down and try and educate us.'

While sometimes criticised for its approach to developing players, the Independent's Phil Shaw wrote in 1993 that more than 40% of graduates had gone on to make their professional debuts. Its alumni would include Nick Barmby, Andy Cole, Sol Campbell and Michael Owen, before the Lilleshall experiment was brought to a close and Centres of Excellence sprung up at clubs across the country.

'I was there for two years until 1986 and played about twelve internationals,' Willo continues. 'We played an international game against Italy on the pitch before the 1985 FA Cup Final. I was at Leicester for two years after that before they said they were going to release me. They then offered me the chance to go on a tournament which I did well in. Pisa came in for me because I was on a free,' he adds wistfully of the once in a lifetime chance to play abroad. 'Then they (Leicester) said "you can't go, it's a hundred grand". I said, "you let me go last week?" but the old system was that if you still had a contract, they had the choice of selling you or letting you go. So I was forced then to sign a 12-month contract, they thought the money was gonna come in and it never materialised and then I moved on to Stockport County.'

Paul's story is a familiar one for players of his era. It was a time when clubs often had the strongest hand and could block moves accordingly if the fee for an out-of-contract player wasn't deemed sufficient. It was a rule that would remain in place until Jean-Marc Bosman's successful legal challenge against RFC Liege, the Belgian FA and UEFA in 1995 – half a decade too late for a young Paul Williams and a potential dream move to Tuscany.

'I struggled in the first year a little bit,' he says of his time at

Stockport, 'and then managed to get in the team towards the end of that season. The following season we got promoted with Andy Preece and Kevin Francis. I was the first to move on to Coventry City and a few of the lads moved on to bigger and better things.

'From there, I was in and out of the first team so they asked if I wanted to go on loan so I went to the Albion (West Bromwich). They were struggling and (we) kept them midtable and I just basically wanted to play and I came back (to Coventry) and was stagnating again because we changed managers from Bobby Gould to Ron Atkinson. Started off alright, then was in and out, so they said, "it's not working out for ya, we want you to go and get some more experience."'

Still only in his early 20s, Paul's solid start at Stockport was beginning to stagnate further up the league ladder. It would take a step back down to reignite his career.

He continues: 'I went to Huddersfield, they were midtable, got promoted there. I just wanted to play and got really frustrated and then, during that year, Plymouth came in and Neil Warnock said, "do you want to come down and play?" and I said, "where the hell is that?"' He lets out a hearty laugh following this recollection. 'He said "it's miles away but it's a nice part of the world."

'So, in the end, I wanted to play and so I went down there and got promoted. I did about three seasons on the bounce, played about 160 consecutive games and really enjoyed my time down there. He was right, it is a nice part of the world. Then Tony Pulis came in and I signed for another two years. But the type of player I was and the way he wanted to play weren't suited and it just wasn't my game. We didn't get on or see eye to eye so I was there for about six months.

'By then, Neil had done all his rounds here, there and everywhere so I ended up (with him again) at Bury,' he recalls, remembering a time when he was a trusted steed of one of football's most loyal managers. 'I played in the Championship for about two seasons. When he moved on, Andy Preece came in and my contract ended. He said, "we can't afford you, we're gonna have to let you go."

'I had a house back down in Leicester by then so went back home, played a bit of non-league for Ilkeston but I just couldn't settle at the time because all my mates were back up here. The house was getting a bit too expensive because I had a spell then where I went back to college to re-educate myself and the money wasn't there so I struggled for a few years and had to sell up. I bought a little house in Darwen for about thirty-five grand, did it up, sold it for about a hundred and twenty and made a killing, but it put me back on my feet,' he says.

While the life of a professional footballer might be perceived from the outside as glamorous, the reality is often quite the opposite. Away from the bright lights of the multi-million pound top flight, Paul's career path hints at the sudden and sharp readjustment to life outside the game experienced by so many.

'I got a job, ended up playing for Hyde and then, the more I worked, the more I ended up going into the coaching side. Then I went up to Ramsbottom because my mate Andy Feeley was up there and asked if I wanted to do a bit of coaching for him. I went up there and helped him out and then he ended up leaving. So from being a coach, I ended up managing for about seven months on my own! No Assistant, nothing.'

Being thrust in at the deep end would give Paul a taste of things to come – and, at the time of us speaking, he had little idea that set of circumstances would come so soon again at Church Lane.

'I was managing, coaching and had a physio and the board behind me and that was it,' he continues, on his time at Ramsbottom. 'They asked me if I could do it and I told them I had no choice as they'd just lobbed me in at the deep end. We were in the bottom three but ended up midtable. After that, I decided to take a bit of respite and went up to Rossendale which is where we joined up together and it took off from there,' he says, nodding in the direction of Garry.

Earning a living away from football for the first time since leaving school must be difficult. Thankfully for Willo, it seems like he's laid solid foundations following his time spent studying and the house renovation that proved so profitable.

'I work for BOC, we're a worldwide company worth about £2.5bn. I used to do the managing side but they changed our role. I used to be office-based but they made me field-based and gave me a bigger pay rise which was nice. But the only downside is I don't know where I'm going from one day to the next, so one day I could roll in and it's Manchester, the next day you're down in Wales,' he says. 'Or back in Plymouth!' I add, which receives a big laugh from Ryan Hopper this time, who you might recall had made our three-way conversation a foursome several chapters ago.

'I get in for 6am, don't know where I'm going. It could be a matchday, I could have 20 calls and I've gotta try and get that done by half past four, get in the car and get back to training. It's an absolute nightmare because Gaz tries to sort things out and I get there and it's tough because I've got two kids as well. My other lad is at FC United so I try and watch him on my days off. Sometimes I don't see the kids for two or three days because they're only young and in bed, so it's tough. If it helps the club and helps some of the lads progress then it's worth it to see some of them moving on.'

As coaches in the ninth tier of English football go, and with respect to the current managerial incumbents, it could almost be said that Willo is over-qualified. There aren't many former Premier League players plying their trade this deep into the football pyramid. What's it like for an ex-Pro of his quality managing at this level?

'It's frustrating because when you're playing, you can do something about it. But when you're watching and you're trying to tell the lads what to do, you get stressed because you end up kicking everything and heading everything and you think you can still do it and then you get on the pitch and you can't,' he laughs. 'Obviously your mind can still do it but your body can't because your body just isn't working with your mind anymore and it's unbelievably frustrating.

'That's why I have all my shirts and all my medals in a box. I hardly have anything out. The missus says she wants to do a memorabilia room but I've said no because it's a chapter that's shut. A few of my lads (I've managed and played with), because they've had it and they can actually see it, they've had depression and stuff like that. I didn't want that so that's why I boxed it up and put it in the loft. It's a chapter of my life that's over and done with and you move on. That's how I've managed to deal with it. But every so often it does get frustrating and you're just sitting there wishing you could do it again but you can't turn back the clock,' he says, quite wistfully.

Willo's honesty about the risk of depression is as refreshing as his methods of avoidance are surprising. His resolute refusal to create a permanent shrine to his playing days, though, certainly seems a logical way of keeping the past where it belongs.

'I was fortunate enough to work with some really good people. Bobby Gould, Dave Sexton, Bobby Robson, but also different extremes like Keith Burkinshaw. So all different styles and I've taken a lot from all those different types of people and then try and put that little bit into the lads. It's stood me in good stead.'

Such an illustrious selection of former managers reinforces Williams' career as a player of genuine quality. With such a level of professional experience, it's hard to imagine his frustration at what he's seeing at times from his side on the pitch, not least when we resume our conversation several weeks later after the Radford defeat – his first game in charge that ended in such bitter disappointment.

'I was basically one of those type of players who, if people didn't pull their weight, I'd be having a go at 'em,' he says, harking back to his own playing days and the old school football dressing room. 'I'd be grabbin' 'em and getting a grip of them to get them to start pulling their weight.

'What Dougie did over there, kicking the bins?' he says, gesturing over to the dugout behind him and his striker's - and also new assistant's - outburst at the final whistle. 'I'd have been like that because I'm driven, like Dougie is. To be successful, you have to be driven and that's the way it is. And if you haven't got that component and that nasty streak about you then you shouldn't be playing the game as far as I'm concerned. That's the reason why I survived so long because I was so aggressive, people hated playing against me because I didn't care how big they were, I was decent in the air, I was quick, so I was quite capable of mixing it, plus I could play, it wasn't a problem for me.

'To play in a Tony Pulis side, Neil Warnock's side, you had to have something about you to play in those sides. I played for Neil Warnock for about four seasons, won two promotions with him. Then I ended up at Bury with him and he said "that's the reason why you play for me because it does what it says on the tin. I know you're aggressive, I know you're quick, I know you're strong and that's why you play for me," and I played two hundred and odd league games for him.'

To end our conversation as we sit on the weathered pub benches outside the clubhouse reflecting on a disappointing afternoon's toil, I try to end on a positive. With so many professional appearances and a brief cameo in the Premiership glory days, who would Willo class as the finest opponent he's ever encountered?

'One of the best players I played against was Ruud Gullit,' his says, his eyes and voice lighting up slightly at the memory. 'I'll always remember it, he was tight in the bottom corner here,' he says, turning round to re-enact the Dutchman's magic in his imagination. 'I think it was me, Ronnie Mauge, Adrian Littlejohn...there were three of us trying to nobble him! It was a pre-season game. He'd not long got World Player of the Year. He bounced us all off and hit an absolute worldie of a pass to the opposite end of the pitch, pinpoint and to their feet and we all just stood there and clapped him. We could not believe how he got out of it and then found time to hit an absolute stormer. We couldn't believe it,' he says, mentally reliving the shock and admiration of witnessing one of the greatest players to ever take the field at such close quarters.

'He was player-manager at Chelsea at the time. So I got his

shirt, got it signed and all that. He was unbelievable. When it comes to stature, he was up there. I played against a few of them though; Peter Beardsley, Andy Cole, Cantona…I played against all of them. But that situation sticks in my mind more than anything else. He still had pace, even at 35, he could move and run with the ball. He did everything. He was the one who stood in my mind, even over Cantona. Always managed to make a lot of time for himself. People like Jan Mølby, he was another one. I played against him at Liverpool and then we played against him in the Masters,' he says, recalling his time representing Coventry City in the indoor pre-season tournament that was once a staple of Sky Sports' summer coverage.

'Everybody thinks it's a nice cushy floor; it's a hard floor with green carpet on it. It's rock hard. And the lighting is big lamps coming down. The shirts are dead thick so you're just sweating buckets, your knees are killing. He never moved out of the centre circle. Just sprayed it about, made it look dead easy. I've been very fortunate to play with the players that people still talk a lot about now – your Paul Scholes and David Beckhams. I've had a very blessed career.'

While a more comfortable retirement might have been nice, Willo seems to take pleasure in developing young players almost as much as Garry. With his own son Jake rising up the ranks of non-league, he's got plenty of constructive advice for those wishing to progress and improve their game.

'I didn't make as much money as I'd have liked to but I was very blessed to play in a good era. The players then in the early Premier are ten times better than what they are now and that's what I say to my lad at FC United. As long as you do the basics well, you can go far. He's got components because he's decent in the air and he's quick. He can play at either right back or right midfield. That's the difference – when he beats someone, he'll cross it. He won't even hesitate. Our lads, take a touch, take a touch. Every time you take a touch, the defender gets closer. It's what I've said to these lads. When you get the ball, you've got to cross it.

'Same as taking a strike. Move it, take a strike, because every time you take a touch, you get closed down. This is the difference between the higher level and lower. Vision is good because they see things earlier. But if something's on, they'll play it. When you train with someone week in, week out, you can play blind to a certain degree because you know where he's gonna be standing. They do the basic stuff well, that's all it is, and they're fitter. And there's really that much difference between this level and the top. They just keep it all day, have that bit of quality, get half a yard in with a bit of backlift, it's in the back of your net and you're thinking "what happened there?"

'They're taking the strike early because the 'keeper's not set and he's bouncing around. That's what I try and explain to our lads. As soon as I think there's a chance, shift it, smash. Same as down the line, if you're running out of pitch, just put it in an area. Our lads will take a touch, look, take a touch look and it's gone. I say to them "the pitch doesn't move. The goals don't move." You've got to have pictures in your mind, do it and trust your instincts. The lads don't do it enough and that's the big difference between when you're playing at the top level and this one.'

Our conversation ends there. Between the two halves of our chat, his circumstances have changed considerably. Once the Assistant to his old friend, he's now the lead figure in a management trio receiving a baptism of fire.

Things would soon get much tougher.

13

AUTUMN LEAVES

October marks the beginning of a busy month, both at Church Lane and at Chez Jones. It begins, though, with a controversial U8s match on the playing fields of Chesterfield. With my son leading the attack once again, this morning we're participating in something of a grudge match against our 'sister' team from the same village and accidental arch rivals, the Wildcats. It doesn't start well.

'Come on lads!' bellows their Assistant Manager at his gaggle of seven and eight-year-olds as we, the opposition, take a very early lead. 'It's not won yet!' We're three minutes into a 40-minute game of kids' football. He's right; it's definitely not won yet. Despite being an otherwise respectable member of society, to say he takes his duties on the sidelines a little too seriously is a bit like suggesting Bob Bradley was about to have a difficult spell in charge of Swansea.

It all started a few years ago. As six-year-olds, the boys (and an encouraging smattering of girls who, sadly, didn't continue) all trained together. At the advent of the Under-7s season, when teams are formed and fixtures are set, the bumper group was split down the middle. That's when the trouble began.

As both sides struggled to win a game in their acclimatisation to a league seemingly made up of better drilled and more experienced teams, we still watched their development with enjoyment. With two separate management teams and petty squabbles brewing over shared training nights and other inconsequential things, our mercifully more laidback managerial duo agreed to a request to begin training separately. This would still occasionally see us run into the odd conflict, but generally kept the trivial fallouts to a minimum. That was until the inaugural 'local derby' reared its ugly head.

I can't deny I probably enjoyed the resulting furore a little too much. Our easy-going style was in stark contrast to the 'win at all costs' approach that also wasn't really paying dividends either across the training field. This was still kids' football, however, with all concerned either committed volunteers or dedicated parents. Hearts were in the right place, by and large, even if egos and noses were sometimes put out of joint. Even now, it's hard to imagine how things became quite so heated.

Having found their feet and a couple of positive results a little earlier than our team did, the Wildcats were openly predicting victory in that first meeting. That's right: like prime Mourinho goading Wenger or Fergie prodding Keegan, the Matlock and Rowsley District U8s league was the stage for pre-match mind games.

With just one win to our name back then, a 1-0 triumph in a 'friendly', it was hard to argue with the common assumption that we were the underdog. Knowing that we had beatable opposition who were a little too confident about their chances, though, made the prospect of victory even more appealing.

'We're gonna win you!' one of their players growled at my son just before kick-off as I tied his shoelace.

'It's 'beat'. And no you're not,' I mumbled back under my breath.

That first match was one of the tensest games of football I've ever witnessed. It might sound ridiculous – in fact, if you've never had the investment of your own child in a game of kids' football while facing a touchline of adults urging their offspring to 'smash' into yours, I guarantee it does – but we really, *really* wanted this victory. In the end, a penalty in our favour settled the match 1-0. As the kids posed in front of their testosterone-pumped management teams with 'Fair Play' t-shirts on at the final whistle, the grudge had been temporarily put to rest; until the opposition claimed that the result wasn't really a victory with it being decided by a penalty, that is.

After drawing the next meeting 1-1, losing the one after 4-2 and then going on to exact revenge with a thumping 6-1 victory in subsequent games, the newfound local dominance of our beloved little Falcons was close to being confirmed when the league's fixture secretary dictated that our paths would cross again in an unfathomably congested fixture list. By this time, parental friendships on Facebook had been culled and harsh words had been spoken – these were largely between the management team of the opposition and some of our parents, many of whom will spend the next decade stood alongside each other at the school gates. It was getting out of control.

'Handball! HANDBALL!' shouts their Assistant Manager, in the latest instalment of our village's answer to Boca/River Plate, as he wills his side to doggedly defend a one-goal lead for the best part of 40 minutes. He's parking the school bus, if you will.

I grimace a little as I realise the significance of the incident. A difficult bouncing ball heads towards my own son, Jacob, who controls it with his chest but sees the ball nudge his left arm on its way to the ground. It's unintentional. It's borderline. The ref plays on. Our resulting attack leads to the equalising goal.

'Ref! Are we playing handball?' shouts their Assistant Manager at the bewildered looking 17-year-old with a whistle, who is unaware of the subtext behind his assignment this morning, as he signals for the match to restart in the centre circle.

'HANDBALL!' he cries again a few minutes later. Thankfully, my son is at the other end of the pitch day-dreaming, although this one looks more nailed on. Again, the ref doesn't give it. Instead, he blows his whistle to momentarily stop the game and takes the Assistant Manager to one side for a chat. For the next excruciating minute, everyone diverts their gaze as far away from the heated exchange as possible as an adolescent explains his decisions to a fully-grown man.

'This is kids' football,' is the only audible line we pick out. Meanwhile, twelve 'not quite yet' adolescents stand dumbstruck on the field, unsure of why there's been a delay in proceedings.

'How much did you pay the ref?' he asks one of our parents a little later, only half-joking. There comes a point when you can't actually reason with a person. When they accuse you of bunging an under-8s match is usually that moment. We went on to win the match 4-2. I dropped a horse's head off at the next teenager reffing our game the following week on my way home, as is customary. It might be kids' football but a win is a win at the end of the day.

Much like the Falcons, October also began promisingly for Paul Williams' men. A 1-0 victory over Squires Gate in the Macron League Cup would make it two wins out of three in the consecutive cup games that have begun his reign to give the new men in charge a little momentum going back into the League campaign. When Tunde Owolabi puts the Millers 2-0 up at Hanley Town after 56 minutes the following midweek, the Radford game is beginning to look like little more than an unfortunate blip on the scorecard.

Goals from Jon Higham and Ben Rowley in the 79th and 81st minutes put paid to the Millers' hopes of a second win on the road for the season and New Mills would have to settle for a 13th point of the campaign.

The fixture list wouldn't be kind when throwing up the first opportunity on home soil to rectify the Radford defeat. Atherton Collieries, fierce contenders for the title and the solitary promotion berth into the Evo-Stik that comes with the trophy, arrive in good form to face a New Mills side missing key man Ollie Martin between the sticks. With the visitors guided by former Manchester United youth player Michael Clegg, there's a very reasonable chance you'd find both of this afternoon's managers in your 94/95 FA Carling Premiership sticker album.

The Millers use the match the showcase their new kit, a stylish early 90s-inspired amber with black stripe design, a winning entry of a summer competition to generate interest with the fans and local community. Its stylish unveiling has been slightly overshadowed by a delay at the suppliers – this being the primary reason it's being launched closer to Bonfire Night than opening weekend.

Atherton show little regard for any sentimentality as they take the lead from the spot in the opening few minutes. A second is added by former Millers striker Darrhyl Mason just before the break.

'He played two games for us and then left,' Fixture Secretary Derek tells me a little disdainfully. 'I'm not his biggest fan.'

The Atherton game is also my introduction to a new fan who will become a regular face at Church Lane in the months to come. He's a larger-than-life character who is quite difficult to miss.

I've never been one to judge a book by its cover but, on the face of things, we wouldn't necessarily be a natural fit for a bond that will continue to grow for the remainder of the season. Despite a significant chill in the air, Jon Warrior stands proud in a deer stalker hat, Liverpool FC shorts and a 'No to the EU' t-shirt. In his early 20s, he strikes the pose of a man at least twice his age with a pipe in one hand and a walking stick in the other. A small dog sits obediently near him.

'I've started coming down here because I had a bit of trouble at County,' he says, referring to his hometown team Stockport. 'I was getting bullied and picked on. But it seems much nicer here,' he confides. Jon introduces me to his care worker, a chap called Alan who doesn't seem overly fond of football but is present all the same. Due to several long-term conditions, Jon is provided with support by his local authority. He's a lovely lad with a booming laugh and a bright outlook on life. Time will tell how long that will last on current form.

Atherton go on to add another three in the second half. Mason is awarded the man of the match. It begins to feel like the clouds are gathering once again over Church Lane.

'If we'd have got that early strike, maybe we could have done something,' muses a dejected looking Paul Williams in the clubhouse later. 'Really though, I always felt it could be damage limitation here. They're paying out a lot of money. Their main striker is on £150 a week. As for their other striker, Darrhyl, we offered him £50 and it wasn't enough so he went to Widnes. We can't compete with that. Having said that, he's had six clubs in four months! So that sums him up maybe!' he says, letting out a huge laugh.

'We'll be playing teams around us in the coming weeks,' he continues, referring to the games against Maine Road and Congleton, the two sides just above them, before a November that sees fixtures against Darwen, Barnton and Squires Gate – all of whom are in marginally more precarious positions than the Millers in a tight battle near the bottom.

'We've got to start picking up points now. It's got to the point where I think I'm gonna have to change the formation in midfield. My four lads in there aren't working hard enough so we're gonna have to work on that in training, so I'll look at it. But we were missing a few lads today as well so we need to get them back. That's the key.'

He remains upbeat, laughing and joking with Atherton striker Mason, a player he's nicknamed 'Tiger', as he leaves the dressing room. There are no outward signs of the pressure building despite the Millers' biggest defeat of the season so far. Ray adopts an increasingly familiar post-match routine of staring glumly into his pint.

Captain Ryan Hopper cuts a desolate figure too. Sometimes picked out as the focus of vocal ire from the chairman, he looks particularly affected by the defeat.

'It hurts,' he says with a pained expression on his face. 'We shouldn't be losing like that. We're better than that.'

'Chin up, Ryan,' says one fan. He forces a smile in reply, but it's etched all over his face. As 23-year-old captain, it's his duty to face the fans after the game. Unlike some of his teammates, though, defeats like this one seem to hurt him more visibly and bring back painful memories of the previous campaign. There's clearly emotional baggage to returning to losing ways for the lads who endured it for over a year.

A 3-2 defeat at home to Maine Road, a Manchester City supporters club side formed in 1955 who play in the same light blue with a traditional crest, follows a creditable midweek 1-1 draw at AFC Liverpool, themselves a supporter-led club set up in 2008 in protest against rising ticket prices at Anfield. As the table begins to take shape, the Millers start to find themselves cut adrift in the bottom five from the comfort and consolidation of midtable.

There are words of encouragement from AFC Liverpool on Twitter at least:

Two entertaining encounters with New Mills. With Tunde and Daniel Douglas-Pringle in your side, you'll do fine.

As the Millers begin to find themselves sucked deeper and deeper into a third consecutive season battling relegation, they had better hope so.

Paul Williams watches on from the dugout

LEAGUE TABLE

		PLD	GS	GC	GD	PTS
1st	Runcorn Town	17	41	21	+20	39
2nd	Atherton Collieries	18	46	19	+27	37
3rd	1874 Northwich	17	36	20	+16	36
4th	Runcorn Linnets	17	37	15	+22	34
5th	Bootle	16	43	28	+15	33
6th	Hanley Town	17	38	25	+13	27
7th	West Didsbury & Chorlton	15	39	26	+13	25
8th	AFC Liverpool	16	33	28	+5	25
9th	Abbey Hey	16	28	25	+3	25
10th	Irlam	15	21	26	-5	24
11th	Padiham	16	26	26	0	23
12th	Barnoldswick Town	15	30	28	+2	19
13th	Congleton Town	15	34	37	-3	19
14th	Squires Gate	15	33	39	-6	19
15th	Maine Road	14	32	24	+8	18
16th	Winsford United	13	19	25	-6	18
17th	Ashton Athletic	14	30	29	+1	17
18th	New Mills	15	26	35	-9	14
19th	AFC Darwen	15	16	42	-26	11
20th	Barnton	16	16	51	-35	10
21st	Nelson	15	15	33	-18	8
22nd	Cammell Laird	17	16	53	-37	5

Correct as of October 22nd

14

A NEW MILLS FAMILY HOLIDAY

The Jones family half-term holidays are generally a stressful time. We love our children, but being two working parents on a limited budget, it usually means juggling a busy week working from home while entertaining the kids with various screens and a sprinkling of arts and crafts.

This October would be different. Like the Waltons on tour, the four of us would be taking our Jack Russell/Shih Tzu cross pup (a Jack-Tzu, not a Jack-Shit if you were wondering) Indiana Jones on his first ever holiday. We'd be squeezing into a two-bedroom static caravan for a week in North Yorkshire for seven days of board games, no Sky TV and a considerable reduction in personal space. Here's how that went:

Saturday:
Time for holidays. Except it wasn't really. First up, my son's Under-8s team have a match. A thrilling 3-2 win completed by two absolute worldies from our midfielder-cum-goalkeeper gets the weekend off to a brilliant start. It's not so great for New Mills who, as previously mentioned, are unfortunate to lose 3-2 against Maine Road by all who witness it. I'm en route to host a gig down south as the final whistle blows.

The comedy night, which takes place in a village hall in rural Cambridgeshire, is so posh that there's a sound sensor in the room for noise pollution that shuts off the electricity if the sound goes above a certain level. It does, twice, at one point leaving TV's Patrick Monahan in the pitch black with 100+ audience members staring in bewilderment in his general direction. I almost hit a young deer which saunters across the road on the way back home. It's not my first near miss on country roads coming home late at night, but it's certainly the closest call I've ever had with inadvertently meeting Barry Venison. I did say it was posh round there.

Sunday:
Peace and quiet. Not the beginning of the holidays, but my own empty house with children, wife and dog already at the caravan. A lay-in, a bacon sandwich and Match of the Day in my pyjamas. An almost zen-like calm at the prospect at a week off work washes over me. This is soon gone after having to pack my own case, load the car up with children's bikes and end up barricading the dodgy patio door after it comes off its rails to ensure my house is secure for the next seven days.

Upon meeting my family in the on-site North Yorkshire pub at 4pm for Chelsea's demolition of Manchester United, I'm somehow convinced into a purchasing a pitcher of cider. Pleasantly merry by bedtime.

Monday:
A first visit to Bowness-on-Windermere since a romantic break in the days before children is marred slightly by the eldest's screen withdrawal symptoms. Our steadfast refusal to allow him to wander around playing Pokémon is, to his mind, the cruellest punishment known to man. His lingering grump eases slightly on a boat trip where we spot Princess Elsa's castle, according to our four-year-old, and our dog optimistically and courageously attempts to mount an Alsatian.

An early return to the car and much grumbling later and we're back at the caravan to enjoy the delights of Freeview.

Tuesday:
A much-needed lazy day. Some Pokémon, but not much. I make a spaghetti bolognese for my beloved family and eat it while

watching Gladiators on Challenge TV. I appear to be regressing back to my own childhood and still most definitely fancy Jet.

Wednesday:

Match day. I'd had New Mills in mind, of course, while booking our family break. It's a relatively slim tight rope to tread when you insist on precious family time being within an hour's drive of a Hallmark Security League team but, thankfully, I have an understanding spouse.

Church Lane was in fact an hour and twenty minutes down the road from our caravan park, making the journey slightly longer than my usual non-league commute, but it was one worth making all the same.

A miniature grudge match in the ninth tier was beginning to take shape against Congleton Town. With one win each in their two meetings so far, and the Cheshire side representing a marker point of the standard at the bottom of the lower midtable spots marked 'comfortable' that New Mills were beginning to crave, tonight was an important match for Paul Williams' men.

'I didn't think I was expecting to see you?' says Sue quizzically as I complete my unfamiliar route to Church Lane and meet her on the turnstile. 'Aren't you on holiday?'

'I am,' I reply, 'but there's only so much time you can spend in a static caravan in early autumn with your family before you need to seek out other forms of punishment.' She lets out a familiar hearty laugh.

In the end, 75 people witness a familiar tale. New Mills go in two down at the break and leak a third shortly after half-time. Sam Marshall's penalty against his former side is followed by a belter from Will Wareing with half an hour still to play. The Millers spend long periods of the rest of the match battering the Congleton goal without success. It's another defeat for the men in amber and black after giving themselves too much to do in the first half.

'It takes us 45 minutes to get going,' rants dejected chairman Ray in the clubhouse after the match. 'We should be at that intensity from the first minute,' he continues. It's hard to argue. Had New Mills spread their second half performance across the entire match, the result would have been comfortable. Instead, the league table is beginning to make increasingly ugly reading as the Millers start to look cut adrift from the sanctuary of midtable.

'I reckon that's twelve points now we could have had where we've been the better side,' he continues, staring into that familiar pint. 'We just need to make sure we beat the sides below us now. That has to happen. As we've always said, in this league, if you don't finish top then it doesn't really matter where you finish. The frustration of running a football club…' he sighs as he takes a few more sips.

I arrive back at the caravan in time to catch the opening credits of Murder She Wrote. My intrigue around the episode grew when Bryan Cranston of Malcolm in the Middle and Breaking Bad fame's name appeared. Went to bed shortly after he appeared on screen so I have absolutely no idea if he did it or not.

Thursday:

A trip to Blackpool to see the illuminations. My impression of Alan Bradley being hit by a tram gets absolutely nothing from my loved ones for the third year running. I also discover I've been cruelly overlooked on the new Comedy Carpet, in what can only be described as an admin error and has absolutely no correlation with my night job being at the stage where I still willingly accept gigs in village halls where you're actively heckled by the electricity supply cutting out.

Friday:

The final full day of our holidays and another relaxing one around the campsite. A game of football with my son turns into a two-stick-three head-to-head with a trio of nine-year-olds. He walks back to the caravan on Cloud Nine as a result of the biggest boy saying, "I can't catch him, he's too quick!" and "he's really good!" It's the first thing he tells his mum before admitting that we lost 4-3.

Saturday:
Home time. As we pack my wife and daughter in the car with the dog and send them on their way, it's a football day for me and my son. First on the agenda is a McDonald's breakfast, which we pick up on our way south in Burnley. Several fans in replica shirts tuck into their Bacon and Egg McMuffin alongside us ahead of the Clarets' short trip down to Old Trafford. With Google Maps suggesting we're just a mile away from Turf Moor, it's a good excuse to drive past a Premier League ground.

After that, we head to the National Football Museum in Manchester. After hearing rave reviews, we spend two brilliant hours there taking in memorabilia as varied as the original documents that set the rules of the game in place back in 1863 to a lock of Robbie Savage's hair. The commentary challenge, where visitors are invited to read an autocue of famous moments from the history of the game, offers Manchester United's 1999 FA Cup semi-final victory for us to recreate, John Motson-style. Jacob's reading is slightly too fast, delivering the line "he's scored a wonderful goal!" as Ryan Giggs is barely on the edge of Arsenal's box. He does muster the requisite level of excitement, however.

We both take on the challenge of beating a virtual goalkeeper in the excellent penalty shootout challenge and lose track of time directing our passes at light-up targets on the wall. It all leads to us failing to set off in the direction of New Mills until 2.15pm as we battle our way through the weekend city centre traffic to reach Church Lane.

Today's visitors for the Macron League Cup tie are Silsden, a West Yorkshire side from the division below. As Ray acknowledges in his programme notes, while the recent few games have been disappointing, he hopes the pressure of not playing for league points will mean "the boys can relax and turn on the football we know they are capable of."

As we arrive at Church Lane almost 15 minutes after kick-off, it's not looking promising. Handing over the bargain £7 that admits one adult and one child through the turnstiles, I ask a fan the score.

'1-1,' he tells me. 'We've only got one bloody outfield substitute. They're either on holiday or injured.'

Looking across the pitch at the barren dugout where Willo and Dougie are already giving instructions in an animated fashion, it becomes clear something has gone very wrong. While the squad list on the back of the programme shows a collective of 24 players, Willo has been let down by four key men overnight and this morning. Alongside the third choice 'keeper, Dougie is the only outfield player on the bench. He's not in the starting line-up as he's carrying a knock.

Silsden re-take the lead soon after our arrival with a well-worked goal picking apart a fragile-looking backline. It's enough to further test the patience of Ray as he stands with his arms folded behind the goal. Jacob makes friends with Ray and Sue's grandson and immediately heads off for the astroturf to recreate a few goals himself.

A simple free-kick into the box lands between the two centre halves and the Silsden forward heads home unchallenged to make it 3-1 minutes later. It's as basic a goal as you're likely to see, even at this level, and things get even worse when Dougie is forced to come on for the limping Ryan Hibbert.

'Come on New Mills,' says Sue, half-heartedly. Ray is less charitable.

'Shambolic,' is his assessment, with volume that's intentionally audible to the players.

Things begin to look worse when stand-in 'keeper Mason Mostyn struggles with a goalkick. He lifts his shorts up and looks accusingly at a heavily bandaged right thigh.

'Why don't you get the defender to take 'em, 'keeper?' a fan behind the goal half-suggests, half-instructs.

'It's fine,' he snaps back, clearly not happy with the unwelcome advice from the stands.

Half-time sees two slightly embarrassed Silsden representatives, who appear to be husband and wife, enjoying the home hospitality. They sip their tea quietly as a frustrated Ray silently seethes. Meanwhile, Secretary Derek buzzes around sending half-time scores to the League and appearing non-plussed by the performance on the pitch. He's undoubtedly dedicated to his role with the Millers but remains the most emotionally detached when things aren't going well.

'Elliott Watson looks like he's out for the season,' he tells me. 'Hopper is on holiday in Vegas. My pre-season prediction for finishing 15th is looking good. We can't defend, we can't score and we give the ball away too much,' he muses. 'We haven't got a goalscorer in the team.'

Sue is less frantic in her duties today, seemingly weighed down by worries on the pitch. A member of the coaching staff uses the moments before the restart to check on whether there's a spare outfield kit in the dressing room; embarrassingly, it's just in case the substitute goalkeeper needs to make an emergency appearance as an outfielder.

'It's a shambles,' she reflects. 'We've got to get to the bottom of it.'

There's reason for cheer immediately in the second half as the Millers pull back a well-worked goal in the opening sixty seconds.

'That's what I've been telling you to do for the last two games,' shouts a previously morose Willo as he makes his way back down the touchline to the dugout. It will be the final moment of hope on a dreadful afternoon.

Silsden make it 4-2 after 55 minutes. The regaining of the two-goal cushion leaves Derek and committee member Roy, a formidable chalk and cheese double act at the best of times, to come to a rare, shared viewpoint on the merits of the competition.

'Might as well go out today anyway,' says Derek. 'No money for going through, we have to pay their fees and for the refs. It's £1.50 a coach mile, you pick up injuries, it ruins the pitch…' he goes on. Roy nods mournfully.

'I think they'll get six today,' he continues, as Silsden break dangerously towards the New Mills half. Seconds later it's 5-2, as Mostyn's increasing lack of mobility appears to be being ruthlessly exploited.

'Derek, why don't you just shut up?' enquires Roy, as the familiar friction returns. Mostyn is immediately subbed, bringing temporary harmony back to Derek and Roy.

'Keeper's coming off injured,' remarks the former.

'He has been all game,' adds the latter.

'6-2. There we go,' says Derek somewhat cheerfully with 20 minutes to go as things get worse. A delightful chip over the third-choice goalkeeper on 74 minutes makes it seven.

'Derek? Derek! You were wrong!' calls Roy, finally getting into the gallows humour of it all. 'It's not six, it's seven!'

A strong, two-footed challenge from Mike Jones on the restart sees the Millers reduced to ten men. He doesn't look up once on the long walk back up the pitch but finds time to square up to the gathering melee of Silsden players who are keen to pass judgement on the tackle. Sue follows him in a bid to prevent further outbursts of frustration.

A rare attack from Dougie in the final minutes sees him ignore the support of Tunde and take on all-comers as he marauds into the box. His determination to pull back a further consolation leads him to blast a ball high over the bar. It hits a hanging basket beside the entrance to the clubhouse which leaves its vantage point of presumed safety and smashes on the concrete. Sue is assisted by a regular fan as she gets out her dustpan and brush. It's been one of those days.

Amidst the goal frenzy, I take a moment to absorb Ray's programme notes. They make uncomfortable reading given the disaster taking place on the pitch:

Chairman's Chat

Well, not the greatest of weeks for the lads.

Looking back on the last three games, we showed at times the good, the not-so-good and the darn right awful traits in our game, while also reflecting on the poor refereeing decision at AFC Liverpool in the last seconds that denied us what would have been a great win.

The last two games, however, we regressed back into making basic errors not just by the defence but collectively through the side. Having said all that, I am sure we can all see the potential to do well.

So welcoming Silsden to Church Lane in the Macron Cup, we hope with the pressure of the league points out of the equation, the boys can relax and turn on the football we know they are capable of. So let's get behind Paul, Dougie and the rest of the team and cheer them into the next round of the cup.

Go Millers

An eighth goal in added time piles on the misery and turns a thrashing into a cricket score.

'Fuckin' embarrassing, this! You're fuckin' embarrassing!' is the scream from one of the lads to his teammates.

'Ray isn't happy,' states Derek somewhat obviously. 'I wonder if he's in sacking mood,' he adds, malevolently.

'We're shit and we're sick of it,' one fan mock sings as he passes Ray on his way to the gates. Willo slowly makes his way up the pitch. It's hard to see such a proud ex-player with a solid professional career behind him being subjected to this.

Peering through the clubhouse window, the final whistle blows at Old Trafford. The Burnley fans we saw this morning have survived 36 shots from Manchester United to grab a point in a 0-0 draw. At Church Lane, with a combined total comfortably less than that, we've seen ten goals. It's a crude measure of entertainment, of course; but it's also not bad with change from a tenner, provided you're not a Millers fan.

The mood in the clubhouse is predictably sombre. Ray sips a pint and looks dumbstruck. Sue scalds the Silsden lads, unsurprisingly out of the dressing room first and tucking into the post-match buffet somewhat earlier than their opponents, when one player launches a bread roll across the room for a teammate.

'Really, lads?' she shouts. The victorious Yorkshiremen

momentarily regress to schoolboys as they quietly get back to their dinner. Alongside her permanently cheery demeanour, Sue has that gravitas.

Next out of the dressing room is physio Claire who gives an insight into the general mood.

'Dougie's givin' 'em a roasting in there. I came out – I'm scared!' she laughs. Ryan Hibbert, already in the clubhouse with a tray of curry following his early withdrawal, rolls up a trouser leg to show me the damage of a stud taken to the knee area. A decent swelling has emerged. He angrily wolfs his food as he openly suggests some of his teammates "don't care enough" about the run they're on.

'Sorry Willo,' is all I can offer to Willo when he does appear. Sue hastily grabs him a drink and jokingly offers added Prozac.

'There's no need for a chat today,' I say. We'd arranged a post-match get together but Willo, ever the pro, is a man of his word and he insists. We head outside where Mike Jones walks out of the dressing room past us and into the clubhouse.

'Sorry mate,' he says as he passes his manager. Willo, somewhat tellingly, doesn't respond. Jones' apology to the player he clattered to gain him early access to the showers is received more positively, though, as Silsden make their way out of the ground.

'Just frustration, lad. No worries,' offers his opponent sportingly as he heads for the gates.

Willo and I take a seat on the wet pub benches outside the clubhouse. A few remains of the stricken hanging basket can be spotted on the floor beside us and it's a little chilly on the derrière but there's nowhere else to go – Dougie hasn't quite finished giving one or two of the players a full going over in the dressing room.

'A couple of lads have had a few home truths,' he begins, downbeat. 'We've had a couple of good results, we've been a bit unlucky, but a lot of the lads dropped out at the last minute today which didn't help. But at the end of the day, we had enough to get something out of this game. Unfortunately, lack of concentration, lack of discipline…' he trails off, shaking his head.

'Dougie, being on the playing staff as well as the coaching staff, has delivered a few harsh words,' he continues. 'I didn't say much purely because we've been going over certain issues about systems, about the way of playing with individual players, and unfortunately I said to them "we can't keep on doing this", so I gave them an ultimatum in this game to try and get something out of it and then the next one (Darwen) which is the ultimate one – if we don't get a result, that's me done pretty much,' he says with a dejected sigh. It's another worrying omen for the long-term stability in the dugout.

'With individual errors, I can't legislate for that. That's the problem and it's boiled down to that really. At the end of the day, they're waltzing through (to score) and that's the reason why I'm bringing four new players in by Monday and hopefully shaking it all up. Plus we've got people coming back as well. It's got to change and it will change,' he adds forcefully.

'I put down for 17 players today, and to only get 12? It's just ridiculous. Certain individuals will get told. When they're not involved, they'll understand why.'

It's been a rocky start to life in the hotseat for Willo. But after so many years in the game, it certainly hasn't fazed him as he explains.

'The change in role (from Assistant to Manager) is not really a massive issue for me. What is an issue for me is when people don't give me 100%. People aren't doing what I ask. That's a problem for me as well. As I explained to them last week, if I can't solve it then not many can. You can't tell me I haven't played the game because I've played in every single position that you've all played in so I've got a decent understanding of every position going. Left back, right back, centre back…cos I played everywhere in the professional game so it's no different.

'The main thing for me is just too many basic errors. Giving the ball away in bad areas where people are counter attacking us which is causing a big problem to us. So yes, it is very frustrating and it's disappointing but I've got to stay positive for everybody.

I'm gonna turn it around and that's why I'm bringing new personnel in.

'It's got to the point where I have to change it,' he continues, 'because I can't rely on people not doing what I want. That's the difference, I must admit, with this level and the higher up you go. You tell an individual to do certain things, they won't argue because they'll say, "you know what, that's what my Gaffer wants, not what I wanna do." That's the difference. That's what I'm finding very frustrating because I'm not asking them to do something which is too complicated. That's the reason why I'm gonna have to change it.

'We're lacking leaders, we're lacking people who haven't got the will to overcome that difficulty and that's the biggest thing for me. Even when you've got your backs against the wall, you can still be offensive. The lads are just too busy sometimes laying down and dying.'

'Apologies,' says Mike Jones for a second time as he leaves the clubhouse and shakes Willo's hand.

'Listen Mike, at the end of the day you were one of the few who cares mate so don't worry,' responds Willo. It's a fair summary of his performance and an example of Willo's man management in action; having at first blanked the player who was arguably the most committed on a sorry afternoon to reflect on his red card, he sends him away with an encouraging word.

'Some of them in there aren't fit enough to wear the shirt,' the stand-in captain says as he heads for the gates.

'We've only got a few of them who actually care which is why we're gonna have to change it round quite a lot,' continues Willo as he watches him leave. 'Mike showed commitment today. We need more of that.'

If Williams had been unsure of the size of the task ahead of him, he surely couldn't be now. Even in the context of a winless season, the atmosphere at New Mills had reached a new low. Shipping eight goals at home to a side from the division below was an embarrassing new bullet point in an increasingly difficult chapter for the Millers.

15

A SIX-POINTER

'Welcome to Darwen' reads the sign as you enter the small Lancashire market town just off the M65 in England's far northwest. 'Proud home of Blackburn Rovers FC'.

If you turn right at the T-junction and you'll find yourself at Ewood Park, home of the 1995 Premiership Champions; but turn left, then left again by the head office of their one-time sponsors Crown Paints, and you'll arrive at the Anchor Ground, home of the Salmoners. While AFC Darwen might not be too thrilled that the name of a Championship club in a neighbouring town takes such pride of place just 500 yards from their front turnstile, there hasn't been much debate on who the biggest fish in the pond is around these parts for quite a while. It wasn't always this way.

One of the pioneers of professional football in the area, Darwen FC were formed in 1870, reaching the FA Cup semi-finals in 1881 and spending almost a decade in the Football League before the turn of the 20th century. That's not quite who today's opponents are, however.

Reformed from the ashes of Darwen FC in 2009/10, AFC Darwen is the phoenix club from the flames of destructive ownership that tore the historic old club apart. With plans for Darwen Council to buy the ground failing, Darwen FC were eventually wound up with £60k of debts after refusing an offer to repay 25p in the pound to a series of breweries, asset investment companies and a local radio station. The 134-year-old club ceased to exist. They've swum in these depths for much of the time before that winding up order and since.

On a bitterly cold Bonfire Night, FA Cup First Round ties are also kicking off around the country with the usual smattering of David vs Goliath meetings. Having followed 'underdogs' for the last few years, I've enjoyed a couple of games at this stage of the competition. It's one of my favourite afternoons in the football calendar, with visits to now extinct Norton FC of Staffordshire hosting Gateshead, as well as Gainsborough Trinity against Shrewsbury Town in the past couple of seasons giving me an insider's insight into just how big an occasion FA Cup First Round day often is for semi-pro sides. A particular highlight had been at Norton, where a large banner reading 'Good luck Mr Skillern' brandished by the P.E. teacher's entire class was clearly visible on Match of the Day later that evening. Dreams are made of this stuff.

Back in the reality of the North West Counties relegation battle, there was no argument that today's meeting was between perennial underdogs, even if the FA Cup First Round was something of a distant dream. Locked in the battle at the bottom, AFC Darwen vs New Mills was beginning to look like one of the Hallmark Security League's first six-pointers of the season. For New Mills, with the return fixture at Church Lane to come in just five weeks' time, it was at the very least 'must not lose'.

I meet Fixture Secretary Derek as I head through the turnstiles who gives me the rundown on the team. Most notable is the tall and graceful looking frame of 17-year-old Jack Taylor, an Academy player for Morecambe who has joined the Club on work experience to help shore up the defence – he's straight into the team at left back this afternoon. It's pretty impressive when you consider I spent a fortnight at a local café making scones for my work experience.

Also back in the team is captain Ryan Hopper. Absent on a holiday to Las Vegas for the mauling against Silsden, he's the kind of experienced head Paul Williams will be pleased to be able to call upon today. His attendance means photographer James has also made an appearance on the long trip north – there was a space in the car.

'Are we gonna get a win today, Underdog?' asks Jon Warrior, also here as part of a healthy travelling party from the High Peak. 'Bloody freezing, innit?' adds Jon. 'I think we should all come in onesies. Have they got them in the club shop?'

As an edgy match gets underway, it's already looking somewhat low on quality as the biting wind interferes with play. Despite that, New Mills are firmly on the front foot with two early attacks and a penalty shout in the opening two minutes. Just the start they need on current form.

'These are no worse than last week,' observes James, referring to Silsden. 'Apparently they sacked their manager the week after,' James adds. I check I haven't misheard him – they sacked their manager after an 8-2 win away at a side from the division above? 'It was on the league website,' he reiterates. 'I'd like to have seen that conversation: "we know you won 8-2 but we're gonna have to let you go."'

Keeping one eye on the FA Cup scores, Spennymoor's trip to Milton Keynes Dons is one that immediately jumps out, as the side who'd so ruthlessly demolished New Mills on their way to promotion last season go three goals down in the opening quarter of an hour.

'That shows the gulf in class,' says James on hearing this. 'They were head and shoulders the best side we played last season. We were miles away from them and it looks like they're miles away today.'

There's the early signs of nerves from the teenage left back who intermittently looks either calm and collected or prone to catastrophic mistakes as he gets his first competitive touches in semi-pro football. Tunde Owolabi looks to be the greatest threat for the Millers with his pace an outlet down the left-hand side. He provides the breakthrough midway through the first half to raise a cheer from the dozen or so Millers faithful who've travelled. It's a lead they take into the break.

The half-time hospitality, a small portacabin that makes Church Lane's look spacious, provides much needed respite from the cold. There are at least two extra Millers fans who've sneaked themselves onto the guest list by hook or by crook.

'Savouries?' asks a member of the Darwen committee as he passes round a tray of beige bitesize pastries. 'They're like sausage rolls but they've got cheese and onion in 'em. They taste better than they look,' he reassures me, his broad Lancashire accent elongating the 'oo' on 'look'. I make do with the mug of strong tea that just about restores feeling in my fingers by the time the game gets back underway.

'Another tea?' I ask James as he pitches up a seat behind the end where New Mills will attack in the second half. 'My round!' I add. It's five minutes in and the coat that I'd previously announced would protect me from the elements regardless of how sub-zero the temperature might be was facing its greatest test to date; it really is a different kind of cold in deepest Lancashire.

The £1 of scalding warmth in a polystyrene cup lasts James and I until around the hour mark, by which point a tactical switch appears to be giving Darwen the upper hand in midfield. It's a changing of the tide that is increasingly making us nervous, and with good reason when Darwen find the equaliser.

With the match on a knife edge, the final ten minutes throws up the most controversial moment of the game. With Darwen over-committing in the search for a winner against a New Mills side being increasingly pushed back, a fine through ball from Ryan Hopper releases sub Robbie Swallow who is through on goal. With defenders making their way back in an attempt to cover the line, Swallow drops his shoulder and attempts to round the goalkeeper before being brought down. Incredibly, the referee waves play on.

James and I jump around behind the goal, partly in disbelief and partly for warmth. Swallow remains sat on the floor with his arms aloft. To add insult to injury, Darwen almost score from the counter attack. It's the final clear-cut chance of the game as both sides settle for a point.

'How is that not a penalty?' asks Ray rhetorically in the clubhouse. He's travelled alone today so I've kept Sue updated via Twitter. 'Everyone in the ground can see it's a penalty except for one man.'

'Can't believe that,' adds Paul Williams as the Millers squad gather in the clubhouse. 'I don't know how we haven't won that with the chances we've created today.' He's left to reflect on another near miss for a much-needed result.

'It's a point, but we need to be beating sides like these,' is captain Hopper's assessment at the full-time whistle. 'We had more chances and looked better than them. We've still got players to come back in as well who'll make a big difference.

'I had an amazing holiday until I touched down and checked to see how the lads were getting on. We touched down in London and it was 5-2, 6-2…my Mrs looked at me and I was fuming. I just showed her my phone. Monday was surprisingly positive in training though and we got the spirits back up which was what we needed. I still think we're in a false position but we'll keep going and keep plugging away.'

'I'm waiting for Hopper,' says James as I make my way to the door. 'Don't look at the table, he adds, analysing the updated Hallmark Security League table as we leave the clubhouse. 'We're in the bottom three.'

LEAGUE TABLE

13th	Maine Road	17	40	30	+10	25
14th	Congleton Town	18	42	46	-4	22
15th	Barnoldswick Town	17	32	30	+2	21
16th	Winsford United	16	26	33	-7	21
17th	Squires Gate	19	38	50	-12	21
18th	Barnton	21	27	64	-37	19
19th	AFC Darwen	20	20	51	-31	16
20th	New Mills	18	31	42	-11	15
21st	Nelson	18	20	40	-20	10
22nd	Cammell Laird	20	17	64	-47	6

16

THE WINTER OF OUR DISCONTENT

After almost a quarter of a century supporting Tottenham Hotspur, I'm relatively used to disappointment. From my very first game in 1994, a destiny that had been set several decades earlier was passed on to me by my own father, as we witnessed a capitulation that would go down in Meadow Lane folklore: Notts County 3 – 0 Tottenham Hotspur. Such is the creativity with which misery has been piled upon us over the years, we regularly refer to this Spurs-related hereditary condition as being 'the family ailment'.

Since taking Jacob along, things appear to have improved. There have been setbacks and the grasping of failure from the jaws of success, of course – it wouldn't be Tottenham without them – but, generally speaking, things have been on the up for a while now. Dele Alli and Harry Kane certainly carry more weight on the playground than Colin Calderwood and Jason Dozzell ever did, for starters.

Much like New Mills, 2015/16 had ultimately ended in disappointment for the Lilywhites. Having looked so convincingly likely to finish above each and every one of their local rivals, they had been unable to surpass eventual champions Leicester City before conjuring up a final day capitulation to allow Arsenal above them for the twenty-something-th consecutive year. Jibes of finishing third in a two-horse race were predictable, if not entirely well-founded, but there was at least some consolation that their achievements would at least see them return to the Champions League automatically for only the second time. And yes, for those with a keen knowledge of 'St Totteringham's Day' and its associated meaning, the beginnings of Tottenham's inability to be North London's premier side just so happened to coincide perfectly with my own obsessive dedication to them back in the mid-90s. How can the things we love hurt us so much?

With White Hart Lane soon pencilled in for a building site, and a reduced capacity already in place, Wembley was identified as the venue of choice for the arrival of Europe's finest teams. It was a sad decision, effectively sealing off the memory of the many famous European nights under the floodlights in N17. However, as someone on a season ticket waiting list for almost a decade, it did at least offer an unmissable opportunity to purchase a three-match package for the group stages and give Jacob a taste of Europe's premier football competition.

An uninspiring group draw took some of the anticipation out of things. Monaco, Bayer Leverkusen and CSKA Moscow were all relatively familiar opponents during the Europa League years, although the missed opportunity of seeing exactly what Bayern or Barca might do to a side with Moussa Sissoko on the right wing took some of the sting out of things. A disappointing opening night against an underrated Monaco side set the tone for things to come, before a 1-0 defeat at home to the Germans and a 2-1 defeat in the Stade Louis-II.

By the time John Lewis were bouncing small animals around on a trampoline to flog their festive wares, the final home game against CSKA Moscow was a dead rubber. With only third place in the group offering a parachute into the Europa League to play for, a competition Tottenham Hotspur Football Club have spent the best part of a decade being magnetically drawn towards, there was a decision to be made on where my allegiances would be on December 7th.

For New Mills, November had been a torrid month. Five league games had delivered zero points, with narrow defeats to Barnton, fellow strugglers Squires Gate and 1874 Northwich proving to be just as fruitless as heavier defeats to Bootle and Runcorn Linnets. More worryingly, their failure to register on the scoresheet in four of those games, with only a 4-2 Church Lane ding-dong against Northwich to show for their attacking efforts, meant things were beginning to look particularly bleak.

As player networks dried up, several new faces came into the team once the addition of coach Dave Potter had been acquired. A familiar face at this level, he'd joined Paul in the dugout in recent weeks and helped bring in players. Unfortunately for them, at a time when quality was desperately needed, it seemed like the common and often vocal consensus of Church Lane regulars, chairman Ray and the committee alike, was that they simply didn't look good enough.

One small light at the end of a darkening tunnel had been the Millers' Derbyshire Senior Cup form. With all other hopes of silverware ended, this long-standing county competition pitted small village teams alongside the likes of League One Chesterfield and National League North side Alfreton Town. It was an opportunity to turn focus away from the misery being endured in the league and to bring some much-needed cheer and local pride back to the town; and it had been working to some degree, with the visits of lesser sides offering rare opportunities to be considered a 'favourite' - not that that meant they weren't making hard work of it, of course. Some parallels with Tottenham are unavoidable.

Against Dronfield Town, their first match following the vital point at Darwen, the Millers would twice give up the lead to trail 3-2 at Church Lane before finding an equaliser that would see them eventually go through to the last sixteen via a penalty shootout.

That match set up another home tie against South Normanton Athletic, a tenth-tier side chasing promotion from the East Midlands Counties First Division – and, for me at least, a fixture clash with Tottenham's Champions League bow at home to CSKA Moscow.

'I'm not going down for that,' was my dad's assessment. Such were expectations these days, the spectacle of a pre-paid ticket to the national stadium against the reigning Russian champions was no longer a pull if there was nothing really riding on it. We'd come a long way since that night at Meadow Lane. Friends had similar reasoning – I literally couldn't give the tickets away – and so, instead, I settled for the trip to the High Peak with one eye on the clubhouse TV screen from Wembley.

I didn't know it at the time, but the perfect metaphor for my decision would be waiting for me at Church Lane. While the millionaire internationals stretched and preened during the BT Sport studio's extended analysis unpicking Tottenham's European failures, a familiar face stood out from the South Normanton squad being put through their paces.

Kenny McEvoy came to some notoriety a few years back. A promising looking prospect in the Tottenham Youth Academy, it would be his uncanny facial likeness to outgoing talisman Gareth Bale that would make him a viral hit. In those times of mourning at seeing one of the handful of truly world-class players to grace White Hart Lane don the famous cockerel for the final time before a move to Madrid, small crumbs of comfort came from having a lookalike in the ranks. Who needs scouts when you've got a successful cloning department? In reality, we actually signed Paulinho and McEvoy went on loan to Peterborough United.

It's important not to forget that, for a long while before he'd hit the heights of the Bernabeu, Bale's talent was almost overlooked. For McEvoy, already working his way up through the ranks to the Ireland under-21 squad, Peterborough could yet prove to be the stepping stone into professional football, the Tottenham first team and, ultimately, the world stage. Unfortunately for Kenny, however, his career was beginning to look like a shit remake of Sliding Doors by comparison, with Tim Sherwood playing the role made famous by Gwyneth Paltrow.

From Peterborough, it was on to Colchester, before a short stay at Stevenage. On paper, it was beginning to look like the worst caravanning holiday of all time, until a loan spell at York

City became permanent and McEvoy had hopefully found his level in the fifth tier. This made it all the more surprising, and also rarer than non-regulars at non-league would think, to find a player of his assumed calibre another five rungs down the ladder.

'He only played for Peterborough a few times,' photographer James informs me as I recognise him with incredulity. 'He was alright. I reckon he'll look pretty good tonight.'

It would be one of two remaining matches that would define the Millers' season – and also the future of Paul Williams and his players. As his former teammates line-up to the sound of the Champions League theme tune emanating from the clubhouse, Kenny McEvoy is plotting the downfall of New Mills' last remaining hope of silverware. It doesn't begin well.

McEvoy opens the scoring in the ninth minute, showing skill that looks beyond this level in doing so. Jack O'Brien adds a second in the fourteenth minute as their Derbyshire neighbours threaten to run riot in the opening stages. As I flit between watching what looks like another forgettable night at Church Lane and the clubhouse, the misery is compounded as Dzagoev puts CSKA Moscow into the lead at Wembley. Callum Collinson pulls one back around the same time for the Millers before Ryan Hopper equalises from the spot to restore pride. I miss the two quick goals that see Tottenham lead 2-1 at the break.

'Bloody rubbish,' moans Ray as he miserably munches a sandwich at half-time. There's not much to be said on nights like this – few crumbs of comfort on offer.

'Entertaining game, though?' I offer. The visiting delegates sip their tea quietly as they consider the opening quarter of the game where South Normanton squandered enough chances to have already booked their spot in the last eight.

The second half is a more even affair as New Mills shake off the toils of the first half and begin to look like the better side. In McEvoy, though, it's clear South Normanton have a match winner who they're keen to get on the ball as often as possible. It's a tactic that will eventually pay dividends.

'What's he done that for?' asks Ray as one of his players brings down McEvoy in the final minute of the game. With another penalty shootout looming, it seems an unnecessary challenge. 'What a pillock!' he adds with disgust.

Kenny McEvoy stands over the ball and analyses the picture in front of him. As South Normanton pile everyone into the box, confident that the whistle will follow the outcome of this set piece, the Millers backline already looks dangerously deep. A Gareth Bale-esque puff of the chest, a short run up and a whipped ball to the back post finds the head of Lee Fell, who heads home powerfully before wheeling away.

'Fucking useless,' shouts one fan in the general direction of the pitch as he heads for the turnstiles. He hasn't even reached it by the time the full-time whistle blows moments after play restarts. There won't be many of tonight's paltry crowd of 47 remaining to cheer the lads back into the dressing room.

****

There's little festive cheer to be found ahead of the Millers' final engagement before Christmas. The Derbyshire Cup defeat was followed by another 4-0 drubbing, this time at the hands of promotion chasing Runcorn Linnets. Just 72 fans are here to see the return game against relegation rivals Darwen just six weeks after their Bonfire Night encounter ended all square. A select few of the familiar faces that have dodged the last-minute Christmas shopping trips look gloomy enough to wish they were at the Trafford Centre as kick-off approaches, such is the current optimism around Church Lane ahead of what is now undeniably a relegation six-pointer.

'We're putting something out about the new developments,' Sue says cheerfully. 'James, will you put this up on the website tonight please. Do you want a copy?' she asks, handing me a bundle of papers. In it, an impressive array of drawings and floor plans are headed up by the following statement:

Following an extraordinary meeting held at New Mills Town Hall on

Wednesday 9th November, both New Mills Juniors and New Mills AFC would like to make available the information given to New Mills Town Council, prior to and at the meeting. The proposal is to develop the land on Ollersett Avenue to facilitate a 3G pitch and Community clubhouse for use by the whole of the community and local schools during term time.

Although the ten Town Councillors were notified about the meeting, only four attended which was a disappointing response. Both New Mills Juniors Chairman and New Mills AFC Chairman gave a brief outline of the need for improved facilities in the area. Morbaine, the proposed developer, gave a brief outline of the background to the proposal and outline of their company. Club Design then gave a more detailed presentation and showed the Town Council the drawings which are attached.

The main points of the presentation are summarised below:

- *New Mills AFC have an ageing Astroturf facility and one grass pitch which during the heart of the winter can and does on a number of occasions become unplayable*
- *The club relies on the income from the Astro and supporters to continue to run whilst competing at the highest possible level which is a battle at all times*
- *The club has four teams using the main grass pitch and, whilst the club wants to develop and run a Ladies and Disabled team, the playing surface is not suitable*
- *New Mills Juniors have two grass pitches and both, during the winter months, become unplayable. Whilst everyone would love to play at Church Lane, the surface will not stand any more games*
- *Both clubs are run on a volunteer basis and more volunteers are needed to maintain the surface and surrounding facilities for both clubs*
- *New Mills Juniors accommodate football from U8's to U18's, however the U8's and U9's have to travel to Glossop to play on a 3G pitch due to lack of available pitches in New Mills, a round trip for parents and players of 20 miles every weekend*

- *A number of the age groups play the majority of their fixtures away over the season due to the playing surfaces at Ollersett and the Rec at Wirksworth Road*
- *New Mills Juniors want to grow and encourage girls to play football and other sports. However, due to the lack of changing facilities and playing surface, this is not possible at the present time*
- *Both clubs are losing players to other clubs who have better facilities and playing surfaces*
- *New Mills Juniors and New Mills AFC represent the town in the Hallmark Security League and Stockport Metro League, playing teams from all over South Manchester through to Macclesfield, Glossop and Buxton. The facilities the town have are not adequate for the number of people in the town and investment is needed*
- *Both clubs are working hard together to develop stronger links and working together to create a Community club for all levels of sports and all age groups. With the present facilities, we are unable to achieve these goals – we are way behind the facilities in other areas.*

At the meeting, New Mills Town Council stated they would draw up a list of questions and forward questions to Morbaine and both clubs. At this time, no communication has been received by Morbaine from New Mills Town Council.

As I stand and analyse each word, I try and read the context behind it. Firstly, the tone reflects the disappointment of the Board that no contact from the Council has been received. A month on from a meeting in which fewer than half the Councillors attended, the silence is deafening. The timing of today's statement is clearly a rallying cry to the local community to support the project.

Secondly, my eyes are drawn to the mention of neighbouring towns, specifically Glossop and Buxton, who are both riding high several tiers above the Millers in the non-league ladder. It's clearly not just on the pitch that New Mills are underdogs, and this statement seeks to highlight that.

Finally, I analyse the drawings. A large space of open fields behind several housing estates appears to offer the perfect space for the car park, pavilion, outdoor gym area and basketball/tennis court. It looks impressive; but with several properties presumably losing unrestricted views from their back gardens to a football stadium, it also looks like a petition waiting to happen. The Millers need the support of the Council to help the PR campaign for their new project or risk it being grounded at the first stage.

On the pitch, there's a very different battle about to take place. It feels like nothing less than a win will do to drag them back into the pack above – a win for the visitors would see the Millers dumped further still into the quagmire at the foot of the table.

As we stand and chat behind the goal, the subs bench warm up on the field. The regular shout of "HEADS!" is an indicator to everyone idling outside the clubhouse that a ball could well be flying in their direction. Thankfully, I've not witnessed a direct hit. That was, at least, until this afternoon. It seemed ominous for the afternoon ahead. Worse still, it connected with velocity to the side of Sue's face.

'What are you bloody doing?' she screams at the pitch as I and several others move towards her to check she's alright. She's clearly shaken by the force and disappears into the clubhouse soon after as the perpetrators wave apologies and point fingers like naughty schoolchildren. Anyone who has ever taken a football to the face will know it's not pleasant; even less so in mid-December.

'We're gonna win 3-0 today,' I confidently predict to James as the teams head out and Sue presumably spends five minutes with an ice pack. James doesn't look convinced. 'Actually, that's a clean sheet isn't it?' I add, correcting myself. '3-2?'

On Sue's return, a clear red mark has emerged on the side of her face.

'Have you applied a cold compress?' I ask, doing my best to be helpful and sympathetic.

'Cold compress?' she repeats. 'I'm gonna bloody punch someone. How many times do we have to tell them about shooting in before the match? All these fans stood here. There's signs up in the changing rooms asking them not to do it,' she grumbles before heading off with a trademark laugh, albeit somewhat forced through the pain of her throbbing jaw.

As we watch the match, James tells me he's halfway through the season as New Mills on football management simulation game Football Manager – all thanks to a dedicated but anonymous football fan who has been unlocking the club by uploading squad details.

'It's got about eight players on there who actually play for the club,' he tells me. 'I actually checked and even things like Hopper's date of birth are correct. He's my top scorer with eight goals.' Back in reality, that's looking less than likely.

'It's over today,' Sue tells me in hushed tones midway through the second half. 'It's going to be Paul's final match. We decided after the last few results that we had to make a change. It's been very hard but we're not going anywhere but down at this rate. We've got to do something,' she tells me with a pained expression of a different kind on her face now. Sworn to secrecy until after the announcement is made, the weight of this knowledge hangs heavy – now, even more than before, I'm desperate for Willo to go out on a high.

On the pitch, meanwhile, the Millers struggle to keep hold of the ball and appear to lack pace, energy and even desire in the opening exchanges. They're punished in the 20th minute as Darwen take the lead. It fails to rouse the team and they trudge into the break a goal behind.

'If you want to warm up, warm up out of the goalmouth, PLEASE!' shouts Ray as the subs bench prove during half-time practise that they still haven't learned to take heed of the signs in the dressing room.

'People ask us why we don't cone the goal off. Because there's a bloody sign up telling them!' chuckles Sue.

New Mills toil throughout the second half without reward. As the minutes tick by, the realisation that they'll end the afternoon seven points adrift of safety, rather than closing the gap down to a point, begins to dawn on James and I. Watching the performance on the pitch, it sadly doesn't look like the same jeopardy is being injected into their play. Willo watches on with a mournful look. Whether he's accepted the inevitable or not, it's a sad end for a well-liked figure at the club. A thumping victory might have given him ammunition to ask for the committee to reconsider; even he would struggle to make a case on the back of a devastating result like this.

As the final whistle blows, the players trudge towards the dressing room. Last off the pitch are Willo and Dave who are met by Sue and Ray. The usual commiserations ensuing before the management team head for the dressing room isn't the order of the day this afternoon – instead, all four head ominously for the portacabin.

A short while later, perhaps less than five minutes, the pair head back out. Both hang their heads and Willo appears to shake his ruefully towards the ground as they make their way into the dressing room. Sue and Ray follow on behind, with the weight of their decision clearly visible in their hangdog expressions.

Sue enters the clubhouse, her face now slowly beginning to return to its normal colour, and heads towards where James and I are sitting. She hands him another piece of paper:

MANAGER PAUL WILLIAMS HAS BEEN RELEASED BY THE CLUB

It is with regret that following a run of disappointing league results and our current league position New Mills AFC have decided to release Paul Williams as their first team manager along with assistant Dave Potter with immediate effect.

In the interim period training will be taken by player and assistant manager Daniel Douglas-Pringle and the club hope to appoint a new manager before the Atherton Collieries game on Boxing Day.

The club would like to place on record a massive thanks to Paul for his tireless work both on and off the field since taking over in September from

Garry Brown. During his time in charge he has made a massive contribution and improvement to the team. However it is unfortunate his efforts have not materialised in the results he deserved.

Paul and Dave leave with the club's best wishes for the future and are always welcome back at Church Lane.

Sue Hyde,
Secretary New Mills AFC

'Stick that on tonight as well please,' she says to James in hushed tones.

'As well as the one about the new development?' he asks.

'Yes. Stick that one on first. The new development one can go on after. Everyone will be on the website looking at that and they'll see about the new development that way,' she says, spotting the unfortunate but canny promotional opportunity.

Willo and Assistant David Potter enter the bar and get a warm hug from Sue. The news hasn't quite spread just yet but you don't need to be a body language expert to see what has happened as several regular faces in the clubhouse clock the interaction. Rather than the usual post-match ritual of a drink and polystyrene tray of Sue's curry, Willo is about to head out of the door for the final time. I shake his hand – it's unspoken but obvious that this is likely to be our final interaction.

A low-key Ray quietly nurses a pint at the bar. Despite the inevitability of the decision, it clearly hasn't been an easy one.

'It's a results business,' says defender Michael Jones, a little less charitably as the players gather. 'If you don't get the results, you've got to go.'

I grab Ray for a chat about the decision and we head to the relative privacy of the portacabin where Fixture Secretary Derek is still finishing his post-match duties.

'We had made up our minds as a Board and Committee that, even if we won today, we were going to make a management change because of the results that have gone prior. We went through a spell when we were playing pretty well and not getting results. We bossed games, we went in front in games and couldn't see it through, so it's been on our minds for a while,' he says.

'Paul probably shot himself in the foot bringing Dave in and he's not really, for this level at least, been up to it with the players he's brought in. We've all had concerns about that. I've been telling Paul for weeks that he needs to bring in a bit of experience; one player could change that whole team and he's not brought him in. It's just been a build-up. If we're gonna get out of this situation then the lads who come in (to replace Paul and Dave) are gonna need at least these 18 games,' he goes on.

'Perhaps they should've had more and we, as a club, may have left it four games too long,' he adds, with a tone that suggests hindsight is already proving to be a wonderful thing now the deed is done.

'You don't want to be seen to be getting rid of managers at the drop of a hat because you're in trouble. It's always the manager's fault. I suppose we should've looked at it a few weeks ago and said, "it's not working". There are 18 games left and if you win six or seven of them then you'll probably survive but we haven't won three out of the last how many so it's a tough task. But when the new manager comes in, they see it as a challenge. Whoever it is wouldn't have wanted us to lose today because a win would've just left it one point and now it's seven.

'The brief for the new manager is "18 games. Bring us a couple of really experienced players in." You've got quite a lot to work with there, some really good players like Sam Marshall and Tunde, and you can name five or six who are good enough to be in that side. The other five or six might be on the verge of it, but we could do with a couple of really good players.

'It's football, isn't it? Paul probably would've gone today anyway. Dave was very disappointed but I don't think he's any reason to be disappointed. Paul trusted him to bring players in and I don't think he's brought us in anything that's exciting. They may turn out to be really good players, but is it what we needed at this time? I'd suggest not.

'Paul knew and said, "if I lose this game, I'll be going". I'll be honest, we'd made the decision beforehand that it'd gone too long and he'd have liked to have left us by giving the next person a little glimmer. Now it's a very little glimmer, but it's there!'

'I need to find my festive jumper,' says Sue cheerfully as we head back into the clubhouse. 'I've got a Christmas party tonight!'

A couple of players remain seated in the quiet surrounds, mournfully poking dinner around their tray.

'Do you not like my curry?' Ray asks. Nobody dare ask if it matches up to Sue's Special. As the last few fans leave, they're replaced by a new group made up of local carers carrying food and balloons in from the car park.

'We've hired it out for a Christmas party,' Ray tells me as I help him shift the pool table. 'It's a local place that looks after mentally handicapped people. They find it very hard to find a venue. I don't know why. They had a booking somewhere else and were let down at the last minute. I mean, if we can't help them out, why are we here?'

While there'll always be difficult decisions to make on the pitch, the extension of Christmas cheer to a neighbouring charity isn't one of them. Wherever New Mills AFC sit in the table and wherever they play their football, now and in the future, they'll remain at the heart of the community.

17

NEW YEAR, NEW NEW MILLS

January is often a time for change. As the Christmas decorations come down, it's an opportunity to reflect on the excesses of the festive period and seek positive transformation. Dry January is a bit of a stretch in our house, and the healthy eating can't really begin until the second half of the leftover brie wheel is consumed, but at least an expedition to rediscover (or at least dust off) the gym membership card must have burnt a couple of calories, surely. Now what to do with the rest of the double Bailey's cream…

Football is no different, of course. At the very top of the pyramid, Swansea and Hull City, two sides having comparable seasons of struggle to the Millers, made changes in their respective managerial hotseats. In Mike Phelan's case in particular, the decision to be relieved of his position on the Humber coast seemed particularly harsh. With pressure on the transfer window coming up, his successor Marco Silva would be expected to salvage the Tiger's Premier League status, starting in the newly opened transfer window.

Dropping eight tiers down the league ladder, the task for whoever the new Millers management team would be wasn't entirely dissimilar. While rules around when players could be recruited were not quite as restrictive in the Hallmark Security League, the choice of which players were available was. As lamented by Garry and Willo, with Church Lane being something of a rural outpost to the cream of Manchester's semi-pro crop, it would undoubtedly be a factor in the recruitment policy for both players and coaching staff.

For Calum Sykes, the fresh-faced and sharply dressed new man in the hotseat, making an eight-mile journey south-east from Stockport Town FC with his assistant, Gareth Cross, alongside a small coaching team, taking over at New Mills looked like a solid move. Having narrowly missed out on promotion into this division with their former side - a club which he'd managed since their formation in early 2014 - he was now tasked with keeping New Mills in it.

With expectations raised at his former employers, he left Stockport sitting just outside the play-off spots in Hallmark Security League Division One – within a few wins of the top six spots, if not quite matching the heights of the previous season. Upon handing in his resignation, Stockport Town released the following, ever-so-slightly passive-aggressive, statement on Saturday 17th December:

CALUM SYKES RESIGNS AS FIRST TEAM MANAGER

Stockport Town can confirm that Calum Sykes resigned as First Team Manager early on Saturday evening. Later the same day he was announced as the manager of New Mills AFC. Also departing the club will be Gareth Cross, Assistant Manager.

Jamie Kay has been appointed as Interim Manager for the next two games against Cheadle Town and City of Liverpool. The process for appointing a permanent manager is already underway.

Sykes was appointed First Team Manager in July 2014 after guiding Glossop North End Reserves to the league title. He subsequently led the Lions to a fourth-place finish in NWCFL Division One in 2015/16 before the team were defeated in the play-off semi-finals.

Chairman Seb Rowe said 'We would like to thank Calum and Gareth for their commitment to the club over the last few years. We wish them all the best in their new venture.

'Although the news is untimely given it's the week before Christmas, the club now have the opportunity to bring in a new manager with fresh ideas. We expect the first team to be challenging for the play-off places. This season the aim was to build on the success of last season, but for one reason or another that hasn't happened so far. Despite a recent turnaround in results, there is still scope for greater improvement. It has been evident that squad morale has been low, so a change in manager will hopefully give the players the boost they need to kick on.

'We will now take steps to bring in a new management team. As was evidenced in the 2-2 draw with Holker yesterday, the club has an extremely talented group of young players who require strong leadership in order for them to fulfil their potential. The new manager will need to share the same ambitions as the board, as well as displaying drive, determination and rounded managerial skills.'

Layered with subtext, it felt like a kick in the teeth to an ambitious young manager who had laid solid foundations before making the decision to move up a division and join the fight at Church Lane. Accusations around low "squad morale" would soon be tested when his former players would enquire about joining him, while digs around "strong leadership", "sharing the same ambitions as the board" and "rounded managerial skills" could all be filed under overly-personal critique in what was supposed to be an official club statement.

By contrast, Sue's confirmation on the incoming appointments was an altogether much warmer affair:

CALUM SYKES ANNOUNCES HIS MANAGEMENT TEAM

Following the departure of Paul Williams and Dave Potter, New Mills AFC Committee are thrilled to welcome Calum Sykes to New Mills AFC.

Calum brings with him an experienced and forward-thinking Management team.

Calum has spent the last three seasons managing at Stockport Town FC in the North West Counties Division One, reaching the play-off semi-final last season. Calum previously worked at Glossop North End and guided their Reserve side to the last NWCFL reserve league title. Calum coaches full time in and around the New Mills area and has been coaching since he was 17 years old. Calum once created his own amateur side Aldwyn Town before stepping up to non-league level.

Gareth Cross began working with Calum two seasons ago. Gareth 'Crossy' Cross had spent the previous 12 years as first team manager of Newton FC before deciding to take some time away, however this lasted just a few months before teaming up with Calum at Stockport Town. Gareth's knowledge and passion is clear for all to see and he is the perfect assistant.

Nick Dowse joined Calum and Crossy at Stockport Town at the start of this season, assisting with the coaching. Previously after retiring from his playing career he started coaching at Denton West End juniors and then managed their open aged team. He also coached at Newton FC with then Manager Gareth Cross before taking the role of Assistant Manager at Denton Town.

Lee McDonagh completes the Management team as physio. He will be busy as the new Management team are looking at training twice during the week preparing for the forthcoming Saturday League fixtures.

The club has 18 games (54 possible points) before the end of the season and we have to turn around the results and build for the future. Calum and his Management team bring knowledge and coaching qualities to the team, and he is excited by the challenge ahead.

'It is a great honour to be appointed as the first team manager of New Mills Football Club. The club have had a difficult period in the last couple of seasons and my immediate aims are to improve our current league position

and climb the table, place by place, and gradually take the club into a position where we can build from.

'There are already so many excellent players at the club I don't feel that wholesale changes is what we require, but to refine their skills and add three or four players to the side to take us to that next level.

'My aims are to restore this club to the levels expected from the fans and produce performances that you can be proud of. We are as one big family, we all have the same hopes for our club and my team and I will be doing all we can to achieve and surpass our targets.

'I would like to take this time to thank Stockport Town FC for the last three seasons and wish them well for the remainder of the season. I'm looking forward to the challenge ahead and enjoying magnificent support from the Millers fans in the coming years.'

Reading into Calum and Crossy's achievements, it felt like reason for cautious optimism at Church Lane. Calum's early assessment on the squad he'd inherited also seemed positive for the lads left behind. At the time of giving that quote, however, he perhaps didn't realise a small stampede of players would be following him out of Stockport Town's back door.

New Mills registered nine Stockport Town players ahead of their Boxing Day fixture at promotion-chasing Atherton Collieries. They included Nathan Neequaye, one of the leading scorers in Division One with 21 goals to his name, and Warren Gaskin, who had played for the Millers back in the Evo-Stik glory days. Gaskin would immediately be installed as club captain, relinquishing Ryan Hopper from his role.

The news was met with some controversy on social media, where weekly lists of player transfers are published by the official League Twitter account. Outside onlookers, observing a provocative looking list of movements that almost exclusively lists players heading out of Calum's former side and into Church Lane, questioned whether Stockport Town were still in business.

Former New Mills Academy Manager James Kinsey, himself an outspoken cheerleader for his own capabilities, publicly berated the decision to bring in half the squad of a midtable team in the league below. Inside the club, Sue pleaded with the players to bite their tongues over the angry war of words brewing between New Mills and Stockport Town, and to do their talking on the pitch. They almost did.

Taking the lead against Atherton Collieries on Boxing Day, a side who'd put five past the Millers at Church Lane earlier in the season, was the first sign of promise in a while. Colls would overturn the deficit to take a 2-1 lead but the game wasn't over there. In the final minutes, Sykes would get a glimpse of the newfound potential in his side when they won an opportunity to salvage a vital point from the penalty spot. Debutant Nathan Neequaye, a strong and athletic presence leading the line, stepped up but was unable to take that opportunity. The Millers were defeated again in the cruellest of fashions.

'He's absolutely gutted,' Calum told Sue after the game. 'He feels like he's let the side down.' It could've been worse; Stockport Town began life after Sykes with a 10-0 defeat at home to AFC Liverpool to further add to the brewing controversy.

With games coming thick and fast over the Christmas period, there was the opportunity to put things right at home to Abbey Hey on December 30th. With Ray and Sue flying out to the Canary Isles to enjoy the New Year in warmer climes, the ingredients were all there for Sue to miss another rare league win - until a pitch inspection following several days of freezing temperatures meant postponement. As the calendar year of 2016 ended, the Millers had posted just three wins and 18 points across two divisions in the League. Despite the best efforts of those who had gone before, it had hardly been a vintage year.

One of Sykes' first media engagements would be with High Peak Radio. Speaking to their sports show, he summarised the task ahead.

'First of all, we've got to get ourselves out of the situation we find ourselves in at the bottom of the table, eight points adrift, so our first thoughts now are to start moving up that table.' A bizarre and misleading suggestion that Calum is the Millers' fifth manager in six months goes uncorrected as Calum continues when asked what he will do differently to his predecessors.

'I can't really talk for how other managers work but I certainly know how I want to run my team. I've got hard-working staff with me and that's what we'll be bringing in. We're going to up our training schedule from one night, one hour to two nights and longer duration. (I'll be) bringing across to the players what my expectations of them are, raising confidence and raising their belief in themselves and getting those extra percentages out of players that perhaps hasn't happened for them in the last few months.

'The performance against Atherton (2-1 defeat) I saw a lot of positives,' he continues. 'I think most people including Atherton wouldn't have expected the performance we put in. I think we scored inside the first fifteen minutes and I felt we were quite unlucky with the two goals we did concede and they would probably say they were lucky to take all three points from the game. We saw players take their performance up a couple of notches and showed us that bit more belief in themselves and that belief that when we go behind, the game's not finished.

'The run of losses the team is on, it's very easy to get into the habit of losing and once you go behind, you feel like the game is done and there's nothing worth fighting for. That's certainly not my way. You can be 2-1 down or even 3-1 down in the 90th minute and if there's two minutes to go I'll say, "we can still get something out of this game." That's the mentality I want to get into the players.'

On the question of bringing in so many of his former recruits after telling fans that he'd felt "wholesale changes" weren't required, Calum's response to what that means for the squad he's inherited is suitably measured.

'I'm not looking to drop players. What became evident is that we need a strong squad. It's not just about the eleven on the pitch or even the sixteen-man squad you can take to the game. At this level, with player availability, it's always going to be difficult to get your best eleven out every week. To maintain what we're hoping to achieve, we're going to need to have a stronger squad overall and that's why we have moved to get more than the three or four I mentioned initially to get that strong twenty-man squad. In terms of other players, opportunities will still be there, but first and foremost we need to get out of the situation we're in before we can do that.'

Calum wraps up the interview by praising the plans for the new stadium – stating his ambition to be part of "a real family club" – and speaking of the wider benefits to the community. It's an impressive and professional first media engagement for the new man in the hotseat.

Alongside the newfound positivity in the local media, 2017 would begin with a win. On Tuesday 3rd January, Calum Sykes began his New Mills career with a 3-1 victory over Chadderton. It was in a friendly, switched from Church Lane at the last minute due to the continuation of the cold snap, but it was a win all the same. With a few new faces added to a side containing a spine of the Millers' stronger players, there was reason for some hope heading to West Didsbury and Chorlton for the first competitive encounter of the New Year.

Hidden down a small private road in the leafy Manchester suburbs, the Brookburn Road ground was premium grassroots football to its core. With cars parked alongside the touchline and a fine clubhouse serving cheese topped sandwich baps and bottled craft beers, the crowd of over 200 was made up of a younger, more metropolitan looking bunch than you might find in New Mills. With more than a few hipster haircuts and a Greek flag hung from one of the stands, it felt more like a haven for a Mancunian Senior Web Developer than two men and a dog by 2.30pm on a Saturday afternoon.

Among the crowd were a healthy and tanned looking Ray and Sue, back refreshed from their jaunts and ready to roll their sleeves up for 2017. Committee member Roy returned after a considerable lay-off from a cough he couldn't shift through

December while Fixture Secretary Derek prowled with his clipboard and grumbled about the player recruitment policy that had dominated conversation in Calum's early weeks. James was flanked by his trusty camera and his equally trusty father.

'I like those,' observes Sue, gesturing towards the West Didsbury volunteer committee creating a walkway from the dressing room to the pitch with fold-away railing on a simple hinge mechanism. 'We could do with some of those ourselves.' I grimace internally at the memory of almost wiping out the Hanley Town first XI back in August.

As the sides emerge, there aren't too many familiar faces in the Millers line-up for the hardcore travelling contingent of away fans joining us. Ryan Hopper still leads the team out as captain, closely followed by Ollie Martin in the green goalkeeper's jersey. Defender Dan Johnson and attacking midfielder Sam Marshall complete the familiar looking core to the side. On the bench, Michael Jones and Dylan Stringer-Moth join Tunde Owolabi, Dom Welsby and Dennis Sherriff.

The mood is lightened as the players await the refereeing team to arrive from the dressing rooms. A tall, athletic bloke in his late-twenties arrives in a sand-coloured wool coat, carrot bottom jeans and suede-looking Caterpillar boots to wish the players luck. He fits right in with the clientele here and is clearly known to the West Didsbury lads, who break from their pre-match concentration to rib what is presumably an immaculately dressed teammate who didn't make this afternoon's squad.

'Look at the ASOS model,' says one.

'You just come in from going out on the town?' asks another. Even a few of the Millers lads break into smiles as they can't ignore the ruthless dressing room banter spilling out onto the sidelines. Soon after, a smartly dressed Calum emerges and makes his way across the pitch.

'I asked him for his measurements so I could get a tracksuit ordered for him,' she tells me, as our attention turns to the new man in charge. 'He said "I don't need a tracksuit. Just a club tie." You don't see many with collared shirts on the touchline at this level.'

New Mills start the game well and look solid with the lively Ruben Abreu, in the position vacated by Owolabi, looking particularly dangerous down the left-hand side. Ollie keeps the visitors in the game with a couple of fantastic saves before the breakthrough comes for New Mills. A ball breaks kindly into the path of Neequaye off the defender's boot that leaves him clean through but with plenty to do. Bearing down on goal with pace, he rounds the 'keeper and, with the ball bobbling along the slippery surface and a chasing defender already breaking from his pursuit to attempt to cover the line, the big striker composes himself to squeeze the ball inside the near post.

'YEEEEEESSSSSS!' screams Sue as the goalscorer celebrates in front of us. Ray congratulates his man as he's mobbed by teammates and he gives a nod of gratitude in return. There's relief in his expression as he puts the frustration of that crucial missed penalty against Atherton to bed.

Soon after, it should be 2-0. A brilliant run down the right-hand side from Sam Marshall is followed by a deep cross to the far post. Neequaye follows its path over the flailing goalkeeper and connects with his head a yard or two out. The ball hits the inside of the post and rolls agonisingly along the line before being claimed by the grateful goalkeeper. Neequaye finds himself in the back of the net, having almost collided with the post. It's a massive moment that would come back to haunt the visitors.

With a rare 1-0 lead at half-time, Sue ponders aloud any little-known league rules that might allow the game to be declared a result at the break. As we file into the busy clubhouse, fans gather around the television in the warmth of the impressive surrounds to see where the FA Cup Third Round shocks might be.

'Did you hear the drum?' enquires loyal travelling fan Jon Warrior who was situated at the opposite end of the stand and is becoming a more familiar face on away days.

'I did!' says Sue. 'I'm not going anywhere bloody near it in the second half, either!'

I enjoy a Coronation Chicken sandwich and a brief chat with

former Millers manager Roy Soule who is in attendance this afternoon. Describing himself as "the last manager before the cuts", his spell was largely a successful one and almost saw him lead the side out of the Evo-Stik and into the heady heights of the seventh tier where the likes of comparative Derbyshire behemoths Buxton and Matlock ply their trade. Here as an observer and friend of the club, he speaks warmly of his time and his relationship with Ray and Sue but hints towards the issues around budget that led to his departure. Now an experienced Scout for several football league sides, his forthright approach suggests there might also have been the occasional locking of horns with the Chairman. After a brief chat, he excuses himself to catch up with the injured Daniel Douglas-Pringle, a player from those comparative glory days, who is also here to observe the new look New Mills.

I catch Sue admiring a canvas the length of the clubhouse wall with the complete history of West Didsbury and Chorlton FC on it.

'I wonder how much that'd cost?' she ponders aloud again. Between the wall art and the safety barriers, she's heading back to Church Lane with more design ideas than Laurence Llewellyn-Bowen who, looking at one or two of the more flamboyant home fans, wouldn't look out of place with a West Didsbury season ticket.

The game is level early in the second half as the home side work their way through a fragile looking backline to slide the ball beyond Ollie into the net.

'Come on Millers! We go again now!' screams Calum from the dugout.

The turning point of the game arrives around the hour mark though. With Ollie withstanding the onslaught with a number of fine saves, West Didsbury's game plan resorts to longer, hopeful balls into the box. One of them is miscontrolled off the boot of a Millers defender deep inside his own box and, under pressure, Ollie claims the ball with his hands.

A roar goes up from behind the goal for a pass-back which the referee gives despite the protestations of the Millers. It's hard to judge how intentional it was from our vantage point but it's naïve defending at best and is indicative of the way in which the visitors are being slowly pinned back as the game progresses. Amidst the usual melee and false starts of an indirect free-kick in the box, West Dids eventually do nudge the ball and blast it towards the eleven-man defensive line across the goalmouth. The ball bounces and ricochets for a split second before a great roar goes up from the stands along the clubhouse entrance. Somehow, despite the entire team camped out on the line, the ball has found its way into the net.

West Didsbury add a third and then a superb fourth from outside the box to give the scoreline a flattering look. The early promise and solidity of the first half has crumbled and it's hard not to wonder what the second goal might have done for the Millers' resolve. The game isn't over just yet however – this is still New Mills, after all.

Neequaye grabs a second in the final ten minutes and Dennis Sherriff, another large and physical striker introduced from the bench, rockets a third in off the crossbar in the dying minutes. From the kick-off, the Millers win the ball back and attack again but they've given themselves too much to do. A knock to winger Sam Marshall that he's struggled to run off blunted their attacking threat midway through the second half and the introduction of Tunde's raw skill and pace had caused issues but it wasn't enough. A slightly deflated Calum confers with Ray and Sue post-match about the chance that could've been in the first half.

'I can't wait to get back in this side!' says Millers veteran Dougie, joining in the conversation. 'He's looking at me going "you're not getting in the side"', he adds, testing the new manager's resolve before laughing infectiously and somewhat nervously at the lack of reassurance coming back the other way.

There's an upbeat nature to the chat, though – the improvements are clearly there – and, as Ray observes, the Millers finally look like they've got goals in them. Concerns over the defence remain and Barnton's 1-0 victory over Darwen means the gap to safety remains static at eight points. More worryingly, it does mean the gap to Barnton, only three places above the final relegation spot currently occupied by the Millers, is now a mammoth fifteen points. Assistant Crossy begins to reel off the fixtures where they need to pick up results.

'Don't forget the Hanley game,' says Ray, listening to the list of teams intently.

'We've already played them twice. 1-1 at our place, 2-2 at theirs,' says Crossy, who thankfully doesn't appear to have heard all about my attempts to kill the opposition that night. 'I know that and I wasn't even there! You're dealing with a statto here, ya know!' he jokes. As Ray leaves, he shakes his hand. 'Sorry boss,' he adds ruefully.

'No need to apologise, the signs are there,' returns Ray, with genuine optimism in his voice.

I find Calum in the clubhouse post-match, nursing a chilled bottle of craft lager with his wife and young daughter. His squad seem in high spirits and, barring the familiar faces of Ollie and Hopper, it's a very different looking group to weeks gone by. Calum is thoughtful in his reflection on the match, noting how his lads were tired due to the tracking required for West Didsbury's movement off the ball.

He already has another friendly lined up for midweek and is upping the training schedule to twice weekly in a bid to get his side ready for the challenge ahead. It's a decision that means Ryan Hibbert, a familiar face and consistent performer, has had to move on due to work commitments outside of football. Congleton Town are first in line to claim a useful addition to their squad sat safely in midtable.

New management, new players, a new training regime and a raft of friendlies to find fitness and form. 2017 was underway with the intensity of a pre-season – it would surely be a defining calendar year for New Mills AFC.

Nathan Neequaye - soon to be a fan favourite - celebrates a goal against West Didsbury and Chorlton

18

THE ROAD TO LITTLE WEMBLEY

Until 1923, Wembley was a fairly unremarkable area in northwest London. Today, it's a word that is synonymous with being inextricably linked to the spiritual birthplace of the modern game and, to some, the very home of football itself.

In the same summer Wembley hosted its first ever match beneath the old twin towers, the famous White Horse Cup Final won by Bolton Wanderers, another Lancashire club were also making history. Nelson FC, a side who had become founder members of the Football League Third Division North two years earlier, having spent their first four decades in the Lancashire and Central Leagues, opted for a tour of Spain in readiness for a season in the Second Division following a promotion winning campaign.

After a 2-1 win over Real Oviedo that was nothing to be sniffed at, they stamped their name in the history books, becoming the first English side to beat Real Madrid on Spanish soil. Their 4-2 win might not have landed them a place in football folklore in quite the same way their Lancashire neighbours' trip to the capital had, but it remains a source of intense local pride here almost a century on. It would prove to be the highlight (so far, at least) of a 130-year history that would see financial troubles and the Second World War confine Nelson FC back into the Lancashire Combination League by 1946. They would never taste Football League action again.

Quite whether this illustrious history has any bearing on the affectionate name of their Victoria Park home – more commonly referred to as 'Little Wembley' – isn't entirely clear. Without meaning to be too unkind, it's certainly a nickname with its tongue firmly in its cheek. Their slightly less ambitious 2009 fundraising campaign to raise £10k for floodlights aside, it's more akin to the Wembley Stadium project just after they knocked the original down.

Parking on a long adjacent street, the walk towards the well-hidden ground takes in old Victorian terraced housing and tall chimneys that point to an industrial past that's as distant as the pre-season tour to Spain for the current inhabitants of Little Wembley. A fiver on the old turnstile is enough to join the small throng who'll witness this afternoon's battle at the bottom of the ninth tier.

'He's here!' says Sue on spotting Jon Warrior. 'And he's brought that bloody drum!'

The big team news is that Nathan Neequaye, the Millers' most prolific source of goals in recent weeks, isn't here. His absence at a university graduation means big striker Dennis Sherriff will fill his considerable boots up front. The omens are good though – today is his birthday.

'He's what every team needs,' says Ray of his big, blonde haired striker. 'He's a good player. Scored plenty of goals at a higher level than this. He's just a nutcase off the pitch!'

'Here we go! Here we go!' says an excited Jon as the teams come out of the tunnel. 'Three points in the bag before the bell has gone!'

'Oh no!' warns Ray. 'No, no. Don't say things like that.'

'It won't be easy because these lads have had some good games,' adds Roy. Jon holds back on any further vocal score predictions before telling us he is sore today having recently had a fall on-board a mini-cruise to Rotterdam.

'Did you do any window shopping?' asks Sue with a glint in her eye.

'No! I did go in one or two of the coffee shops though. How's the book going anyway Underdog? Have you devoted a chapter to the drum yet?' he says, quickly changing the subject.

The familiar war cries from the Millers line-up can be heard as they fire themselves up. The Little Wembley pitch is covered in leaves as the lads enter the field.

'Fancy us today?' I ask Fixture Secretary Derek as the game gets underway.

'I'm not so sure,' he replies, in his trademark dour tones. 'My opinion hasn't changed much. I still don't think the changes are going to make too much difference. But I'm a pessimist. You're never disappointed that way, are you?'

Derek's outlook is vindicated as New Mills concede a penalty inside the opening six minutes following a shove in the box that's converted well by Jason Hart.

'Ollie Martin continues his record of never saving a penalty,' observes Derek with trademark timing. As the words leave his lips, the ever-dangerous Sam Marshall races down the right flank, rounds the goalkeeper and slots in from a tight angle to level things up.

The goal-scoring frenzy doesn't stop there. Almost from the restart, Nelson make their way up the field to restore their lead. With a penalty shout not being given, the free-kick on the edge of the box is delivered into Ollie's top corner with unerring accuracy. After 13 minutes, it's 2-1 to the home side.

'Come on Millers!' shouts Jon as he bangs his drum. 'I stopped at Burger King and a music shop on the way up as I'd lost my drumsticks. I asked them for the cheapest and the loudest! Come on Millers!' he continues as he tries to get a beat going.

Nelson make it 3-1 on 27 minutes with a good volley from a cross. It's 4-1 on 36 minutes in a carbon copy of the previous free-kick. It's looking like another horrendous away day.

There's the feeling of queuing up at the buffet table of a wake as we enter the portacabin for half-time hospitality. Ray and Sue chat quietly to each other as Ray mutters under his breath and shakes his head. He doesn't have the words to quite summarise what he's witnessed in the first 45 minutes.

'We could do with a light on,' says an elderly Nelson fan to the chap serving much needed hot drinks. The old portacabin is quickly darkening in the fading light of the cold and dismal midwinter afternoon as he carefully pours boiling water into polystyrene cups. A commemorative frame from that famous game against Real Madrid hangs quietly on a damp looking wall.

'We couldn't get it going this morning. I think something tripped,' he replies, suggesting a last-minute electrical issue being the reason why we're all struggling to see our sandwiches.

'It's been off for two or three weeks!' corrects the old gent as he stirs a sugar into his tea. We fill our plates in the dusk light and eat quietly in the darkness.

'Darwen are winning,' is the unwelcome news for both sides at half-time. 'Beating West Didsbury 1-0,' says James as he necks a cheese sandwich.

'This pork pie is nice,' says the old chap. 'I think it's pork pie, anyway. I can't see it.'

While the hospitality is soundtracked by a hubbub of laughter and chat from the home contingent in the fading light, Sue looks on at Ray with concern. He sits slumped in the corner of the room staring glumly at a cup of coffee, barely uttering a word throughout the entire fifteen minutes. There's not much to be said to improve his mood so I instead make my way to the outdoor toilet around the back of the somewhat basic clubhouse as the effects of a warm tea on a cold afternoon take effect.

The lads are making their way out as I walk past the entrance to the pitch. I hear the referee's whistle restart play to the sound of Jon's drum as I enter the toilet block. By the time I'm midway through making full use of the facilities, New Mills are 5-1 down. It's taken them 54 seconds of the second half to concede.

'What are they doing?' is Roy's incredulous observation as I make my way back round the pitch to join the travelling New Mills clan. Luckily, Ray and Sue are much further down the line. 'What ARE they doing? Just giving the ball away too much. Absolutely ridiculous. I just don't know what the hell is up with them. Giving them far too much time to play. I don't know if they're nervous or what the bloody hell it is,' Roy continues.

'They're not good enough,' chips in Derek. 'It's as simple as that. How we can bring so many players up from the division below and make them good enough, I don't know. If they were that good, why would they be in that division to begin with?'

It's a painful one to admit but, as they face obliteration against one of only two sides with a worse record than themselves, it's difficult to make an argument against this point of view.

The balance of the game takes a swing back in the Millers' favour in a crazy three-minute spell for Nelson that illustrates just how capable they also might be at shooting themselves in the foot with a cannon.

Joe Armstrong pulls one back in the 52nd minute for New Mills before a second yellow card for a Nelson midfielder is issued after kicking Ryan Hopper. His first yellow was for kicking the ball away. As of the 55th minute, the Millers have a three-goal deficit to close against ten men. On recent showings, when they've only tended to get going after a game has looked beyond them, it feels as promising as it has done for most of the afternoon.

That is until the 59th minute when, with New Mills already throwing the kitchen sink at their opponents, Hart adds a second by breaking the offside trap by virtue of being inside his own half.

'Come on Calum, you've gotta change this! Fuckin' shite!' says Roy, unable to hide his disappointment from the players on the pitch any longer as they trudge back to the centre circle to restart play. 'This is embarrassing boys.'

In the 62nd minute, captain Warren Gaskin rises highest to bag the ninth goal of the game. The tenth soon follows but is ruled offside, denying the Millers a 6-4 scoreline. In the 72nd minute, Sam Marshall takes on half the Nelson team on a mazy run before dragging a shot just wide. It's a moment of quality the game doesn't deserve as it threatens to descend into farce.

'Come on! 25 minutes left, I want another 20%!' screams Warren Gaskin from the back. 'Come on! I want more!'

The game gets its 10th goal with just under a quarter of an hour to go as Hart completes his hat-trick. The previously animated travelling support which I'm a part of, still contesting every 50/50 decision and screaming on encouragement for the lads, falls silent. In the twenty minutes since the red card, Nelson are effectively winning 2-1.

Dennis Sherriff grabs a fourth for the Millers to mark his birthday and the smallest crumb of comfort and respectability onto the scoreline. It's a great header from a Sam Marshall free-kick that sees his marker turn away and remonstrate with his teammates in fury. The defender has a top knot and a deep tan, I notice, something he most certainly didn't attain naturally living in Nelson in January.

Despite the late consolation, though, it's another very difficult afternoon to explain or excuse from the boys in amber and black. New Mills have lost a topsy turvy game 7-4, a ridiculous scoreline that actually flatters them. A modest crowd of 52 fans have witnessed 11 goals. That's more than a goal each for every five fans in the ground. At £5 a ticket, it's less than 50p a goal. No wonder they can't afford to put the lights on in the portacabin.

Ray and Sue wait impatiently to greet the management team at the end of the game. Elsewhere, Darwen's 3-0 win has opened up an 11-point gap to safety.

'Ugh!' says Sue, letting out a massive sigh. '15 games left. 45 points to play for. Think of the positives. I know that's quite difficult at the moment. A bad day at the office,' she tells me. 'Giz a hug anyway, I think we all need one today. We're gonna make a move as I've got a hot date with a quiz,' she adds, referring to a long arranged fundraising quiz taking place back in the New Mills clubhouse tonight. 'We'll probably lose at that as well,' she jokes.

'We can't defend like that!' says the ever-honest Crossy as the management team emerge. 'That first penalty? If we didn't have a referee and they'd have come to me and asked what I thought, I'd have given it! We just can't defend like that. We've actually created more chances today. We just haven't converted them.'

As Crossy chats, Calum wanders away to make a short phone call before beginning a solitary circuit of the empty stadium, running his hand through his hair and holding his head throughout. There can be no doubting how much this afternoon's defeat has hurt him personally and professionally. I time my exit to catch him on the return down the touchline.

'What can you say?' he begins despondently in a quiet voice. 'They drove us down the middle. Overran us in midfield. I don't think they were worthy of seven goals when they maybe had nine or ten chances. We've scored seven goals in two games but conceded eleven. That's gotta change. Pitch didn't help. Ref didn't help. But that's just looking for excuses.

'Are you up at the club tonight?' he asks me, dejectedly. I'm not. 'I've got to be there tonight, all smiles. There's nowhere else I'd rather not be, I can tell you that.' With that, he heads back towards the changing rooms to gather his bags and his thoughts. There'll be plenty of time for that on the long road home from Little Wembley.

The Millers toil at Little Wembley

LEAGUE TABLE

16	Barnton	30	41	77	-36	33
17	Congleton Town	28	49	61	-12	31
18	Barnoldswick Town	24	40	37	3	29
19	AFC Darwen	27	30	65	-35	26
20	Nelson	25	36	58	-22	15
21	New Mills	27	41	70	-29	15
22	Cammell Laird 1907	30	22	112	-90	6

19

A POINT TO PROVE

'Commitment' and 'character' are two overused cliches in football. It's the sort of phrase the TV pundits use to question a poor result or explain away a downturn in form after a head is turned by another club. Are the players showing enough character? Is the manager committed to the club? The word 'commitment' is defined as being the state or quality of being dedicated to a cause. Where commitment exists, there's a pledge to get the job done no matter what. Character is the mental and moral qualities distinctive to an individual.

Commitment can be tested, though, and character must sometimes be discovered when faced with adversity. So it would prove for me at Buxton Pavilion Gardens, as you join me on stage on Friday 3rd February 2017.

'Where did you go on a stag do mate?' I ask the man seated on the front row.

'Erm…errrr….'

'Yeah…' I add, encouragingly, feeling the energy and momentum draining from the room as he stalls on an answer to this simplest of questions.

I'm hosting the monthly comedy night at Buxton's Pavilion Gardens, a grand venue at the rear of the famous Opera House where some of Theatre's greatest names have performed. It's my first attempt at audience interaction of the night and I feel absolutely dreadful. Despite this, it's my job to get the atmosphere going and the assembled audience laughing.

The reason for my ailment might be linked to my line of

questioning. A week earlier, I'd spent several hedonistic days on a stag do in Krakow while New Mills' scheduled trip to midtable Maine Road had been postponed. On returning, I was struck down by a plague my family had passed around in my absence that meant spending Wednesday evening and most of Thursday bed-ridden. Having convinced myself that gig adrenalin kicking in would do me good by Friday evening, I was beginning to have second thoughts.

'I went to erm…it was…', he continues, stumbling over his words to my increasing alarm.

'Bloody hell mate, how good was this stag do?', I enquire, momentarily generating a bit of a laugh to get both of us through an exchange that it's difficult to tell who is enjoying least.

'I don't mean to break the comedy atmosphere,' he says, ominously, 'but I do actually suffer from memory issues.'

It was a long night.

Undeterred, I rose on Saturday morning, still a fever-ridden mess but ready for Church Lane. After a stormy drive home, there was every possibility Calum Sykes' long-awaited first home game might fall foul to the weather yet again. The man himself put paid to those concerns.

'Today's New Mills AFC game does not require a pitch inspection,' he tweeted. 'Game ON!!!! C'mon the MILLERS!'

While I don't seek sympathy, dear reader, I must confess that the severity of my germ jockeying was so serious that I almost didn't make it to Church Lane. Arsenal's capitulation at Stamford Bridge beneath a blanket was, for a short while, proving to be a more attractive option. Like the prospect of 'bantering' in front of paying onlookers with a man with medium to long term memory issues, though, the thrill of the chase kicked in and adrenalin did indeed get me out of the door.

As I reached Church Lane, kick off had already happened. Armed with several layers of clothing and a generous lump of Snuffle Babe applied to most of the upper half of my torso, I got out of the car to hear the cheer of a larger than average crowd. High-flying Runcorn Linnets had made the hour-long trip inland from the banks of the Mersey in big numbers to contribute to a bumper gate of 181. I peer through the gap in the fence as the anticipation of the crowd suggests a building attack. Not for the first time this season, it's converted. The Millers are 1-0 down and I'm not even through the turnstile yet.

A solid first half performance is undermined late on by a second yellow for recent recruit Sam Scott, a wiry presence in midfield. He's unlucky for at least one of the cards. A goal down at the break is probably a fair summation of the game but it feels a long way back with ten men. Ray joins the team poking the sodden turf at the interval as the pitch begins to show signs of cutting up. A second goal and a second red card, this time for left-back Jamie Kay in a 50/50 challenge on the halfway line that he was judged to have gone into two-footed, and it looks like disaster again for the Millers.

Instead, something wonderful happens.

The nine men begin to protect the ball. Linnets, who've been playing a high intensity pressing game to close down their opponents try to impose their numerical advantage even more but are undone when a seeking ball out to the right wing finds Sam Marshall. Often the main attacking outlet, he drives into the box before being brought down by one of the two defenders tasked with stopping him. Nathan Neequaye steps up to finish the job from twelve yards in the 64th minute and banish his Church Lane penalty spot demons.

Four minutes later, New Mills push forward again. With the side out of shape, defender Warren Gaskin pushes forward and finds himself on the edge of the box surrounded by three men. He holds off their challenges individually with a Cruyff-style pirouette that sees him turn all three of his markers in a 360-degree motion, before smashing the ball with his right foot. It cannons off the underside of the crossbar and into the back of the net.

The cheers are long and raucous. A busy Church Lane is witnessing something special. I feel a rush of energy course through me that overrides lingering infection and I'm convinced

Sue is about to have an aneurysm as her guttural roar sends her face redder than when she inadvertently controlled a stray ball with her skull against Darwen.

A full team celebration is completed by Ollie Martin, who has made numerous excellent saves once again to keep the game alive and now sprints the length of the pitch to mob the goalscorer.

Jamie Kay, who had kicked and screamed his way down the touchline on the way back to the dressing room following his dismissal re-emerges now, showered and gloomy looking.

'They're playing loads better without me,' he jokes wryly.

The game takes a further swing on 70 minutes when Linnets go down to ten men, and again in stoppage time when the referee levels things up to nine aside with his fourth flash of red. Dennis Sherriff's 35-yard effort from the resulting free-kick dips just over the bar after encouragement to shoot from his manager in what turns out to be the last kick of the game.

The players receive rapturous applause as they leave the field. The circumstances overcome to retrieve a point against one of the better sides in the division are hard to believe. That it's the Millers' first league point since Darwen on Bonfire Night makes it all the more incredible.

'MILLERS!' shouts a jubilant Sam Scott on entering the busy clubhouse post-match. He's clearly facing less of an internal struggle with his red card than teammate Jamie Kay who has already made a getaway.

One by one, each player enters the clubhouse for their tray of Sue's slow cooker special with a big smile. Calum and his coaching team find their own table and relive a rollercoaster afternoon. After a while, Sue turns talk towards a proposed comedy night she's asked me to host the Thursday before Easter. While the players are enthusiastic, manager Calum turns pale. He's no intention of letting his players have a piss-up just a few weeks from the end of the season, and espccially not on a training night. The plan will need a rethink.

As Ryan Hopper reaches the bar, a shout goes up from the team.

'Drink for Chesney-esta!'

It's in reference to the ginger haired former skipper's supposed likeness to the Coronation Street character and draws a huge laugh which Hopper just about shrugs off. The culprit is Sam Scott, who then turns to a woman in her 60s and repeatedly tells her she has dementia. It turns out it's his slightly inebriated nan who has come to watch her pride and joy take an early bath this afternoon.

'Chesney?' repeats Hopper under his breath. 'Cheeky bastard!'

'Oi Fellaini! Fellaini!' shouts the ever-exuberant Sam Scott from across the bar in reference to my head of thick and curly hair. He has the energy of a kid in detention who refuses to be tamed, and as I suspect his radar might be turning towards me, I remind him that I've dealt with rowdier audiences than him before.

'I hear you're doing a comedy night?' he asks pointedly. 'If anyone picks on me, they'll be choosing which window they're going out of.'

He's an interesting character who certainly adds colour to the clubhouse, even if it does feel like he isn't entirely in control of his emotions, as his double booking this afternoon testifies. He refers to me as 'Fellaini' several more times before spotting something shiny and becoming distracted.

Meanwhile, Sue is drawing the prizes for the 100 Club, the competition players and fans alike are encouraged to pay into as a fundraiser, with a top prize of a literal ton of cash that would keep anyone well-watered in the reasonably priced surrounds of the New Mills clubhouse.

'Michael Jones? Where's Jonesy?' she says, looking round the clubhouse. The centre half has also made a relatively quick departure this afternoon.

'What's he won?' is the shout from his teammates. 'He can't have won the £100 can he? The jammy bastard.'

Sue begins to laugh uproariously as she checks the prize list.

'No!' she says. 'It's not the money he's won. It's a half-season ticket!'

20

FEELING SYKESED

With the feel-good factor back at Church Lane, it seemed like a good time to finally speak to Calum Sykes. I've sensed his guardedness about my presence since he took on the hotseat – understandably, given the difficult transition from Stockport Town and the controversy it courted – and with the bold move representing a risk to a growing reputation, it was also perhaps logical that he might want to keep a low profile until he'd had the opportunity to make an impact on results.

As he arrives at Robinson College in Gorton, where the Millers' training sessions now take place on a rented pitch, he's almost unrecognisable in boxing training gear; it's the first time I've seen him out of his trademark suit. As we find a seat in a quiet area upstairs with an instant coffee from the machine, there's only one place to start.

'Saturday was a funny one,' he begins, softly spoken as if sharing trade secrets with me, but letting out a small smile at the recollection of a memorable first point against the odds in his first game at Church Lane. 'I'd spent all week coming up with how I would alter things leading into the game to make sure I'd made changes following the Nelson game. So as soon as they walk in, everything was up. All the set pieces were up, all the team sheets were up, new motivational posters all around because it was our first home game as well so I just wanted everything to be absolutely spot on.

'I got to the ground at half twelve, they all arrive at half one and everything is magic for them. As the game starts, I couldn't ask for any more from them really. The first two or three minutes, Runcorn Linnets come at us as you'd expect but we settled into the game really well and we were breaking everything up from them. From where I was, their goal certainly appeared to be offside,' he says. I don't have the heart to tell him I'd only seen it through a crack in the fence and therefore can't confirm or deny.

'I think on the first 42 minutes,' he continues, 'we were right in the game and certainly didn't feel the one goal was gonna be an issue for us. 42nd minute we get a second yellow for Sam Scott, red card, and you start thinking this is going to be a difficult afternoon. The feeling when we got in the dressing room was full of positivity – you do your team talks and you look around because you just wanna see "am I on my own? Are you sat with your head down or are you with me?" and when I say we can go out with ten men and get something out of this game, that's what they were saying back to me.

'We go out in the second half, start reasonably well. Ten, fifteen minutes in we concede again from an error that comes from the pitch in that the ball should have bounced and it didn't, it just completely died and it was a lovely finish to pass it in the way he did round Ollie Martin. So we're two down but I still felt like they kept going, still felt like they kept believing that we could still do something,' he continues, the passion building in his voice now.

'Part of the team talk was about it being the first home game and we wanted to show what characters we had with the negativity that had gone around following the Nelson game as well. We definitely wanted to show that we had better team spirit than that and better character individually. The other hammer blow goes in with the straight red card for a bad tackle – but I think the other lad who has gone in against him is equally as bad. Another day and it perhaps goes the other way.

'I made two substitutions after that,' continues Calum, picking up enthusiasm for the tale, 'and, if anything, it opened the game up for us. I got Luke Podmore ready to go on to play…' he says, before hesitating and chuckling at the recollection. 'The comment to him as he went on was actually "Luke, you're gonna play left…side! You're gonna play all that line!" And they didn't deal with that.

'So Sam Marshall gets the penalty, they couldn't deal with Luke when they got their man sent off. Their manager kept their right back at right back, which meant Luke had thirty or forty yards to run into before he was engaged. If their manager had put a right winger on instead of a right back, we wouldn't have been able to get out. He didn't, which led to us getting the second goal which is possibly the best goal I've ever seen!' he beams, referring to his captain Warren Gaskin's strike from the edge of the box.

'The way he's gone in to intercept the ball, the way he's took two men,' Calum continues, somewhat giddy at the recollection. 'The fact he does a spin, a bit of a Maradona turn, and then just unleashes it. And when it hits the bar, it's so exciting to see bar, boom, in! And he's been texting me this week, he's still absolutely buzzin'. Someone whose never scored a goal in open play for me and what a time to get your first one.'

Calum is really animated now, reliving every moment of the game. The relief it brought, too, especially after the Nelson result, is palpable in his retelling as he continues.

'They get another man sent off, nine-a-side, and I really thought we could, with another five minutes, we could have nicked something, got the three points and the whole league would be thinking "New Mills have done that to Runcorn Linnets". I think a lot of the teams are wondering how New Mills have done that. That's what we want people to see. Alright, we're in a difficult position but we're gonna fight to get ourselves out of the position we're in.'

That message for the rest of the League – and perhaps detractors at his former club, too – is clearly an important one for Calum. Inheriting a side in freefall, there was always a big risk in overhauling the squad, especially given his early assessment that he wouldn't necessarily need to do so. But with games running out and more experience and leadership brought in, it felt like the long overdue confidence boost of Saturday's performance had restored some belief back into the dressing room.

He continues: 'Following the Nelson game, we got the whole team together. We had a full team meeting which, considering we'd only had one when I'd first got the job, was quite quick to have another full team meeting. The performance against Nelson was unacceptable. The feeling I went away with was that I couldn't have personally done any more as a manager, the staff couldn't really have done more. It was down to them. What I actually put it down to was that there are that many new players here now, they almost don't consider themselves to be in the bottom three. You're not a team that is aware they've not been doing great, this is a new team. It's like half a season for this group.

'They look at it and go "Nelson are at the bottom, so mentally this team are a lot worse than us" which isn't the case at all. So because these players were mentally unprepared and Nelson were well prepared and aware that they're bottom three and fighting, this team that should've performed and had performed against West Didsbury and Chorlton who are a top team, went out against Nelson and thought "this'll be easy."'

It's an honest assessment of his side's shortcomings but points to the encouragement it gives for the testing schedule ahead – something which the manager is already given plenty of thought to.

'In the team meeting we went through the fifteen games we have left. Five are against teams that are in the top six positions, the others are against teams that are tenth and below. So I explained to the team that, with the group of players we have, tenth would be the minimum expectation I would have for that group. So when I consider that, every team we have left to play in that ten are below where my expectation for us would be. So all those games become winnable games.

'Of those ten games, I'm expecting we get 25 points. Of the top five teams, I'm expecting five points. That's your thirty points. That puts us nineteen points ahead of where (21st-placed) Darwen currently are. Are Darwen gonna get nineteen points? Our hope and belief is they won't and I've gone through their fixtures as well. It would take a massive surge from them to accomplish that, they haven't brought in a new manager or group of players, so it's our hope that that won't occur.

'Saturday, the first one of the top five, and we get the one point. We have Padiham to play twice who are in that top six and we certainly think we can get four points just from them. We do think we've got players who are good enough and I think we saw glimpses of that last Saturday; glimpses of the quality that we have on what was a difficult pitch to play on. Until it's mathematically impossible, we will believe that we can get out of it.'

It all sounds like a daunting task but there's something about Calum's enthusiasm that makes you believe it. It will be a vital ingredient in the dressing room if the Millers are to still pull of a great escape, but it's certainly not one that fazes the charismatic young manager.

'I genuinely wouldn't have taken the job on if I didn't think I could get 'em out of it,' he continues. 'My reputation as a manager, obviously because I'm so young, is based upon getting Stockport Town to the play-off semi-final last season in Division One and having a reasonably decent start to the season this year. I wouldn't wanna ruin what's only a small reputation by getting New Mills their third consecutive relegation. So I do believe I can get 'em out of it.

'I do believe in the Atherton Colls game (where New Mills lost 2-1 on Boxing Day) that I can get more from players. I only had two new players out of the sixteen-man squad and we got an unbelievable performance from them. That'd be my aim.'

Calum's route to Church Lane is our next avenue of conversation. Starting at this level with Stockport Town two seasons ago, he'd been building an impressive managerial C.V from a young age that led him to the newly formed side just a short journey north towards Manchester.

'I'd previously worked at Glossop North End, where we won

the Reserve League and the First Team won the (North West) Counties (League). At this point, New Mills were in the Evo-Stik. Glossop then have to make a decision on finances and pitch protection; obviously it's just around the corner and they're getting the same bad weather. So they made the decision that there wouldn't be a Reserves team anymore. So my group of players who've just had a fantastic season, runners-up in the cup competition as well - now there's twenty players who've got nowhere to go and play.

'So I was looking for a Club who are looking for a manager or at least trying to get a team into the Counties. That was the level I wanted to be at, I wanted to be in the Premier Division of the Manchester league, the Mid-Cheshire Prem and with a club that was saying "we want to go to the Counties".

'I did have a conversation with one club who were really interested in me coming in and I asked if they were going for the Counties. The answer was "in the next five years". There was nothing at this club stopping them other than the bigger financial burden, fines are so much more, and you'll have seen on matchday how much Sue and Ray are buzzing around and that's because there's so much more to do.

'So Stockport Town wanted to form a club, I knew a guy that was involved and, at the time, there was a lot of people involved at the Club, maybe fifteen people involved setting it up. And I said it to the guy at the time "they must have a manager! Who is gonna create a club and not have a gaffer?" and they said "no, they've not got a gaffer!" And I'm thinking "Stockport, this could be perfect, pretty much on my doorstep and I've got a team that's ready". I got in contact and it took about two weeks for them to confirm it. I took training sessions, interviewed with about three different people, and they were like "yes, you are the gaffer!"

'The club started and when I took the job, it was on the premise that we were gonna get in the Counties,' he continues, of the process of applying to the League for a place. 'That is what the club was set up for. And then we didn't get in so we appealed it in the summer. I've got this big group of players - and players coming in to trial on top of the players I already had - and I had to sit 'em all down right at the end of July and say, "we're not in". So all these players who've worked so hard for seven or eight weeks of pre-season training...' he trails off, the disappointment of that decision fresh in his expression and body language.

Abandoned by Glossop North End and shunned by the North West Counties League with his newly formed club, Calum needs a plan.

'So we decided we're gonna have a season of friendlies,' he says, almost visibly wincing at the memory. 'And that's what we did.' I think back to the summer and Sue's less than enthusiastic approach to friendlies – it matches Calum's perfectly.

'For development as a manager, it was amazing. We played FC United, we played Mossley, Droylsden – we played teams that were much higher than where we were. As a manager, I had to somehow persuade and motivate players to train twice a week, turn up on Saturdays or Fridays or Tuesday nights and play to their best to beat these oppositions when, in theory, they had nothing to play for other than pride of not losing. We did really well; I think we played just shy of 40 games and won maybe 34 of them.

'From that, we do get into the Counties League and it was another step up as a manager, understanding how oppositions were set up and how other managers would behave. I think it's probably in the friendly season, other managers aren't doing quite the same thing as it's a friendly, whereas for us it meant everything. So that was a learning curve for me, having to understand that unattractive football still wins football matches. Playing against that, how do you combat that? Players telling me "these are rubbish, can't play football!" – no, they can't, but they've still scored four goals!'

Calum's first season proper at the helm of Stockport Town would be a successful one, even though it would ultimately end in disappointment.

'We got to the semi-final of the play-offs, finished fourth. We know we could have finished third if results had gone better. We wouldn't have got second (an automatic promotion berth), the points total Irlam got was too much, but I still think we could have got third. We played against Bacup who had a really good side that year, a very experienced side. We had maybe 300 people come to watch that game and I think our average was about 40. So I think for the players it was about being in awe of the crowd and the experience of Bacup was just that bit better.

'They scored (from) two corners in the 20th and 25th minute and just defended; which you would! They wanted to get through to that final, we couldn't find the answer to that problem. And that was that' he says, with a hint of regret. A promotion in their debut season would have only enhanced a burgeoning reputation.

'So when I started back there this year, there were changes from behind the scenes. My objectives given from the club were still the same but what I had available to me wasn't the same. Trying to manage that was really difficult and, I feel like I've said it a few times, but 'mentality' – the players who are at this level are at this level for a reason and something as little as being unhappy about something like money…it might be a fiver, a tenner, so tiny, but that mentally would affect them so much. And that was what we saw in the performances for Stockport, a general unhappiness, and I'm working my socks off to get that right but ultimately the players were getting frustrated with things happening behind the scenes that were beyond my control.

'Eventually, it just became too much for me. You give up your time and you wouldn't do it if you weren't passionate and weren't enjoying it. For me, I've got three kids, a wife, two houses and this takes up so much time. It's not just when I'm here, it's when I'm on the phone to players, texting players, you're like their big brother or even to some of the kids like a dad. And it's not just an age thing, it's the same for some of the players older than me. That is the role you're put in and you can't say to players "I'm with the wife tonight, you just go and be upset on your own,"' he says. It's fascinating insight into the all-encompassing nature of what is essentially a voluntary role and echoes some of the concerns and pressures Garry had spoken of at the start of the season.

He continues: 'There's a lot of time commitments, which I love, but if you're not happy with everything then that's when you start thinking: "Why? Why am I doing this?" And then the opportunity with New Mills comes around and it's just too good to not be involved in a club that has such history, such experience.

'Sue and Ray are the exact sort of people I wanna work for. The sort of people that, if you're honest with them, they'll be honest back with you. I'm more than aware that if things aren't going good, if I'm out of line, then they'll be there to tell me so. At the same time, they'll be there to fully support me when things are going well. That's what you need, that's what you want. They've got this family club feel which is a massive thing for me.'

The family feel of New Mills is another hallmark of his short managerial career so far. In his early 20s, Calum had started his own club – a venture that would start him on his path to management. And, according to Calum, It's also a vital ingredient in bringing the fans back, building an atmosphere at Church Lane and helping the Millers dig their way out of trouble.

'We'd play Saturday mornings and I'd get all the players to go back to the pub straight after,' he laughs, recalling the memories of his first venture into grassroots football. 'We had a link-up where they'd put food on for us afterwards and we'd be in there for half twelve and in there until four or five o'clock. People would bring their girlfriends, their children in, mums and dads, and this was an open age team, not kids. It was massive to get this family feel about the place. That's the potential we've got at New Mills. And Saturday, two-nil down with nine men and you see that fightback and hunger from these players. Those fans are seeing this for the first time. And these fans are thinking "I'll come back in two weeks against Nelson because you lads have got some fight about ya."

'When I see the crowd statistics for three years ago, there's probably 190. On Saturday, even if we split it down the middle, there were probably 80 or 90. But hopefully they're gonna go tell

Jim, Jane and Bob to come down 'cos it was a great game!'

My final question is a difficult one. Having sensed Calum's guarded nature about my reasons for speaking to him, I'm keen to cover the way his departure from Stockport had been handled by his former club. It feels like a question that could go either way and his eye contact with me intensifies midway through his answer before he seems to relax slightly.

'The way in which Stockport Town dealt with it, not only to me via texts but also on social media, is extremely disappointing,' he says after a pause to compose a diplomatic answer. 'I did work hard. Whether or not I was successful or ultimately what they wanted, the time I was there, I gave everything. I've no doubt that I did all I could and left them in a decent position.

'The manner in which I resigned probably wasn't exactly as I wanted to as it was over an email. The reason why it was over email was because I was in Barrow-in-Furness where we'd just played Holker, a game which in all honesty I probably didn't have to go to. But I wouldn't have left the club in that way and left them to not have a team and not have a manager. I took a young side there because a lot of the players were frustrated with the backroom and the Board weren't willing to go.

'I get a text message telling me I've taken the New Mills job. I'm three hours away on a minibus full of players that don't know and I'm not willing to tell them in this manner – "by the way lads, that's my last game. Sorry."

'I wasn't gonna do that. So I'm thinking how to let the Board know before this source that's texting me. So I'll construct an email, send that on and then I'll ring them. Later on that night they (Stockport Town) announced it on their Twitter that I'd gone to New Mills which wasn't great. They (New Mills) had just come out and said they'd parted company with Paul, an announcement will be made in due course and then Stockport say, "Calum has gone to New Mills". It's not their news to share really. "Calum has resigned" but not "Calum has gone to New Mills".

'I spoke to the Chairman and the Secretary, explained my

decision and they were alright with me. We spoke on the phone, the Chairman actually said he had no issue over email. It is what it is, you've worked hard, wish you the best of luck. They then mention that a lot of players had asked to leave the Club.

'My words to both were that it's your choice. It's your choice as a Club whether you wish to release them. I'll be dead straight, I'd pick up my team and bring them with me because I've brought all those footballers in. It's not like pro football where a manager comes in and he has to have certain players because that's who the sporting director has bought. You're bringing in players you've pulled from somewhere else and I'd worked really hard in the summer to bring a lot of these players together.

'When player x, y and z are saying "I want to be at New Mills and I've asked the club to release me," for me it's "why would I not want you to be at the club when you've been released". All the Stockport players realise it's more serious here. They've gone up a notch, *I've* gone up a notch, so everything goes up that little bit more. Two of my players on Saturday didn't make the squad because they'd not adhered to some of the new rules. We're not just chasing promotion, we're not just chasing the play-offs, we're in a relegation battle that we've got to get out of.'

With the drama and chaos surrounding his exit, Calum also saves a few words for the official channels that stoked the fires – perhaps inadvertently – and created additional controversy around the move.

'The North West Counties (League) doesn't help the situation,' Calum says, consciously choosing his words carefully. 'Every week, they post player movements. (The) Player movements (in this instance) were all de-registrations, someone who was no longer signed and then they signed for New Mills. You'll see every week that players you know were at another club don't appear in 'move from', they just appear under the new club's name. They've agreed to release him and then he signs for another club. Now Joe Armstrong was the only player who appeared in the correct bracket: Joe Armstrong – New Mills.

'The other players all appeared in the top bracket, so then it says *x moves from Stockport Town to New Mills*. Everyone is screenshotting it on Twitter and it became a bit unsavoury. It didn't look good on the club (New Mills) that we've taken all these players and done a mass transfer. The club (Stockport Town) have then decided to attack me on social media, personal insults, and they attacked Sue as well so it was all quite sad. I think the worst night was Christmas Eve when I'm trying to be there with my wife and kids. I don't really need it and I probably don't really deserve it. I haven't asked you to release these players, I haven't bad-mouthed the club, but that was how they chose to go with it. In a way, that sort of shows why I moved from there to New Mills,' he says, unable to resist a tiny dig.

'Even on Saturday, they wrote on Twitter "Our best ever first half performance since we were formed" and you just think it's still very bitter.'

I joke that it's akin to an ex posting on social media about how wonderful everything with the new rebound boy/girlfriend is.

'If I was so bad…? They called all the players (that left) "charity shop", taking all the unwanted gifts to the charity shop. Obviously those unwanted gifts would've helped them not get beat 10-0 on New Year's Eve,' he adds with a twinkle, in another glimpse of him allowing his true feelings to sneak beyond his professionalism. 'If I'd have been so bad then why did I last so long in the job? Surely they should've released me from what I was doing?

'I fully expect that if my team don't fight our way from relegation, don't show any signs of fighting our way away from relegation, I fully expect to lose the job in May. I wouldn't expect Sue and Ray to say "well don't worry, you'll get us promoted next season" because you expect to see what you've hired. Although as a manager at this level you're not being paid, it's still a job. I talk to friends who just don't get it, they're like: "can't you just have a holiday?" It's the middle of the season, this is my team. It's my team!'

It's the most animated and passionate Calum has been throughout the whole chat. Usually quite a cool, calm and collected character, he allows himself a little more therapy in the final few minutes of our chat as we become mindful of the players beginning to arrive downstairs.

'The worst thing was…you sign a player and at the bottom of the form there are two sections: 'witnessed by' and 'club person'. On my computer I have the scanned copy and text boxes. The copy we had would have the Secretary's signature pre-signed on there. He never had to handwrite any. When the release forms were done, they were sent to me rather than the players. Not really the way, but never mind. I send them two forms back for everyone in the same way I have for every player that I've signed at the club. Hand on heart, I've sent them back for his convenience because otherwise he has to print them off, sign them, scan them back in. I've saved him the job. It's his signature we've used for 40 or 50 players.

'He chooses to go on Twitter and tag in the FA and Derbyshire FA, saying I was fraudulently using his signature. I know people at the FA because I'm such a young coach and it makes me look so bad. And he's writing that knowing I've only sent it to him. If I'd sent it to the Counties, I agree, I'd have been out of order. I've sent it just to you, it's your choice. Subsequently he has deleted all this stuff but they did put a report into the FA to say I'd tapped players up.'

With that off his chest, it's clear Calum has no regrets in either his move or the subsequent signings of players he'd worked with before. It's the nature of the beast at this level, it seems, as he explains further.

'When a manager leaves, unless you've formed a great bond then you might stay because you're loyal to that club. But a lot of times players go because they love a manager and there are players that play for me and are purely playing for me.

'Playing for no money or next to no money and doing it because they see - I hope it's because they see - I work hard and they think "do you know what, he works hard and he does it all for free and I want to do that for him to be successful, for us to be successful together" and I think that's why they still wanted to be a part of that, to help us out of that situation and I think that's why we saw some top performances at the weekend. New Mills had some top players beforehand as well and that's why I believe we can do it.'

As the lads arrive for training and Calum and I finish off our chat, you can't help but be won over by his passion and enthusiasm. With more performances like the one against Linnets, there could be life in the Millers' relegation fight yet.

Calum Sykes, surrounded by his coaching team, watches on from the Church Lane dugout

21

PUTTING THE BOOTLE IN

There was once a time when the only way to 'watch' a match you couldn't attend was via Teletext or Ceefax. They were wondrous days, filled with anticipation. As the pages scrolled, expectation swelled, as you awaited the appearance of your team to see if they'd grabbed that all-important equaliser in the intervening forty-five seconds since they were last on your screen.

One of my fondest memories of Teletext was in 1997, when my beloved and relegation-haunted Tottenham announced a new marquee signing. The living room television was out of bounds on that particular afternoon during the Christmas holidays as we had visiting guests, but I can still remember exploding with delight before they'd even got their shoes back on in the hallway as the TV displayed the most wondrous news my 12-year-old eyes had ever seen: *Klinsmann re-signs for Spurs*. My mum still scalds me for my manners in front of house guests to this day.

Nowadays, such a signing would be all over social media within minutes. Dozens of 'in the know' accounts might have predicted the signing weeks in advance, alongside outlandish claims that Ronaldo and Batistuta were also planning to pitch in with the North London relegation battle. Viral videos of Christian Gross's infamous brandishing of a London Underground ticket at his introductory press conference would be 'GIF'ed and mashed up with the unveiling of the return of a hero while Twitter would go into overdrive over the perceived bad blood between the German international and the future employer on The Apprentice.

For better or worse, social media has revolutionised how we follow football. And, while dodgy streams of the Premier League are readily available, it also offers a vital link for non-league sides to build a fan base and keep them engaged. Some might say a little too engaged…

One of the most familiar faces at Church Lane on a Saturday these days is Jon Warrior. Tonight, New Mills are making the not inconsiderable trip north to league leaders Bootle of Merseyside. It's a four-hour round trip I can't cram into a weekday evening without missing most of the first half but Jon is on the train – no drums, for once - and is tweeting his heroes as he makes his way north.

'New Mills ultras on there (sic) way no drum' he tweets at 4.30pm, tagging in Club Secretary Sue, midfielder Ryan Hopper and Manager Calum Sykes for good measure. All know him on first name terms and are no doubt pleased to hear the away fans are travelling to support the side, percussion or no percussion, in what looks like a daunting fixture on paper. The Thursday night fixture has been rearranged to slip into the schedule with a free weekend coming up for the Millers, even if it does offer slim hope of a points return against the division's in-form side.

'Whys they (sic) no water in the trains had a pee can't wash me hand rank' he tweets again ten minutes later. He's included the same audience as before, but this time helpfully tags in East Midlands Trains. There's no clarification as to which hand he was planning to wash but, once I've painted the picture with words, dear reader, it really is your job to fill in the blanks.

An hour passes and an all-important update follows.

'finally got to wash my hands at Liverpool south parkway hope it (sic) a good result for millers tonight :)'

I picture Calum preparing his team as his phone notification pings and he's momentarily distracted by the post-lavatory hygiene issues of the travelling faithful.

As the game gets underway, I'm glued to the coverage via Twitter. Tonight, this is my Teletext. The first update is a positive one.

'New Mills 1 Bootle 0. Get in Sam MARSHALL.'

I make a small, emphatic noise from the sofa but it's not even half-time yet and we've been here before. Best to keep a lid on things early doors. The next one follows some twenty minutes later.

'Great first half performance from the Millers half time 0 1'

It makes great reading as I sip a mug of decaffeinated tea from the comfort of my sofa. The full-strength stuff will keep me awake until the early hours at any point after Emmerdale. If you've ever struggled with insomnia, try it. I don't mean Emmerdale. Well, that might work as well.

Fifteen minutes into the second half, the seemingly inevitable follows.

'Bootle 1. New Mills 1'

It's blunt in both its assessment and delivery. I slump back a little. A couple of substitutions follow and then, four minutes from time, the ping of my phone notification goes again.

'Get in Darcy. Bootle 1 New Mills 2'

I literally leap from the sofa. I pace the living room, unsure of what to do. I'm watching New Mills beat the league leaders on social media and now all I want to do is be there at the game. Another notification. A description of the goal, perhaps?

'3rd sub Ruben off Joe Armstrong on'

There's clearly no time for dwelling on how the potential winner has been scored. It's understandably a melee of activity, I imagine, as Bootle see their promotion hopes dashed against a side who haven't won in five months and rally for the point. That's when the next notification follows.

'Bootle 2 New Mills 2'

I stare at my phone for a second. It's hard to take in but reality soon rises to the surface. Calum had set the target of a point per game against the top sides and this is a point. It might feel like a defeat but it's still a point. A point towards safety against one of the best sides in the division who are well-placed for promotion because they fight for every point themselves, play until the very last minute, work and press and pressure and…PING!

'*Bootle 3 New Mills 2*'

I stare again, this time in utter shock. While gauging the minutes played is difficult via Twitter, the time itself suggests the goal has come deep into injury time. The pictures would later confirm that everyone including the Bootle goalkeeper mobbed the goalscorer for what would turn out to be a winning goal that would maintain the Merseyside club's place at the top of the division.

'*Great performance from the Millers tonight. Full time Bootle 3 New Mills 2*'

This tweet arrives less than two minutes after the previous one. Bootle have stolen the points with the last kick of the game. The Millers account falls silent for the rest of the evening. There isn't much else to say.

'*My head is well and truly gone*' tweets Ollie Martin just before midnight. His dad would tell me later that the 'keeper, a mature and vocal presence in the team despite his relatively young age, was close to tears on returning home having felt his decision to punch when he might have caught for the decisive third goal had cost his side the draw. The reality was that he'd kept the Millers in more than a few games over the years, even if his overly harsh self-assessment had been correct.

Meanwhile, with freshly cleansed hands, Jon Warrior was happy to announce to the world that he was home safe and sound.

'*@calumsykes home now thanks to derek and sue and thanks to @calumsykes and the millers for a wonderful effort tonight #proudmiller*' he tweets just after midnight. It's been an 8-hour round trip and he's finally made it back.

'*Thank you for your support it really means a lot*' comes the reply from Calum just after 1am. Whether he's just home or struggling to sleep while dwelling on an unbelievable game isn't entirely clear. The effort of his side can't be doubted though, and it's already winning support from the faithful. The last word goes to Jon, who travelled home in the car with Sue, such is his integral part of matchday now.

'no bother millers is my home hope your (sic) staying whatever happens after April mate #proudmiller #miller4life #millersaremyteam :)'

You couldn't have given the manager your vote of confidence over Teletext back in the day, nor could you have arranged a lift home with the Club Secretary. Maybe it is progress after all.

As if Bootle away hadn't been enough of a kick, February would end with even more disappointment:

New Mills FC chairman Ray Coverley has expressed his dismay and frustration at the town council's decision to veto a planned redevelopment of Ollersett Fields, begins an article in the Advertiser.

A new and exciting facility had been proposed for the site, which included 3G pitches and facilities for not only New Mills FC to use but also junior and girls teams from across the town. However, despite the pitches at Ollersett Fields currently being in a poor condition, New Mills Town Council decided at a meeting last week to turn down the proposals.

Coverley said: 'The council say that the new facilities will have no real benefit to the community, only to New Mills FC itself, which is staggering really given it's an entirely community-based proposal and designed to benefit everyone.

'We've been putting the plans together for a long time now with developers Morbaine and this would have cost the council nothing given Morbaine would have organised all of the public consultations and so on, but we've not even been allowed to get to that stage.

'It's been a very sudden end to quite a drawn out process and we're desperately disappointed, as are our junior coaches and players as they currently don't have anywhere suitable to play regularly. It's a huge setback. I could understand if consultations had taken place and there were suitable enough objections to it all, but it has been nipped in the bud before the plans had been made fully public.'

Morbaine had also put accompanying plans in place to develop the playing fields at Quarry Road, currently used by school teams but which are also in a poor condition. Coverley added: 'Everything we had planned was with a view to improving current facilities to provide a fantastic community resource and yet the council have, for some reason, not seen that and dismissed it out of hand.

'Everything was being financed and literally the only thing the council had to do was give us the OK to do it. We've had widespread support from across the town for what we wanted to do.

'I've been involved with this club for 30 years and wanted this development to be my legacy so I'm very frustrated at the way this has happened. Both sites are going to rack and ruin and it's such a huge waste when you consider both what could be put in place instead and just how many people will benefit. I can't understand how the council believe the community won't reap the rewards.

'Our only option now would seem to be developing our current home at Church Lane but we have limited space there and the end result wouldn't be as useful.' Coverley added that a petition may now be started to encourage the council to look again at the plans. The Town Council have been approached by the Advertiser for comment.

Back to the drawing board.

22

HOME IS WHERE THE HEART IS

March had begun in all too familiar fashion for New Mills. Well hidden behind a busy main road in south Manchester, Maine Road Football Club would be the venue of their latest defeat. Formed in 1955 as a Sunday League side of Manchester City supporters, the familiar light blue shirts and club emblem displayed proudly on the front of a matchday programme left little doubt of their allegiances despite being just a couple of short miles from Old Trafford.

Despite an early Ryan Hopper goal and a merry band of travelling supporters with flags, songs and Jon's trusty drum, the Millers would succumb to a 4-2 defeat in the soggy conditions. Leading the chants of the self-styled 'Millers Ultras', consisting of Jon Warrior and a band of enthusiastic teenagers, was Jon himself.

'We love you Millers, we do. We love you Millers, we do,' he sang, trusting others to take care of the drum. 'Come on! Get a beat going!'

With the lead Hopper's goal had given the Millers both cancelled out and then reversed by half-time, a glum looking Ray made conversation with the Hallmark Security League Fixtures Secretary who in attendance this afternoon. With Ray and Sue having travelled with the supporters by coach to the game, the familiar sniff of impending defeat at the break was soured further by the lack of a bar in the clubhouse, thwarting the Chairman's planned half-time pint. Rarely has a man stared so dejectedly at a mug of complimentary tea.

To make matters worse, the scores from elsewhere are desperate. Given the likely 'two from three' scenario forming at the division's trapdoor, with Cammell Laird cast adrift at the bottom and the rest of the division beginning to pull away, scorelines from Nelson and Darwen are of increasing importance as the games run out. Both are winning. As it stands, New Mills are 13 points from safety. Anyone for a beer?

'Carl's writing a book about us,' Sue begins as she introduces me to the League Fixtures Secretary over Ray's increasingly glum demeanour. He listens with interest at the project.

'Did you not want to write a book about a successful side?' he quips. I catch Ray's shoulder's hunch slightly in my peripheral vision like a cat about to pounce. Instead, he takes a deep breath and impatiently reiterates the limitations his club work under. The League official smiles. His bait was taken. I move away from the conversation.

'Sykesey, give us a wave! Sykesey, Syksey give us a wave!' sings Jon midway through the second half. The rain is pouring and New Mills are 3-1 down.

'He might not be in the mood,' suggests a younger member of the Ultras, wisely.

'It cheers 'em up!' replies Jon with confidence.

'You sure?' comes the reply.

'We used to do it all the time at Stalybridge to Keith Briggs. Even when we were 5-0 down.'

A 78th minute goal from Nathan Neequaye gives the familiar feeling of hope before Maine Road see the job through by adding a fourth.

'I've passed my radio qualification,' Jon tells me as he heads for the bus home. 'Sue's asked me to be matchday announcer next weekend.' No fan deserves it more, or is likely to appreciate the gesture quite as much, as Jon. It's a rare bright spot on an utterly miserable afternoon.

Back in the clubhouse, Derek finishes his duties but the supporter coach hasn't hung around. Within minutes of the final whistle, it's loaded and away with Sue and Ray on-board with it.

A dejected Calum arrives through the double doors, seemingly in search of his employers before turning back to begin the post-mortem with his team. There's little I can offer in consolation so I remain quiet. It's been a demoralising day as it is, even before the confirmation comes through that both Nelson and Darwen have hung on for three points apiece.

'Another chapter for the book?' queries the League official, with a glint in his eye, as I depart. However poor the performance, it's an unwelcome return to New Mills threatening to become the easy punchline once again.

****

There's a received wisdom in football that relegated sides perform better once their fate is sealed. With the pressure valve released, so the theory goes, teams find a new freedom and cohesion they've seemingly spent months trying to find. Wigan Athletic's 2013 FA Cup final victory over the giants of Manchester City might be one such example.

On the 11th of March, as Calum Sykes prepared Church Lane for only his second home game despite almost three months in charge thanks to the High Peak's microclimate putting paid to half the fixture list since Christmas, New Mills were still far from relegated mathematically. There was certainly a resigned feeling among many within the Club, though, that a demotion to the tenth tier of English football was beginning to look inevitable.

'Lining up for the Millers today, number 1, Ollie Martin!' comes a familiar voice over the tannoy. It's a new noise and, while it might sound strange, it's almost taken up until this moment to realise that the familiar sound of the line-ups being read over a tinny speaker has been missing from the Church Lane experience thus far. Up until now, I've only heard the P.A used to announce the lucky winner of a bottle of wine on the half-time raffle.

'He's doing well, isn't he?' beams Sue, as Jon proudly steps out of the portacabin holding a microphone.

'Not bad for someone with dyspraxia, ADHD and dyslexia!' he replies, equally pleased with himself. 'Did I read the names out right?'

Today's visit of in-form Winsford United suggests another tough afternoon in store for the Millers. It also represents an opportunity. With today's game marking the first of three consecutive matches at Church Lane, the unfortunate fixture backlog offers a glimmer of hope to close the gap.

'Eleven cup finals,' was how one fan described the remainder of the season. Helpfully, seven of them were on the saturated, repair-strewn home soil New Mills were running onto. The comeback starts now.

Watching the promising opening exchanges with me is Ollie Martin's dad. A stranger to Church Lane for the past few months, he begins to pass judgement on a side almost unrecognisable from the one we'd watched together in 2016, barring Ryan Hopper and his own son between the posts. In good news for both of us, he also appears to have stopped calling me 'Craig', ending any need for me to have to meekly correct him months later.

'Offside! OFFSIDE! Lino, who was on then? Who was on?' screams Warren Gaskin at the back as the Millers survive an early scare. 'I need to know so I can bollock him!' The referee's assistant unconvincingly nods in the general direction of the right back before lowering both his flag and his head to indicate a corner.

At the opposite end of the ground, the New Mills Ultras are once again out in force. Made up of six or seven young lads with a flag and a sense of humour, they chant throughout the first half and even manage to antagonise the small band of travelling fans with some good-natured ribbing.

'Oh dear…' says Ollie's dad as his son makes a rare mistake. With the ball played back, he slices the clearance horribly and it flukily bounces beyond the on-rushing striker and into the path of Millers left back Kiarno Samms.

'He's got the biggest arse in football, that lad. But he's looking quite fit at the moment,' says Fixture Secretary Derek, as the attacking full-back begins his run up the wing. As space opens up, he continues to run, jinking in field.

'He's done well here,' is the chorus of approval as we watch him continue. 'He's done very well!' we continue as he slips a ball through to Nathan Neequaye. The big striker takes the ball in his stride and unleashes a composed finish across the 'keeper and into the bottom corner. The players celebrate in front of the New Mills Ultras just before the half hour mark.

'Goal for the Millers, number 9, NATHAN NEEQUAYE!' comes Jon's voice from the tannoy. Another cheer goes up.

The lead doesn't last long. Sharp play from Winsford on the edge of the box sees their dangerous right winger thread a superb ball across the box when all expected him to shoot. It's a cross that you might expect to see at a higher level and shows great vision that appears to catch out the entire back four. A few half-hearted offside appeals go up as the striker on the far post slots the ball underneath the onrushing Martin but it's as good a goal as you're likely to see at this level and involves most of Winsford's attacking players.

Once pegged back, there's always the risk that a game can get away from the Millers before they kick back into gear. Not today, it seems, with Samms continuing his lung busting runs up the flank and D'Arcy O'Connor, a late inclusion out of position at centre half for the injured Mike Jones, clearing everything in sight alongside Warren Gaskin.

Just before the break, New Mills win a penalty. Neequaye steps up and converts to give the home side a deserved lead for a dominant first half performance. For once, there's plenty to cheer with the half-time brew and sandwich platter in the Chairman's portacabin.

'How am I doing?' asks Jon as a busy entourage from Winsford jostle for egg mayo cobs.

'Sounds brilliant mate,' I reply, honestly.

'It's a bit nerve-wracking!' he laughs. 'I think I've pronounced their names right. Not bad for a lad with dyslexia!' he repeats. It's fantastic to see him growing into his new role and I make sure not to distract him as he successfully reveals the winning ticket on the raffle to the masses. All 102 of them.

I watch the second half from just outside the portacabin. It's a thoroughfare that sees players to and fro after substitutions back to the dressing room but, most enjoyable of all, it offers the opportunity to observe the double act of Roy and Derek close-up.

'Who was that yellow card for?' asks Derek as he makes notes on his pad.

'Can't you read that?' snaps Roy, testily, as the player's name and number is being taken in clear sight on the halfway line.

'No,' he retorts.

'You need to get your bloody eyes tested!' replies Roy, the more senior of the two gentlemen. There's a pregnant pause. Derek squints a little harder.

'Substitution for New Mills…' announces Jon, as the excellent Neequaye's number is raised. There's some confusion over his replacement as the number 21 is raised. Both squads only go up to 17 and are defined by where you're located on either the pitch or the bench – there are no trendy shirt numbers in the ninth tier. A number higher than 18 will probably see you targeted as a fancy dan.

'9 off, 21 on,' says Roy helpfully.

'There is no 21,' comes Derek's retort. Another pause.

'Maybe 12? It definitely said 21. My eyes aren't that bad!'

'…number 12, Callum Scott!' continues Jon into the microphone.

'If they score a third here, I'm having a wine tonight' muses Sue, as New Mills continue to push forward instead of protecting what they've got. 'And I'm definitely having a wine if they concede a second,' she continues thoughtfully. 'Oh, sod it. It's Saturday. I'll have one anyway,' she concludes, dismissing the potential result altogether.

There's a moment of concern for D'Arcy O'Connor, who is

putting a solid performance in at the back, as he limps heavily after a collision with the post.

'How's your leg?' enquires his defensive partner Gaskin, during a brief break in play.

'I twatted the post,' is along the lines of his reply.

'How's the post?' asks Gaskin.

Tensions spill over when a horrendously late tackle from Winsford's number 10 sends Ryan Hopper into the advertising hoardings. With less than ten minutes to play, it's a sign of just how rattled the Millers have their visitors, although that's little consolation to Hopper.

With the assailant bearing a striking resemblance to his own slight build and short, ginger hair to the point that they could be mistaken for brothers playing a little too rough on the back garden, both teams pile in to join the melee that follows the needless sliding tackle. The Winsford player made the challenge after the ball was out of play, sending Hopper into the metal railings with some velocity.

'Oh, for fuck's sake!' says Sue as she heads down the touchline to be peacemaker. The level-headed and calm Hopper has truly lost his head, as he admits later, flying into the crowd of shirts to seek retribution for a truly awful challenge.

'Ryan! RYAN! Calm down! Calm down!' shouts Sue from over the hoardings. As the brawl separates, Hopper shakes his head as he runs off and his remorseless assailant jogs away. He's jeered by the New Mills lads for the remainder of the game.

'No man too big for Sue!' several of them repeat as the offender's five-foot eight frame jogs back into position. There wouldn't be many who wouldn't back Sue with the gloves off.

The dying minutes were as tense as you might expect for a side looking to close out their first win in six months. When sub Dennis Sherriff tried his luck from the halfway line after Winsford sent their 'keeper up for the corner, rather than running the ball towards the corner flag, there was only muted frustration that his opportunity had given the away side another last-ditch opportunity to attack. With a late Winsford corner successfully defended, the sound of the final whistle was greeted with the same euphoria experienced on that August afternoon against Cammell Laird. New Mills had recorded just their fourth league win of the season.

As shell-shocked Winsford left the field, the home side lingered on their way back to the dressing room to soak up the adulation. Each player was given a guard of honour by the fans with special praise saved for the last two off the field – fan's favourites Ollie Martin and Ryan Hopper.

It's little coincidence Calum doesn't linger for long in the dressing room after a win and the manager soon emerges to meet his public. Sue is jubilant and more than a few fans have hung around to share the celebrations. There's a temporary and unfortunate interruption to proceedings, however, when one of the Winsford representatives also emerges early from the dressing rooms to complain of cold showers. Sue's face drops as she heads in to sort it out but she quickly admits culpability; she's forgot to put the heating on.

'I'm having nothing to do with this one,' says Ray, grasping a rare celebratory pint. 'Nothing to do with me.' As the water heaters kick in and the opposition grumpily stomp out of the changing rooms, I take the opportunity to grab Calum for a more positive post-match chat than our usual chinwags.

'It's been a long time coming to see us play ninety minutes instead of one good half,' he begins. 'Individually today, every player has put a performance in that they can be proud of. We've got eleven games remaining and seven of those are at home. We discussed as a group that we want to make this place somewhere the fans can be proud of and (give them) performances they want to come back and see. I think we did that against Runcorn Linnets and today, getting the three points, will be something they'll be pleased with.'

Our chat is momentarily interrupted as a girl of around ten years old walks past in a goalkeeping shirt.

'See you tomorrow,' she says cheerfully. She plays for Calum's Junior side and, such is her talent, has now become a key player for the majority boys' team. 'We'll win now because you've won!' she adds. Chatting to my dictaphone is hardly Match of the Day but it's a nice moment as, blushing a little, he diverts from 'media duties' for a moment to wish one of his youngest players farewell before regaining his composure and professionalism despite allowing himself a chuckle at the interruption.

'If I had to pick someone out today,' he continues, 'I'd pick out D'Arcy O'Connor. Having to come in and play in a position he hasn't played in for a long time – he plays much further forward, certainly since he's played with me at New Mills – I think he did an excellent job today. The whole defence played really well but I think for him playing out of position he was brilliant.'

He reserved final praise, though, for the fans. There haven't been many three-figure gates down Church Lane of late and even fewer of them ended with the team getting a guard of honour off the pitch.

'Hopefully that'll bring them back for the game against Irlam,' he adds, 'which is a tough game, and also Nelson, which we know is important in terms of leaping over them. If we can get the fans to come down for those games, they are like the twelfth man roaring you on and it lifts the players. Getting clapped off at the end makes the players' day and makes it all worthwhile for them.'

A busy clubhouse makes for a happy end to the afternoon. Sue is busy in her duties again, a little more sheepish than usual, as the defeated Winsford lads head in from the cold showers.

'I can't do everything,' she says as she heads outside following a tender kiss of consolation from Ray. 'I'm trying to get myself sacked. Will you sack me?'

But, as the day ends in high spirits ahead of the flurry of upcoming home games, the weather forecast has other plans.

The New Mills Ultras, including your esteemed author and the inimitable Jon Warrior, watch on at Maine Road FC

23

THE LEAGUE TABLE DOESN'T LIE

In the fortnight that followed New Mills' impressive win over Winsford, Mother Nature got involved. With two winnable looking home games offering Calum a chance to extend his unbeaten home record and inject some momentum into his side's relegation battle, heavy rain across the north-west made Church Lane less of a fortress and more of a reservoir. In the intervening period, the battle at the bottom went crazy.

Firstly, AFC Darwen grab a point away at Abbey Hey. Not an unusual result in its own right, but enough to extend the gap to safety for the Millers back to eleven points. Cammell Laird 1907, the Premier League's basement team, win their first game of the season on a weekend that sees more than half of the division's games called off due to waterlogged pitches. Their victory is all the more stunning in how emphatic it is; AFC Darwen, the side the rest of the bottom three are chasing in the fight against relegation, find themselves on the wrong end of a 4-1 thrashing. It's the first win in any competition for Lairds since an FA Cup Qualifying game in August. Against? AFC Darwen. *That's* what you call a bogey team.

Cammell Laird follow their stunning victory with another. A 2-1 win over Hanley Town, a side comfortably situated in sixth and largely considered the 'best of the rest' when the runaway top five are removed, takes the Birkenhead team onto 14 points with six games to play and staves off relegation for another week. Their Twitter feed is abuzz with talk of the great escape. AFC Darwen remain their target destination, fourth bottom on 30 points. They'll need to win all of their remaining games and hope the Lancashire side don't find another win.

Ah. AFC Darwen seal all three points on a Friday night visit to AFC Liverpool. Cammell Laird 1907 are officially relegated, but it's a devastating blow for New Mills, as the gap to safety now extends to a massive fourteen points.

Given the rollercoaster of results at the bottom, the Millers' trip to Runcorn Town takes on new urgency. It's labelled 'must-win' on Twitter by the official account against a side almost fifty points above them in the table. It's an optimistic target for the afternoon ahead. Unfortunately, so it proves.

A 5-0 defeat does not tell the whole story, especially when a missed penalty just after half-time by Nathan Neequaye at 2-0 is considered, but it feels like it could well be the moment that New Mills truly stare down the barrel of the gun at their likely fate. Freak results have conspired with heavy rain to continue to drain all momentum from their recent threat of a rally, and while some inside the club have already written off their chances, Calum remains tight-lipped. There'll be no waving of the white flag until a voluptuous lady has sung, and there's no karaoke nights advertised in the clubhouse just yet.

Fourteen points is the gap to safety for the midweek fixture against Abbey Hey under the floodlights, then. Originally scheduled for the Wednesday, both sides agree to move the match forward a day with one eye on the forecast. As the fixture list compresses with the final month of the season approaching, it seems like a wise idea despite the near torrential downpour I encounter on the edge of Buxton while travelling across.

The change of date is useful given the Wednesday night would have clashed with my son's U8s game. A friendly against a team who are playing their first ever match offers our boys the chance to go into a game as favourites for once. They look the part as they warm up in their kits while their opponents arrive in an assortment of miniature Premier League replicas and pull on their fluorescent bibs before tentatively knocking the ball around.

Our lads race into a 4-0 half-time lead with the kind of authority they've had inflicted on them so many times before. As the opposition shuffle their side for the second half, a young girl, who was perhaps the smallest player on the pitch in the first half, dons a pair of gloves and takes her place in goal.

It's an increasingly common and refreshing sight at this level of kids' football as more and more girls become interested in the game at the same time as their male peers, although it does present a noticeable dilemma for our lads. Now reaching an age where they're happy to throw in the odd blood and thunder tackle, even our more physical players seem reluctant to do the same against a girl. Whether it's a misguided but ingrained sense of chivalry is unclear, but it only lasted until a long blonde ponytailed striker ran rings around them a few weeks earlier. She was too quick and skilful for them to get close enough to tackle her, never mind actually win the ball.

'Keep doing what you're doing,' I try to tell my son encouragingly. He looks slightly downbeat at not being able to get in amongst the goal rout so far in the first half. 'You're making all the right runs. One will drop for you,' I add.

The second half isn't quite as one-sided as the first. They concede a goal, in fact, giving the newly assembled team, their manager and the assorted parents huddled under umbrellas a moment they'll never forget. Our team's collective of adults smile knowingly as we recall that long-awaited moment in our own debut season.

The main highlight for the Jones family comes late on, when a ball drops to my son who connects with it on the half volley to see the ball flash through a crowd of players and be pushed around the post by the goalkeeper. It's one of several great saves she makes in an eventual 6-1 defeat, which she clearly seems to have taken to heart as she walks past me and my son with her parents after the match.

'Well played, 'keeper,' I say. 'Some great saves in there.'

'Yeah, that was a good one from my shot,' Jacob chips in, charitably.

'Thank you!' says her mum. 'Thank you very much. See, I told you…' she says as they continue through the sludge towards the car park. We've been denied a goal but maybe our words of encouragement have encouraged a child of waning enthusiasm into a slightly longer-term commitment to a sport she clearly has talent in.

Turning back the clock 24 hours, Jon Warrior is back on the mic and has assembled a 'Millers Mega Mix'. He's been chasing requests all week, so my choice of *Stand By Me* by Oasis, a fitting tune, I feel, for the fearless faithful of a small community team on the edges of Greater Manchester, are joined by Jon's own choices: *Waterloo* by ABBA - an amusingly melodramatic choice; *Don't Leave Me This Way* by The Communards; *Just Can't Get Enough* by Depeche Mode, in reference to a popular Millers Ultras chant, and *Mamma Mia* by ABBA. It was fairly ABBA heavy, all told.

The Millers Mega Mix is rounded off just before kick-off by Meghan Trainor's *All About That Bass*. Roy or Derek must have picked that one.

It's a below average gate at Church Lane – maybe word didn't quite reach everyone about the late change of date? – but the car park is busier than usual, by virtue of the astroturf adjacent to the pitch being hired out to bring in a bit of extra revenue. The Millers Mega Mix is reaching its conclusion as I arrive.

'You missed it, Underdog!' says Jon. 'I put three Oasis songs on for you.' I feel guilty. It sounds like Liam and Noel outnumbered Benny and Björn thanks to me and I wasn't even around to hear it.

There's no *S.O.S* (sorry…) on the pitch though. The Millers take the lead through Nathan Neequaye, thanks to a title winning Tony Adams at Highbury-style moment from captain Warren Gaskin with the assist. The centre half marauds upfield and slips a ball through for his striker to finish expertly.

The muscular build of Ollie Martin, donning a short-sleeved goalkeeping jersey for the first time on a mild evening, stands untroubled watching the game pass by as New Mills get an impressive grip on the tie from the off.

'Looks good, that shirt,' observes Jon.

'Better on him, I imagine,' I add.

'I'm not sure I could get into it unless they do it in 6XL!' says Jon before letting out his familiar unrestrained laughter.

On the pitch, Ryan Hopper is dictating the game with his usual industrious energy mixed with a range of passing out wide to the dangerous wingmen. Since giving up the captain's armband following Calum's appointment, he appears to be playing with a newfound freedom that has seen his performances raise. Still just 23, the midfielder is no longer one of the squad's more senior players on age at least - even if he might still be one of the more experienced - and the removal of that pressure appears to be helping his game. As ever, the pacey Sam Marshall offers the primary threat down the right-hand side.

A penalty is awarded to the home side after Marshall is sent *Head Over Heels* (I had to Google that one) and up steps Ryan Hopper, back on spot kick duty. His low and powerful shot to the left of the 'keeper squirms in, giving New Mills a two-goal lead at the break.

'*2-0 Nathan again penalty*' reads the official Twitter feed. Jon, Roy, Derek and I all look at each other. With no James around, nobody knows who the mystery tweeter is or how they've misidentified the penalty taker so dramatically, especially given their markedly different appearance. I even have to recheck a video of the penalty I've posted to Twitter to double check I haven't mistaken the diminutive ginger haired Hopper for the tall and well-built target man.

'That was me,' clarifies Sue at half-time. 'Trying to do too many jobs at once. I didn't even see it.'

The Abbey Hey entourage is bigger than the usual visiting party. Roy finds himself serving hot drinks faster than Starbucks as the portacabin fills up and the sandwich tray is demolished. It's a downbeat and somewhat resigned mood in there but, for once, that's dictated by the visiting team after an abject first half performance rather than the New Mills committee drowning their sorrows.

As the match gets back underway, there's an element of game

management in the opening period of the second half. As chairman Ray bellows at the lads to pick up the energy on the hour mark, they look comfortable for long periods. As a rare shot flies across the box, the rollicking continues. There'd be no excuse for letting a lead that looks this comfortable slip away.

Meanwhile, the New Mills Ultras are away with a new take on an old chant:

'Oh Ryan Hopper, you are the light of my life. Oh Ryan Hopper, I'd let you shag my wife…'

Derek allows himself a rare chuckle.

'What are they singing?' asks Jon. 'I think I'm too refined for these songs. What are they singing?'

'They're singing…' I begin, unsure how to politely explain the gist of the song. 'They're offering Hopper…shall we say 'first dibs' on their as yet unidentified future spouse. Which, given most of them aren't old enough to be married yet, could be a while off.'

Jon laughs.

'That reminds me,' he replies. 'I went on a date with Letitia Dean once.'

It perhaps gives an idea of the entertainment on the pitch that the next few minutes are enriched by Jon's recollections of how he ended up going for dinner with the original Sharon from Eastenders after bumping into her at Piccadilly Station. As New Mills see the game out, he enlightens us with the unlikely tale.

'Shit Ryan Hopper! You're just a shit Ryan Hopper! Shit Ryan Hoooooopper…' sing the Ultras behind the goal during a late corner for Abbey Hey. They elicit a small reaction from the corner taker and cheer again. It potentially inspires their next song.

'We are staying up, say we are staying up! We are staying up, say we are staying up! School in the morning! We've got school in the morning…'

The response to their contribution is just about unanimously positive from all inside Church Lane by the final whistle. As they make their way along the main stand to join the crowd applauding the side off the pitch, they get warm pats on the back from fellow fans plus special attention from the players and manager. Once again, the New Mills Ultras have been the twelfth 'man', even if half of them aren't shaving regularly yet.

As the jubilant atmosphere continues, no one dare discuss the actual possibility of survival. But a win's a win, and it lifts the clubhouse to a place where laughter can be heard and a pint is enjoyed alongside the traditional post-match cauldron of Sue's Special.

'He's in a better mood than Runcorn,' observes Sue as Ray stands beaming with a pint in his hand. 'Someone asked him the other day if he regretted going up through the leagues and he went up like a bottle of pop,' she tells me. 'He's had that question quite a few times and it really gets on his nerves. I could see him going. 'Well what's the bloody point in doing it then?' he said! 'Don't you do it to win the league?'

'But he was right,' she continues. 'If you don't go and try and win the league and get to the next level, what's the point in doing it?' Ray later takes up his side of the story to the unwelcome question of whether reaching for the stars left New Mills in the gutter.

'The guy there forgets I've been around a lot longer than him. I know he's got three players in his side who'll not play for less than £200 (a week). He's got one on the bench who'll be on £300 (a week) and he's not even playing and he's going "our lads are local". Well they're not local, they're paying players, we paid players and that's how we went up to a higher league. That's why we've come down. That's what happens at this level.

'At the time, pubs were busy, we could give a bit more to the manager. They'd demand a bit more and you get carried away with it. I hold my hands up, we did, you get the buzz. We've done it, we've been there and had it and had some good times. And the good times will come back. Now we've got to regroup and see how far we come down. We'll probably be relegated and we're prepared for it. If it happens, it happens.'

Given the resigned tone over their chances of survival, despite another three points this afternoon, Ray remains confident that the division below holds little for them to worry about – not least because of the standard of side that awaits them there.

'We played in the next division below and made it out. We can do it again. I've been to a lot of the grounds and a lot of them shouldn't be at this level. There should be a certain standard, it shouldn't be all singing, all dancing but I put a lot into what we do for hospitality. You go to some grounds and wipe your feet on the way out. We went in one that was a shed with a one bar fire once. There were drainpipes on the inside.'

As I head out of the doors, I briefly catch Ollie's dad.

'Good result that, Craig,' he says. We discuss the recent upturn in results and the brighter atmosphere about the place. I miss the opportunity to tell him my name is Carl. That boat has sailed, docked, set off again and is possibly now hurtling towards an iceberg.

'There was even a bit of music before the game,' he observes. I tell him about the Millers Mega Mix and we briefly discuss the merits of ABBA over Oasis. For the Millers, though, there's no contest. It will need quite a few more results like this in the final weeks to make it happen, but it could yet prove to be a case of *The Winner Takes It All* (you've got this far, please don't put the book down now…)

The New Mills Ultras gather behind the goal to cheer on their heroes

24

A TOUGH CROWD

There's an old joke in stand-up. It goes something like this.

Two comedians are catching up.

'How are things going with you at the moment?' asks the first.

'Pretty good,' replies the second. 'I've been supporting Michael McIntyre's latest tour. 10,000 people at the O2 every night hanging on my every word. The money is fantastic and I've been booked to do some TV work off the back of it.'

'That's brilliant!' says the first, teeth gritted. 'I had no idea!'

'Yeah! It's a far cry from when I died on my arse in the corner of a pub in front of fifteen people in Droylsden,' beams the second.

'Yes, I heard about that…' replies the first. Well, on Thursday 6th April, I had my Droylsden.

I suppose the same could be said for footballers. Outside the all-time greats, there are many more respectable decade long careers remembered for the glaring miss of an empty net, the slippery gloves on an easy cross or perhaps the acrobatic clearance that became a spectacular own goal. Ronnie Rosenthal, Massimo Taibi and Frank Sinclair all had lengthy careers most players would kill for, but upon hearing their names, what do you think of first?

There were several aspects of my own infamous evening which only added to the injustice of it all. The first was that I wasn't alone to privately bury the memory. Instead, a friend had asked if she could join me to see me perform for the first time. Warning light number one.

'Do you ever get nervous before a gig?' she asked over dinner. It's a question I've been asked many times and, in truth, the answer is quite often 'no'. With six years on the circuit under my belt, I've played rooms and crowds of all shapes and sizes. There are plenty more rungs still ahead of me on the ladder of course, but I'm generally pretty comfortable with the ones I've already conquered.

'I only get a bit nervous when someone who has never seen me before comes to see me,' I reply truthfully. 'You're only as good as your last gig and there's always that chance of someone new coming along and going 'oh! *This* is how well the comedy is going, is it?''

It might sound like tempting fate but it's an answer I've given a version of to more than a few first-timer friends before thankfully managing to get out of a gig with a score draw at the very least. Stand-up comedy can be a lonely game sometimes, and the only thing more pleasing than thumping a gig 5-0 is when there are mates there to witness it.

The second aspect of my evening that hadn't gone to plan was our choice of cuisine. Finding an Italian restaurant around half past six, we scoured the menu outside to see a very reasonably priced selection. As we were seated, a realisation hit us that we'd missed a fairly crucial piece of information. We'd inadvertently discovered an Italian tapas restaurant.

'We recommend you order five to six dishes, sir. Water for the table?' enquired one of the impossibly good-looking service staff. We plumped for just the four at an average of £8 per dish. More tap water please, garçon.

As the food arrived, a further error of judgement was revealed. The portions were still massive. Our inexpensive menu that was full of miniature food turned out to be full of ordinarily priced portions of regular-sized food. Had we taken the waiter's advice and ordered six dishes, I'd quite possibly still be sat there now. I'm getting stitch just thinking about it.

Half an hour, half a 9" pizza and a more than considerable sized plate of black ravioli in a crab and prawn sauce later, I looked at my watch. 7.30pm. An hour to go until my gig and I was bloated beyond optimum performance. If you've ever over-inflated your tyres and then felt the handling on a wet dual carriageway, that's sort of what it's like. I think mild indigestion might have clouded the quality of this metaphor.

All of the above was insignificant by comparison to the third issue, however. As I unwrapped a complimentary mint that I wished was a Rennie, I checked my phone for team news. Most terrible of all, beyond the over ordering or the pressure of a friend watching me try to make strangers laugh in person for the first time, was that New Mills were playing at home and I would not be there.

I've missed the occasional game throughout the season, of course, but none as big as this one. Tonight they'd go head-to-head with Nelson in a game that had been rearranged for a second time due to a particularly wet winter. With the Millers still second bottom, they'd first have to leapfrog Nelson to truly begin to see any light at the end of the tunnel. Nelson themselves had seen a recent upsurge that included an incredible 5-1 away victory at AFC Liverpool. Sebastian Julien, an exotically named striker for a Lancashire non-league side, scored all five and would be the man to watch tonight. Or, in my case, not watch.

Arriving in Droylsden, a place I had visited only once for a chat with former Millers manager Garry Brown, I circled the housing estates surrounding the pub several times trying to find a place to park before entering the room where my fate would be sealed. In retrospect, maybe the busy streets were urging me to abandon the gig and make my way to the floodlights half an hour away in the High Peak. Or maybe I just haven't recovered emotionally from the experience yet and am projecting an unlikely personality onto a busy residential area. It's hard to tell.

I didn't know it yet, but as Calum Sykes' men kicked off against the Lancashire side that had put seven past them just a few months earlier, tonight would be my action replay. Droylsden would be my 'Nelson away'.

It started off reasonably well. The crowd were in high spirits, in more ways than one, as the entertainment kicked off in earnest. Two road workers, still wearing the high-vis jackets they'd presumably put on to leave the house early that morning, sat eating a plate of fried beige food and downing pints of Carling on the front row. Occasionally they'd chip in with increasing joviality as the evening wore on, and the opening act worked them into his set, did the business and moved on. Better still, New Mills were leading at the break through captain Warren Gaskin. All going well so far.

The middle section would be where I found myself. With this section normally consisting of just one 20-minute act, the promoter had added a short 10-minute open spot – an unpaid comedian still finding their feet – to open the section. He's a novelty character act who the audience go with for sections of his set but their patience begins to test towards the end of his elongated quarter of an hour. Nelson equalise. It's 1-1 at Church Lane. Sebastian Julien. At a time when my mind should be focusing on my own big match, I'm beginning to tot up what that does to the table and whether Julien is actually French or if he was just conceived by two Mancunian holiday reps at a Brittany Eurocamp in 1987. I suppose I'll never know now.

As I'm introduced to the stage, it's abundantly clear the crowd are losing concentration fast. By the time I've got the microphone out of the stand, the mouthier of the two men wearing hi-vis has his eyes closed as he applauds me to the stage. He's downed so much Carling and scampi in a basket after a 15-hour working day that he's now essentially sleep clapping.

I start with an observation about a building I'd seen on the way in. Always a risk to open with untested material, but I've started the last three gigs like this to good effect – just a little local observation to break the ice - and it's a habit I'm beginning to enjoy. The audience stare back at me, uncertain of the reference. I begin to question if I've remembered it correctly until one lone heckle rises from the back.

'Oh yeah, I know where he means,' it agrees.

It's a factually helpful response, even if it does drain the remaining energy I've now failed to whip up. It's a tough start.

Scalding myself for not opening with a banker at a tricky gig, I fall back onto my failsafe opener, a joke I've told a hundred times and had a great response for at ninety-nine of them. It gets a lukewarm response. A small amount of chatter begins to build. It's heading south fast and I'm too full of quattro formaggio and pasta to be on my toes to do much about it. The taste of fear mixed with heavy garlic fills my mouth.

My second joke wins them back momentarily. Mouthy hi-vis laughs, opens one eye to check I'm still there, then closes it again. It's a momentary reprieve. I'm two minutes into my twenty. It's like a plucky lower league side going 1-0 up at Old Trafford in the first five minutes of an FA Cup tie. Sure, it's good news, but don't get too ahead of yourself.

The next eighteen minutes are a bit of a blur. A woman on the front row, who'd previously been friendly at the bar, tries to egg me on with random outbursts of support that trample punchlines that are destined to fail anyway. I try not to be too venomous in any retort when she sees fit to interrupt a joke to announce to the room that she's taking the bloke she's sat next to home with her tonight. Hi-vis number one laughs along in his sleep at random intervals.

'That was a tough one,' observes my mate with an equal amount of understatement and sympathy as I reach the back of the room.

'I think we'll get off now,' I reply. On observing the tricky nature of the gig when we arrived, I'd joked that, should it not go well, I should meet her back at the car. As she nips off to the ladies while I get paid, there's an uncomfortable moment where I begin to wonder if she thinks I was serious.

There is one vital reprieve for the evening, however. Not unlike the woman on the front row with the fella she's taking home, New Mills score for the 55th time this season. Jake Pollard's 84th minute winner lifts the Millers into 20th and nine points from safety with six to play. It's another splutter and a gasp from the Millers' fightback that boosts an inkling of hope that survival could yet be in reach.

With their midweek commitments complete, momentum maintained and pressure put on the teams above, it would be a football-less Saturday for Calum Sykes' men. With all of the sides around them playing at home, it would be a nervous watch on social media before knowing how results elsewhere would affect his own side's chances.

****

'Things could've just gone a tiny bit better,' is the slightly pained summary of the weekend's eventual results, as Calum watches his side warm up for the tough task of Irlam under the Church Lane floodlights the following Tuesday night. In truth, they could have also gone much, much worse.

By far the best news of the afternoon was AFC Darwen's 3-0 home defeat to Runcorn Linnets. Nelson's late equaliser after losing the lead against basement club Cammell Laird in the battle of the bottom two eased any pressure coming from the rear and meant the Millers could continue to focus solely on closing the gap ahead of them.

Of the other two sides still in catching distance for what now appeared to be the final relegation spot, Barnton's 1-0 victory over Barnoldswick followed by a further point at home to Abbey Hey two days later moved the Cheshire side towards almost certain safety. They had found form at exactly the right moment and their tally of 38 points looked too ambitious a target for any of the current bottom three to reach and would now surely take them out of the Millers' sights.

Squires Gate, on the other hand, had spent the months since the turn of the year dropping off their perch of midtable safety towards the bottom three. Only the ineffective form of New Mills and their rivals had kept them looking safe. Now they were beginning to look nervously over their shoulder, with a crucial point by virtue of an 89th minute equaliser against Congleton Town easing the pressure a little. It's still a big gap to close, but with the Blackpool side due to visit Church Lane on the final weekend of the season, it threw up the faint proposition of what might effectively be a mouth-watering relegation play-off on home soil.

'If we can win tonight then it rolls on perfectly to Saturday against Lairds,' continues Calum. 'Squires Gate is the one though,' he adds with determination. 'People have mentioned other teams but Barnton have picked up points in 2017; Darwen are looking much better now. Squires Gate have struggled – they were 3-0 up recently and drew 3-3 so they're struggling to win games – so I look at them and think "if we're gonna catch anyone, it's gonna be them."

'The way we've looked at the results, if we go into that two points behind them then it's a case of a win and we stay up. We can't get carried away though. We need to keep winning. Five from six is 40 points and that should be enough. If it's not, we've come as close as we can. The last two home games we've turned up, been bouncing and had two good performances. Fingers crossed we get the same tonight.'

James is back with his trusty camera for the game. His recent absence is easily explained; he's been on a good run with his darts team and has had several clashes of interest lately. We catch up on the recent wins he appears to have managed to dodge.

Church Lane is abuzz with youth tonight as the Easter holidays have clearly had an impact. A bumper gate of 125 is boosted significantly by a large group of £1 admissions behind the goal. Far from being the usual Ultras, it appears most of New Mills' adolescent teen population has turned out in support.

'I've got to get a photo of Ollie for his gloves sponsor and Hopper with the opposition's number 8. It's his best mate,' James tells me. As we make our way to the side of the pitch, Ollie fluffs an ill-advised back-pass on the bobbly pitch that puts him in immediate trouble on the edge of his box. A sharp block followed by a lunging save means he gets the action shot he's after in the opening minutes. It's an early scare for the Millers.

Down the far end, the swollen group of Ultras are a little less friendly in their banter than usual. Each Irlam attack is greeted with abuse for the opposition players. Every goal kick is an opportunity to distract the visiting 'keeper by any means necessary. Even the Millers players come in for a bit of light ribbing.

'That is a proper peachy bum,' shouts one as Kiarno Samms makes his way back up the pitch following a foray down the left-hand side. The full back turns around to make eye contact before slapping his generous derriere for effect.

There's a flat feeling to the performance and the atmosphere at Church Lane that is worrying tonight. The vim and vigour of recent displays where New Mills haven't given the opposition a minute is lacking and the result is a fairly pedestrian encounter for long periods of the first half.

Ollie's mis-kick aside, and a speculative long range shot from Irlam that cannons off the crossbar, the first clear cut chance of the game comes minutes before half-time. As the Millers attack down the left, a deflected cross is flashed into the box from Sam Marshall that appears to catch the defence off-guard. As the trajectory of the ball changes, one defender after another is left flat-footed. The ball continues at pace beyond the goalkeeper and towards the back post where Nathan Neequaye appears to have the simplest of finishes, albeit under some pressure.

James and I explode with delight as he connects with the ball and we see the net ripple. It's the reaction of his teammates, however, that first reveals that he's somehow missed the target completely. It's an agonising end to the half.

I try and warm up with a pie, peas and gravy at half-time. It's an anomaly of this entire book that I haven't managed one so far – maybe it's lure of the half-time catering in the portacabin? – but it represents an excellent £2.50 investment. Each mouthful warms me a little more as the biting wind blows in over the peaks and I wrestle a slightly over-crisp pastry with a flimsy plastic fork.

'I used to write a blog about food at football,' James tells me as he observes my struggle. 'It was pretty good. I got a free pie out of it once. I used to crown the winner of the best pie each season. I think it was Chorley one year. That was a good pie,' he remembers fondly.

My polystyrene tray still isn't empty when Irlam take the lead in the 52nd minute. They've looked the better side with the ball on the floor and a sharp break sees them spread the play quickly into space to leave Ollie exposed. A sharp finish across the face of the goal into the far corner is a cruel blow.

Worse still, it appears that the fairweather Ultras have seen enough. At least thirty of them file out of the gate behind the goal before the hour mark. Matt Boland, the opposition's number 8 and childhood friend of Hopper, gets the killer second twelve minutes later. For more than a few seconds, there is absolute silence in Church Lane. It certainly feels that way, at least. I look across at the dugout and see Calum stood forlornly. There's a pause and then the shouts of encouragement emerge from deep within him.

'Come on! Half an hour, keep going!' he shouts. It's a valiant attempt to keep his side motivated but, in truth, they've looked off the pace since kick-off. There's no doubting the opposition are stronger than them. Perhaps there are only so many times you can approach each game like the metaphoric Cup Final before you just run out of steam. It looks like tonight is the night.

For the first time in Calum's reign, which has delivered 10 points out of 12 at home, there are the first small signs of animosity from the stands. Several players come in for a modicum of stick in circumstances where they might have previously received encouragement. It appears the patience of the home crowd has been tested and every loose ball is criticised by a vocal few. It's unlikely the players escape the sentiment in such quiet surrounds this evening, even if it feels unfair. The reality of yet another relegation is beginning to sink in.

'That's it,' says one fan to his wife as they head for the gates at the final whistle. 'We're toast.'

'Relegated,' says another as he passes me. It's hard to argue.

Of the fifteen points from six games that were required, tonight's defeat means the Millers will have to almost double their wins total for the season in their final five games to stand any chance of survival. If it had been slim hope before, it was paper-thin now.

There's a sinking feeling in the clubhouse post-match that hasn't been so heavy since that pivotal December evening that ultimately led to Paul Williams' departure. Glum faces look down into their pints to avoid eye contact as the players make their way in for food. As I sit down with James, Hopper and Ollie join our table rather than that of their teammates. Ryan in particular can't hide his disappointment at the performance.

'It's like we didn't care tonight,' he says, none-too-quietly. 'I don't know if one or two of these know what it means to be relegated. I don't know if they understand how much it hurts.'

We purr at the finishing of Juventus as the TV screen replays their three-goal win over Barcelona in the Champions League quarter finals. It almost looks like a different sport by comparison to tonight's showing, such is the gulf in quality, so I change the subject.

'I wish I could've made it for Nelson, lads, but I was too busy dying on my arse,' I confess before recounting some of the story of my unfortunate recent gig. I can't imagine it makes them feel a great deal better but it's cathartic for me at least. It raises more laughs in its retelling than I probably got at the gig itself.

'Right, we best get going,' says Hopper as he gives James the nod that he's got a lift most of the way home.

'You better not tell him where you're taking me, Hopper,' says James as he picks up his bag.

'Why?' I ask.

Hopper looks confused for a second, then laughs as the penny drops. 'Oh!' he says. 'I live in Droylsden.'

25

NO SUCH THING AS AN EASY THREE POINTS

They say there's nothing more certain in life than death and taxes; and, for large swathes of the 2016/17 season at least, you could also include three points against Cammell Laird 1907 FC on that list. On a run not dissimilar to the Millers' infamous previous campaign, the Birkenhead club had barely broken a double figures points tally until recent weeks – right up until the point that relegation became almost mathematically inevitable.

Since then, Cammell Laird's fresh-faced team of young academy lads have strung together a four-match unbeaten run that has seen them pick up almost as many points in a month as they had in all of their previous games combined. In a season where their loyal band of supporters have endured two separate nine and ten game losing streaks, Lairds had finally become difficult to beat just as demotion to the tenth tier was confirmed.

If you've been paying close attention, you might recall one of those defeats coming at Church Lane on the opening day of the season. As they raced into a two-goal lead against the newly relegated Millers, just a few days after defeating AFC Darwen in the FA Cup's Extra Preliminary round, there was probably just cause for optimism as autumn approached. After relinquishing that two-goal lead to hand New Mills a first league win in over a year, they'd go on to collect just three points from their opening thirteen games. It truly is the hope that kills you.

'They'll probably want revenge for that result,' says media manager James. 'We probably ruined their season.'

As I began the two-hour journey through the Peak District and around the Manchester ring road to Kirklands in Birkenhead,

I was already running late. With Tottenham playing Bournemouth in the Premier League's lunchtime kick-off, I'd planned to set off early and had visions of finding myself a nice pub within walking distance of the ground to watch the game. Perhaps I'd order a half pint of local beer to enjoy with a Ploughman's before making my way through the turnstiles for my second portion of football of the afternoon.

What actually happened was that, after setting off too late for any of the above to be a reality, I instead spent most of the first half swearing at the pathetic signal on my in-car AM radio as I strained my ears at the commentary before eventually pulling up at Chester Services to watch buffering coverage on Sky Go while 'enjoying' a Happy Meal. Another successful morning.

With caravans and heavily loaded boots of estate cars aplenty, I had time to consider how few people other than me were spending their Easter weekend on a two-hundred-mile round trip to watch non-league football. Happy Meal aside, however, I was still pretty content with my decision.

The long, straight road into Birkenhead offered little appeal for an Easter mini-break and Cammell Laird's small ground with rusty blue gates wasn't much of a holiday destination. With the clubhouse situated across the road from the ground, even enjoying an Easter pint involved a pedestrian crossing.

'Here he is!' shouts Jon as I pay my fiver at the turnstile and join him and his support worker. 'You weren't at Padiham, were you? Did you hear about 'the incident?" It's an impressive opening gambit, as he goes on to tell me how his self-styled "Ultras" – youngsters of school age who had become regulars at every match – had parked themselves behind the goal of the opposition goalkeeper and riled him to the point that he'd offered to "bang them out".

With Jon today is a different care worker to his usual companion. A friendly chap, he appears to be happy to be here and is readying himself to enjoy the match as well. It's not bad work if you can get it.

'Don't you think he looks like a chubby Ryan Hopper?'

enquires Jon. 'Did I tell you about my mobility scooter?' he continues, barely stopping for breath or to gauge my startled response. 'I've written it off! Crashed into a bollard.'

Jon's company is never less than entertaining as we laugh for a full ten minutes about his array of recent adventures and on a smorgasbord of topics, the highlight being his enquiry on our culinary choices over the Easter break so far.

'You have to eat fish on Good Friday, don't ya?' he goes on to tell me. His revelation that he also had Filet-o-Fish for lunch and fish fingers for tea is almost enough to induce a hernia, such is the hilarity in his earnest retelling.

'I've got myself a Scouse Pie,' says one of the travelling supporters as he briefly joins our group. Intrigued at the discovery of this brand-new take on the popular pastry-based snack, our attention eagerly turns to what exactly is "Scouse" within the golden crust. 'It appears to just be a meat and potato pie with extra pepper in it,' he reveals, somewhat underwhelmingly.

There's a poignant minute's silence before the game to mark the anniversary of the Hillsborough Disaster. Sue tells me one regular face at Lairds is missing today having lost a son on that fateful day. It remains a solemn annual reminder of the many things more important than football for supporters at stadiums across the country.

As more travelling Millers filter in at kick-off, they're followed by a handful of Lairds fans. With discounted entry for Liverpool, Everton and Tranmere supporters on offer, only the Toffees are at home today. It's not reflected in what remains a very small gate of hardcore fans, though – the ones who've hung on long enough to see the upturn in form, presumably.

'I sense three points,' says Jon confidently as kick off approaches.

'We can't leave with anything less,' I reply. With games running out fast, it's crunch time for the Millers this afternoon.

'You're not gonna play that are ya?' asks one home fan in a thick Scouse accent as he gestures towards Jon's drum.

'Course I am!' replies Jon defiantly, standing as the lone member of what is otherwise usually a raucous travelling band. 'I'm the New Mills Ultra!'

As play gets underway, it's hard to ignore just how uneven the goalmouth of the end New Mills are attacking really is. With a dip outside the box that you could ride a skateboard down, the gradient continues north to the penalty spot before descending back down the other side.

'Are they called 1907 because that's when they were formed?' enquires Jon.

'I imagine so,' I reply. 'It looks like the original team are buried under that 18-yard box.'

Cammell Laird's side is noticeably young. Some of their players, including a tall and lanky defender, don't look much older than schoolboys. After picking up almost as many points in their last four games as they had in the previous thirty, it would appear trusting in youth is paying off for Lairds.

The first test of their resolve comes early when a tough and late challenge from Millers captain Warren Gaskin leaves his young opponent screaming in agony on the turf. It's an uncomfortable wait for the physio as his reaction leaves us fearing genuine serious injury. Thankfully, he's back up with a heavy limp a few minutes later.

It's a rare occurrence in recent years, even on current form, for New Mills to enter a game as favourites. Despite this, they look the part in the opening stages playing with a strong wind at their backs. It would come in handy in the 27th minute when full back Kiarno Samms converts from close range following confusion from a deep corner.

'What's the area code around here? 0151?' enquires Jon out of the blue.

'I'm not sure mate,' I reply. 'Who are you ringing? It's a bit early for a taxi even by our standards.' I'm still not sure why he wanted to know.

As the half-time whistle blows, there's a feeling amongst the travelling support that the Millers' dominance with the wind behind them should have perhaps been rewarded with more than one goal. It's the main talking point over a half time cup of tea as the last of the Scouse Pies are consumed and the nerves set in before the second half.

I take a seat in the stands with Ray and Sue as the game gets back underway. Behind us, the injured Sam Scott sits with his partner and daughter, a very sweet little girl of around four-years-old, who insists on walking her dad around the pitch during play. It's a far cry from his tough tackling persona on the field or Jack the lad personality in the clubhouse.

'We could have done with him today,' says Sue as we watch him walk off. 'Someone who can really impose themselves on the game.'

One notable feature of Lairds' tactics is their ability, in unison, to claim for decisions from the referee. It's something the Millers don't tend to do – some might argue that they don't do enough – even though it proves to quite often be a useful tactic in helping the referee make his mind up at this level.

'FOOOOOUUUUUULLLLLLL!' scream around five of the Lairds team.

'Don't they whinge?' Sue exclaims as another decision goes against the Millers early on in the second half.

'I've never heard so much moaning in my life,' Ray adds.

'Have you noticed when they all shout together, it sounds like seagulls going over?' I enquire.

'Anything in a Scouse accent sounds like interference on the radio,' Ray chips in, beefing up his Mancunian slightly in the process.

Jon Warrior slowly makes his way down the touchline to set up camp behind the goal as we chat. His care worker dutifully carries his drum kit behind, places it down and stands back each time there's a goal kick so Jon can do his best to put off the 'keeper. One man, his drum and his carer, quite literally never missing a beat in an attempt to gain an advantage.

With the wind behind them, Lairds are looking more dangerous. The by-product appears to be New Mills dropping deeper and deeper to defend the long balls forward. It pays off for the home side on the hour mark, with a mix up between Samms and Martin leaving the big 'keeper off his line. He's lobbed with accuracy and Cammell Laird are level. We sink back into our seats. Sue and Ray don't say a word.

It's not an overstatement to say it. New Mills have half an hour to save their season.

The Millers' one main source of attacking intent remains the ever-dangerous Sam Marshall who is clearly the best player on the pitch. His pace, skill and directness receives the attention it deserves with two markers who are largely keeping him out of the game.

'I don't know how he survives some games, I honestly don't,' says Sue. 'They clatter him.' No sooner have the words left her lips, the winger takes a heavy tackle that he struggles to get up from. He's replaced a short time later by defender Mike Jones – not the sort of change any manager would want to make in a must-win match, but one that is forced upon him based on the lack of options on the bench.

'How long before Jonesy gets booked?' asks Ray. 'I'll give him five minutes.'

'WOZZA! Get into 'em! Come on! Get 'em going!' screams Sam Scott from the stands to his captain on the pitch.

The news gets much worse elsewhere in the 85th minute as Darwen take the lead against Hanley Town. With the Millers looking toothless, the table makes extremely bleak reading.

'It doesn't matter with the way we're playing,' says Ray. 'It's us that needs the goal.'

On the breeze, the haunting sound of an ice-cream van's tune being distorted by the echo of the wind makes its way around the cul-de-sacs and housing estates that surround the ground. It feels like the ghost of happier times, making way for another season of disappointment for both of these sides, hurtling towards relegation against a slate grey, overcast sky.

A goal line scramble almost finds a winner for the visitors that even the most ardent New Mills fan would struggle to argue they deserve. It's cleared away as the Darwen Twitter account announces Hanley Town's equaliser in the final minute of the match. As the full-time whistle blows at both games, the sense of disappointment in the Millers camp at the missed opportunity to close the gap feels terminal. Sue and Ray don't hang around for long as they cross the road to the clubhouse car park and begin the long journey home.

'Missed chances again. I think that's it now,' says one of the travelling fans as the last few remaining Millers congregate near the dressing rooms. 'We needed three points today.'

'Just little things pissed me off today,' admits joint Assistant Manager Nick Dowse. 'Some of the attitudes weren't good enough. We had a couple of them turn up at twenty-five to,' he tells Roy.

'Twenty-five to three?' Roy repeats disbelievingly. 'You're joking?'

'Whether it was the attitude subconsciously that we got beat on Tuesday night so that was it, I don't know,' continues Dowsey, pondering aloud if some of his players had absorbed the importance of this afternoon's game. 'Maybe I'm being unfair on the lads. Maybe you get to the point where you can't keep lifting yourself for a Cup Final each time.'

Calum's post-match comment is somewhat shorter as he leaves the dressing room looking fuming with the performance and the result.

'Thanks for travelling, gents,' he says as he makes his way past. 'Safe journey home, everyone.' There'll be plenty of time to contemplate the ramifications for the Millers on that long journey.

'How did they get on?' asks my wife as I fight through the throng in a Birkenhead Asda to reach the bank holiday deals on the wine aisle.

'Drew. Had to win. Could be all over on Monday now,' I reply, downheartedly.

'Never mind,' she replies half-heartedly. 'Did you say the prosecco is two for a tenner?'

26

WE'VE GOT HOPPER/THERE'S ONLY ONE OLLIE MARTIN

Whatever the result, there are two constants of almost every game at Church Lane. The first is Sue's laugh. It can be heard anywhere within the ground and quite possibly from the bell tower that overlooks the Millers' picturesque old ground.

The second is more subtle but remains fairly constant; the last two players off the pitch are almost always Ryan Hopper and Oliver Martin. These two fans' favourites share a kinship that goes beyond the rest of the group. Having stood by the club during a time when offers were likely to have come in for both, their dedication is often recognised and rewarded with an extra burst of applause from the Millers faithful.

Easter weekend would provide the breathing space in a busy season to catch up with Church Lane's golden boys – and also the two players I've struck up the closest bond with – and find out more about how they came to wear the New Mills badge.

'I was quite a late starter,' begins Ollie Martin, 'and I only started playing when I was 12. I had a couple of seasons in Sunday League but then I had a few clubs offer me trials. Bolton was the first one but I broke my knee while I was on trial there so that sort of petered away. Then I went for a trial at Man United, Liverpool then finally Man City who I signed for. From there it sort of became "let's try and make a career out of this" - that's when I got my scholarship at Fleetwood Town.'

Ollie's story is far from unique for a lot of players at this level.

Spotted as a kid with talent, they move around the big clubs trying to find a place. As lower league clubs spot the ones with potential churned out at 18, these vocational offerings as part of contracts are becoming more and more common to attract talented youngsters.

'After a couple of years being involved in the first team and a couple of bench appearances in my first year, they told me,' he says, hesitating as he recalls the memory. 'They told me I wasn't good enough,' he continues, his voice noticeably wincing slightly as the words leave his mouth. 'So I dropped into non-league. I felt that the way I progressed was fine but obviously that's opinions, I am obviously going to say that. But I am happy that I am playing. My first season I wasn't playing but then my second season I came to New Mills.'

There are nods of familiarity throughout from teammate Hopper who takes up the conversation with his road to Church Lane.

'It all started for me when I got scouted for Man United at six. I was very young playing for Medlock Rangers in Droylsden - I know you're gonna shiver at that,' he jokes, my aversion to Droylsden now well-known. 'I was there from six until 14 so I spent a lot of time there. It was fantastic, not only for football development but how they made you as a person. It was manners like shaking everyone's hands when you come into a room and it sets you up in life so I really enjoyed my time, not just for my football development but also as a person.

'When I left United at 14, I went to Blackburn Rovers from fourteen to sixteen. I enjoyed my time there but, similar to Oll, when it comes to the scholarship time they have to make decisions. It's opinions and they go with certain things that you probably disagree with yourself 'cos you think that you are better than some of the people that go through but that's football and it is just opinions at the end of the day.'

The description of metaphorically falling off the end of the conveyor belt is common with young players at this level but from hearing the retelling first-hand, it's clear to see how hard it hits the players. The similarities between their stories points to the wider problem of the sheer number of players churned back out on an industrial scale.

Hopper continues: 'So from there, I was quite fortunate with Accrington Stanley being down the road from Blackburn. The first team manager was coming to the games because he wanted the sort of talent that doesn't make it at Blackburn. In League Two at Accrington they will have a bit of a punt on players. So he must have liked me, I signed a two-year scholarship and in the second year I broke into the first team.

'I made my debut against Oxford coming on in the 70th minute, and for those 20 minutes I did well. The next game after that was Torquay away and that was when I got my first start. I played 75 minutes, loved it, wanted more and after that they offered me a one-year professional contract. Played two or three more games that season coming on and got one more start. I enjoyed it, got the taste of it and then a new manager came in during the pre-season, which was an absolute killer for me. This gaffer had put their trust in me, gave me a lot of opportunities starting at 18 in League Two in front of a crowd like Bristol Rovers away playing to 8000 people, shitting myself but enjoying it. I mean, don't put that in the book!' he laughs. Ooops.

It's a familiar story for footballers up and down the league ladder when a change of management comes about. At the basement of League Two, though, there aren't many places left to go if you're deemed surplus to requirements; fewer still, as a fresh-faced youngster only just breaking into the starting XI.

Ryan continues: 'At 18, it's what dreams are made of. Any young lad growing up wants to play in front of big crowds. The new gaffer started his pre-season and 'cos I'm quite a fit lad, I worked hard over the summer, smashed pre-season and even all the Pros are saying "you are doing well". It comes to the pre-season games and I'm playing well and then on the first game of the season I'm not even in the squad,' he says. Like Ollie, there's a hint of the rawness of the rejection still lingering in his voice as he appears to bring a previously suppressed memory back to the surface.

'You're obviously asking questions if you're not in the squad. I got sent on loan to Droylsden for three months who were in the Conference North at the time. Went there, did well, came back and then the gaffer got me in his office and said "listen, you're not part of my plans, I am bringing experience in" and obviously that was disappointing from my point of view. It was a mutual agreement; I didn't feel like there was anything I could do could change his decision and I actually asked him if there was anything I could do to prove him wrong. He said no.

'So we mutually agreed that they pay my contract off which is when I went to Mossley in the Evo-Stik Division One North. They were at the top of the league at the time, played the rest of the season and got into the play-offs. Unfortunately we got beat in the play-offs by Cammell Laird which, after Saturday as well, is not a very good ground for me!' he laughs.

'Then Mossley played New Mills the following season. I impressed the manager Roy Souley who was the gaffer in charge here at the time. They put seven days in for me and I'm a club legend now, do you know what I mean?' he jokes again in his strong Mancunian tones. '160 league appearances and all that, the big dog! So they'll be getting a stand and a statue at the new ground,' he laughs.

'But Ollie will back me up, it's a fantastic environment, they are nice people. It's a shame what's happened to the club, we won't go into that and it is what it is, but there are lovely people here. The fans are fantastic, they make you feel so welcome like me and Oll, they love us and sing our names.'

As we sit and chat, the professionalism of both players becomes ever more apparent. With both having frequently shown consistent leadership skills on the pitch despite their relatively tender age, there's a level-headedness about their approach that sets them apart from the rest of the group. With that in mind, we discuss the recent trend of non-league players breaking back into the upper echelons of the league ladder – most prominently, Birmingham City's Che Adams who found his way back to the Championship via Ilkeston and, of course, former Stocksbridge Steels striker Jamie Vardy, whose story is destined for Hollywood, metaphorically and literally. What advice do the lads have for young players who might find themselves churned out by the system?

'I think if you were to get released at scholarship level, you can't rest on your laurels with it,' says Ollie with familiar maturity. 'You have to be out there getting your C.V. into clubs. Don't be scared to send them into football league clubs. Just because you don't suit one team, there's 92 clubs out there in the league that you might. But if you keep your temperament right and keep working hard at it, some club will take you whether it's in the league or at non-league which is still a good level. The level we are at is a good level, you know, semi-professional. You never know who could be watching you.

'You only have to have one good game in front of the right people. Vardy got in with Fleetwood and from there to Leicester and now he's smashing it in the Premier League. You've just got to have the right temperament, stay as professional as you can with it. It is hard, combining part-time or full-time work at the same time. But if you back yourself and believe in yourself that you are going to be back there where you think you should be, then why not?'

It's solid advice from the big 'keeper who works in a digital role for the Professional Footballers' Association. Hopper works in a school.

'I think just to add to what Ollie said, that when you start off in Academy you are in that bubble. That's all you can think about - I want to be a footballer. There's a lot more to academies than just the football. They want you to have a good education, they get in good contact with your school and make sure you're doing all the right things. Like I said about Manchester United, they mould you into a person so I think that's the positive to not only the footballing development but as a person as well.

'On the flip side when it comes to make or break scholarship times, there are a lot of good players that don't get the right thing or the right contract and then they just nose dive 'cos they think "that's it now, I can't do it, I can't be a footballer". Like Ollie said, it's do or die, and it takes your attitude, mentality, everything that you've learnt; it makes you as a person and if you want it that much then you carry on playing.'

It's clear Hopper and Ollie both value the experience gained from playing over sitting on the bench at a higher level. With both being almost ever-present barring Ollie's unfortunate hand injury that saw the Millers' worst patch of the season including the 8-2 home defeat to Silsden, it's experience they've picked up in spades over the past two seasons. It's notable to add that Hopper was also unavailable for selection in the 8-2 capitulation. These boys are key players in a struggling side who play with their heart on their sleeves and leave it all out on the pitch. With eleven of them in the team, it would be hard to imagine New Mills finding themselves in the mire they're currently in.

Hopper continues: 'Even if you have to go a step or two down - and we are playing at a good level now - but even if you have to go down and through the highs and the lows to go back up where we wanna go then that's what we've gotta do. It moulds you as a person but it makes you want it a little bit more. Like if you ask Vardy, when he was playing in the Evo-Stik, going to grounds midweek where the showers don't work and he worked hard, he maybe got off work a little bit early and sacrificed. He's done all of his extra outdoor training, I know Ollie does it, I do it. Practise and practise, then you are going to get to where you want to go.

'Now Vardy is where he wanted to be, he was on the shortlist for World Player of the Year! He's just took off but if you ask him, he's probably been through all of what we are going through now and he's out the other side. I think the Academy systems are a very good thing for young people and for young players but on the flip side if you are not mentally strong or you've not got the right family system or the right people around you and it doesn't work out, it's not 'it', that's not the end. You've got to keep going and keep going.

'But if I had I young lad I would encourage them to go but I would say to them "if it doesn't work out, don't give up, if you have to go down there to come back up, then do it", 'cos it's vital experience and will put you in good stead for the rest of your footballing career and life as well.'

Having been two of the only players to have come through the difficulty of the previous season and be retained by each new manager for the current campaign as well, I'm keen to find out what that experience was like for the players, especially given that both appear to take defeats harder than most others in the group. Ollie takes up his experience first.

'It was frustrating at times,' he says. 'But as that was my first season playing open age men's football, I was focusing a bit more on my personal performances. I understood I was going to be busy every game so if I try and work on certain aspects of my game like, for example, my distribution last year. I'm trying to build that up. Personal performances wise I was happy with how I played, albeit when you talk to your mates at work and they ask how you got on, it's hard to say "we got beat 6-0 but I played well" - it's a bit of an iffy one!

'I was quite honoured to get the Player of the Year awards last season. That was almost a reward for all the hard work. I ticked a box for myself.'

'He had a great year last year,' chips in Hopper. 'It would have been very easy for me and Oll to say, "listen Gaz, we can't do this anymore,"' he continues, in reference to previous manager Garry Brown. 'But that's not the sort of people we are. We wanna play football, we wanna develop as footballers. It's a nice club, there are a lot of great people. I think it was a little bit unfair, the tag of 'the worst team in England', there are divisions below.

'We are playing against Spennymoor with a wage budget of three or four grand and it's New Mills with a £300 wage bill. You can't compete with those sorts of teams so I think it was a little bit harsh. Gaz was the gaffer at the time and he's took quite a lot of it of it as well. Ollie will back me up, Gaz is an absolutely fantastic man, a proud man, who did a lot for me and Ollie and he did a lot for this football club. He deserves to be recognised because there are not many managers that would have put up with the rubbish he had to put up with,' he says in reference to the damning media attention the club received.

'He had a very demanding job as well and he did fantastic. If it wasn't for him and it wasn't for the club and for your mates, it would be very easy to jack it in.'

Ryan Hopper is bolt upright in his seat now, speaking with even more passion than before. His maturity and sensitivity to just how bad the situation was is obvious; as an old head on young shoulders, it's clear to see the qualities that made him Garry's choice as club captain.

He continues: 'In terms of a footballer's development, and me and Oll often speak about this, you've got to have those bad times to appreciate the good ones. I know it's been another difficult year, but there is nothing better than that winning feeling in a football match. I know we didn't really have a lot of it last year…' he says.

'No. We didn't,' interrupts Ollie dryly. As we chuckle, there's no stopping Hopper who is on a roll.

'But you have got to take the positives out of it. When we got a draw at home against Witton, everyone was dead happy,' he continues, in reference to the first of New Mills' three individual points in the league that made up their tally for the whole of last season. 'It was a very difficult time and I think the football club and Ray and Sue, they dealt with it fantastically well, and we've come through that now. I think there was one team in the Southern league that had a worse record than us so it was all a bit silly but, like I said, Gaz was a rock and was making the point of it in the dressing room saying, "don't listen to that, it's a load of rubbish,"' he continues as Ollie nods along.

'He's a great man and he deserves a lot and if you can write that in your book…' he laughs. The respect both have for their former manager couldn't be clearer.

I remind the lads that the point of writing the book was to tell the authentic account behind the headlines of people like Garry. Having spent so much time in and around non-league, it was my goal to try and write the real story behind what had happened to the club, in no small part out of respect for the volunteers who ensured it could continue to run. Unsurprisingly given their dedication to the cause, both are conscious of how fortunate they are to have such a dedicated team off the field as well as on it.

'Volunteers like Roy and Derek. I know Derek can be a bit annoying,' Hopper laughs, in reference to Derek's 'glass half empty' outlook. 'But it's the people like Sue and Ray, the groundsman Les who we know is poorly at the moment and the lads are wondering how he is. It's a community football club, we need to do a little bit more with that at New Mills. We need to get the Juniors in, even if it's as mascot or ball boy, just get 'em in. That's what non-league football is about, they do it for nothing and we are privileged to get paid a little bit for playing football.

'The groundsmen have been on today from 7 o'clock in the morning cutting it, rolling it...I was in bed at 7! There are hundreds around non-league that don't get recognised and that deserve to get recognised.'

As we move on to the predicament the side find themselves in, both lads remain cautiously optimistic of their chances of escaping the drop. Ollie goes first.

'We obviously do believe we can do it. As long as it's mathematically possible then you have to feel positive about it. It helps a lot that we only have one away game left and the rest are at home. I believe we can win all the games that we have left. We do all we can do and then, touch wood, luck falls our way and the likes of Squires Gate don't get the results they need. With us being one of them for Squires Gate on the last game of the season, that's a huge game. If it comes to it then we will have to do the business then.'

Hopper adds: 'There are times this season where we have played really well and not got anything out of it. The Bootle game *(where New Mills saw a 2-1 lead overturned to a 3-2 defeat in injury time)* away at the Northwich game *(where a narrow defeat was compounded by a nailed on late penalty claim being turned down*) at the start of the season. All little things like that and a bit more luck, it might be different. But that's football, that's why we love it.'

'When you are down there, the luck is not there,' adds Ollie. Once again, the two young players are talking like hardened old pros.

Never far from a joke to lighten the mood, Hopper recounts a missed penalty against Champions elect Atherton Collieries that was missed.

'We have a pen to draw the match,' he says, 'and the main man's not on to put it away!' he laughs, referring to himself, and also in turn to Nathan Neequaye's unfortunate miss on his debut. 'That's why the gaffer has put me back on them and now look at it!'

Finally, I ask the lads to use their crystal balls – given the time they've both spent at some of the country's very best Academies, which players should we be looking out for in the future?

'Tough one,' begins Ollie as he gives it some thought. 'In my time at City I played with the likes of Brandon Barker who's currently on loan in Holland as well as Ashley Smith-Brown. Both constant England players at the lower age groups and around the Man City first team where they can. Hopefully they'll ply their trade in Holland, get some first team experience and then when their loan finishes next season they will be fine in the Prem. They are both good enough to do it.

'They just need a chance, don't they? And it would be difficult at City because of the fortune they've got, are they as good at pushing them through?' queries Hopper. 'For me, though, and Ollie might laugh at this, but my mate Joe Rothwell,' he says as Ollie fakes a yawn. 'Yeah, look at him!' Hopper continues. It's clearly a name he's dropped before and shouldn't be confused with his namesake who recently joined the Millers from Bury.

'He's my best mate, I played with him at Medlock since I was six, he went to United and progressed all the way through the 18s, the 21s and on the bench for the first team and he signed for Oxford at the start of this season,' he gushes about the midfielder who has represented at England at every level up to U20s.

'This season he's played at Wembley and got the Man of the Match at Wembley at the Checkatrade Trophy Final. He's a very close mate of mine and I wish him the best of luck. Hopefully he gets a move as he's had a taste of it and he's doing really well at the moment. Also when I was at Accrington, Connor Mahoney, he went to Blackburn Rovers and he's a fan favourite at the moment, he's only a young lad and they want him to get a new contract.'

To an outsider of the game, it might seem insensitive to ask the lads to name their successful mates. As both demonstrate such clear ambition, there could be room for a little jealousy as they speak of success on a level that, to date, has eluded them in their early careers. It's not the case though, as Hopper continues.

'These are lovely lads and you wish them the best of luck. If I see Connor, he will always come over. Some people think that when they get to a certain stage they forget about people but they are grounded. They even come watch our games, they are interested and they just love football. Whether you're playing at Wembley, they are still not too big time to come to New Mills!'

There's no hint of jealousy – just genuine admiration for friends achieving boyhood dreams. Hopper, however, does have one final observation about the lifestyle of his long-time pal before they head off: 'I just wish I was on the money he is!'

27

DON'T STOP BELIEVIN'

Easter Monday would provide the opportunity for New Mills to inject much-needed life back into their league campaign. Following a hard-fought but ultimately disappointing point on the Wirral, only a win would do against midtable Barnoldswick Town to keep their hopes of resurrection from the relegation zone alive. There's a religious metaphor in there somewhere.

With just one week and three games to go until the season's end after the conclusion of this afternoon's match, the Millers were already just about playing for snookers. But on arriving at an eerily quiet Church Lane some three hours before kick-off, there was good early news to report. Relegation rivals AFC Darwen, kicking off early, were already 2-0 down.

'Hello!' says Sue with genuine surprise and delight as I walk through the clubhouse entrance. 'I wasn't expecting you this early. I'm just about to make up the butties.'

There's plenty to do in preparation for matchday as Sue surrounds herself with ham, bread cobs and a massive tub of margarine after she's finished unlocking various gates around the ground. With Ray on catering duties for the players today, Sue is making cobs to sell from the hut. It leads to a surprising revelation – this will be Ray and Sue's final game of the season due to an upcoming return to the Canary Isles.

'When we booked it, it was the beginning of the season,' says Ray. 'I retired a couple of years ago and we usually go around my birthday. We hadn't actually got a game the week we were away

– next week, that is - apart from the last game of the season which, when we booked it, we didn't think would matter too much! Had we won against Cammell Laird, we might have had half a chance of staying up,' he adds, solemnly.

'It means beating Irlam now. We obviously have to win today as well. And then, if Squires Gate haven't picked anything up, it's on the cards. That two points dropped was so vital though. It could get to the stage where we need four points on the final day when we might have only needed three. I'm resigned to it though, even if they do keep giving us a glimmer of hope. They build you up and kick you down!'

'With the way Irlam played here, I thought they were one of the best sides we've seen,' Sue adds. 'We went to watch them with Calum as well and they look like a proper man's team. We have to win them all now but it'll be tough. There are so many games we could have got more from. But that's football, isn't it? There's only so many of those you can keep going back to.'

With the butties buttered and the gates open, it's also my final opportunity to sit down with the Chairman before the end of the season and get his thoughts on another difficult campaign. He begins by reflecting on where the Millers were a year ago and the commitment of Garry Brown, a man he was clearly fond of, as their relegation from the Evo-Stik was confirmed.

'Garry kept us afloat, kept putting a team out,' Ray begins. 'He was nearly in tears sometimes at the results but he kept us going until the end of the season. I was inundated a little bit when we were relegated, people saying "oh, you're gonna sack him because he's taken you down." But he'd earned the right to start this season.

'He started this season, we didn't do too bad, and then it went downhill a little bit. He decided he couldn't do it anymore. I went to Paul and asked him what his take was on it and he said he'd take the job. We stuck by him, he's a great lad, but we just weren't getting anywhere.

'We got to the point in the season where I'd decided that, whatever happened that afternoon, we had to change the manager and bring in new ideas. We lost to Darwen when we should have beat them. Calum spoke with us and he did what he had to do and resigned. He took them (Stockport Town) up to Holker when he didn't have to, did it right. He got a lot of stick for it but that's how it all came about.

'In fairness, I blame myself because we should have done it probably a month sooner. I was still confident that Paul could have kept us up. If I'd have been more ruthless, I might have done it sooner and he'd (Calum) have got more games. Probably too loyal. I still felt there was a lot of games to go to get us out of it but that's all hindsight.'

Hearing Ray reflect like this is a reminder that it's a difficult balance to find, whatever level you're at. In the upper echelons of the game, where great sums of money balance on every result and managers are recruited on seven-figure contracts, a ruthless streak is a pre-requisite. At New Mills, though, where passionate and dedicated football men like Garry and Paul pour their heart and soul into every Saturday afternoon, terminating the contracts linked to their voluntary contributions is understandably more difficult, even if it's sometimes just as necessary.

'Paul and Garry were getting their expenses. Garry resigned, Paul we let go reluctantly,' Ray continues. 'He was such a gentleman. I never had a cross word with him. I had a few with Garry! The best coach we ever had was Ally (Pickering) though. He could change a game with the click of a finger. He had the money of course but he was great tactically.'

As Ray looks out of the window across the Church Lane pitch and ponders the future as positively as he can, there's a nagging feeling that the prospect of returning to the tenth tier feels like a kick in the teeth for a club that flew a little too close to the sun without applying their factor 50. What's undeniable, though, is how far the club has progressed off the field during that time.

'I'm not getting any younger,' Ray continues, 'but I want to leave us in a better position than I found it. There are a lot of predators about at this level who'd come in and take it over without caring about what it means. When I got here, it was a scrapyard and a ploughed field. There was nothing here.

'As you've seen with the plans to get the new ground going, it's been a hard slog. We're trying to get football coaching going over the summer and we're having a beer festival. We're still looking to relocate as well; we have to. It looks like the one with the Council has gone but there are other places.'

For a man who has fulfilled almost every role going from player, manager, committee member and now a decade as chairman, Ray has enough experience to be reflective on the future.

'We have looked a better side under Calum. It was a bit chaotic when he took over and some of the players that he let go were probably a little bit better than the ones we brought in. But there's a lot of heart in the lads here now and the club's heart is beating a little better.

'I'd like to think we can get a side back together that can do well and is sustainable. Time has gone quick. We've had some fantastic times in here. But we've also had some sad times. It looks like we're going back to where we started, and if it happens then it happens. It's not that bad a thing and we'll survive it. We'll come back stronger.'

A bumper crowd of 108 begin to pile through the turnstiles from 2pm as the clubhouse starts to look busy. While the Chairman might fear the worst, it seems like word has reached the Millers faithful that their support is needed this afternoon. On an unseasonably pleasant day for a Bank Holiday, there's a buzz about Church Lane watching the players warming up that suggests there could be something in the air. With Darwen also falling to a 5-1 defeat in the afternoon's early kick off, there's further reason for optimism.

'Warren Gaskin plays for a Sunday League team so this is three games in three days for him,' begins Calum Sykes as we greet each other and watch over his side warming up on the Church Lane pitch. 'He's sore and aching. We know what the situation is today. Anything but a win and we're done. It's like I've been telling the lads though, it's not over yet. I'll show you,' he says, leading me to the dressing room. The pungent smell of sweat and muscle rub resonates as we walk through the door.

'I don't see those points totals going much higher,' says Calum as he points to the whiteboard in the dressing room where a mini league table is on display, showing the gap to safety and laying bare the size of the task at hand for the Millers. 'I still see Squires Gate as being the ones to catch. I've said to the boys that we don't want to see those points totals not move and we haven't closed the gap. It will have been over some of their heads but I need them to care. I was so disappointed on Saturday with the display. There was just no passion, no drive and no belief. As soon as that goal went in, we didn't kick on.'

As we chat, Jon Warrior's playlist is bleeding through the dressing room walls from the P.A system outside. Calum is calm and too focused on the job in hand to notice a fitting backing track of S Club 7's *Reach For The Stars*.

'It's difficult for us today because there's no Sam Marshall, no Nathan. We've changed the shape,' he says, gesturing towards the formations on the board. 'It's a strong team on paper, they're not gonna be getting past Jonesy at the back. We're strong at full back. It just puts that pressure on the front to create. When you play 4-4-2, you're easier to break through, so you've got to make your chances count. We could have got away with dropping points somewhere but we've done that at Lairds when we could have done with saving that for Padiham or Irlam. But we've got to go for it, haven't we?

'I can't sugarcoat it today. I can't say "don't worry about it, lads" - fucking do worry about it! When you look at the eighteen games we've had, the first six or seven games are almost what I'd class as the pre-season bit of it. Then we found some form. If you look at it now, if we'd come in six games earlier, it could have looked very different.'

We head back outside as S Club 7 finishes and Gina G's *Ooh Ah Just A Little Bit* continues Jon's pop anthem theme.

'That's my plan for the team talk,' he says as we head back outside and he watches the lads train. 'Get 'em fired up. Because they don't look fired up right now,' he adds, shaking his head at the warm-up. 'Squires Gate aren't looking like they're picking up any more points so win our next three and it's on. But it's just maths. After Saturday, it just wasn't good enough and I apologised to Ray and Sue. As long as we turn up today, I'll be happy.'

With that, he heads off for final preparations. As the teams head out, ABBA's *Mamma Mia* plays. It's the second time *The Winner Takes It All* would have been a more appropriate choice, but I'm not one to criticise the sterling work of the excellent Jon Warrior who announces the teams with aplomb as is now customary.

From minute one, there's an energy and verve about the Millers that suggests they're up for this. Given Calum was less than convinced about their warm-up, it certainly looks like he's found the words to motivate them before kick-off.

'This is the best I've seen them,' says James, who by his own admission, has been a slightly less frequent visitor to Church Lane in recent weeks, in part due to his university studies but also as a blossoming darts player which has seen him take the crown of Lancashire U21 player of the year. Before too long, the Millers have a lead to back up his praise.

In the 18th minute, a scuffed shot from Callum Scott causes problems in the Barnoldswick box. The ball falls to Dennis Sherriff, deputising for Nathan Neequaye today, who scuffs it again. This time, it somehow gently rolls into the net. The hundred-plus crowd in Church Lane go crazy.

'That's possibly the worst goal I've ever seen,' laughs James. 'It didn't even go in the direction he kicked it!'

'Ohhhhhhhhhhhhhhh....WAAAAAAAAAAY!' shout the New Mills Ultras each time the goalkeeper takes his goal kicks.

'I'm not sure they should be abusing him,' observes James as the wiry teenage frames of the Millers tormentors stand just a few yards away behind his goal. 'He's got a neck tattoo.'

The next seventy or so minutes are some of the tensest Church Lane has witnessed in a while. Although New Mills look comfortable, and even in control for large parts of the game, they are unable to find a killer second to put the result out of reach. That is until the 89th minute, when substitute Callum Collinson, filling in at full back, intercepts a cross-field pass between defender and goalkeeper to direct the ball into the net and send the crowd into raptures.

As Church Lane calms down, New Mills win the ball back again and pile into the opposition once more. When a searching ball forward causes confusion, a poor attempted pass-back from a Barnoldswick defender leaves his neck tattooed goalkeeper charging out of his box to clear with a diving header. As he lands on the turf, finding himself on the edge of the 18-yard box, he begins to pick himself up off the floor to charge back towards his unguarded goal. It would prove to be the perfect vantage point to see a moment of footballing magic that his rush of blood to the head had played a key part in.

His half-clearance falls to the feet of 17-year-old Joe Rothwell. One of the first loan signings of promising young players gaining first team experience as part of New Mills' partnership with Bury FC, his family have become regular faces in recent weeks with a particularly adorable Bassett Hound the star attraction. Today, however, it will be his mum and little sister who'll witness a moment the youngster will never forget.

Brought on for his competitive debut as fresh legs for the final quarter of an hour or so, he composes himself before lobbing the bouncing ball over the head of the retreating goalie and into the empty net. It's a wonderful cherry on top of a very satisfying cake as the entire New Mills bench explodes onto the pitch to celebrate and the teenager is mobbed by every single one of his teammates.

'I've got to call his dad,' shrieks Sue in floods of tears as she comes past us. 'I can't believe he's done that when his dad isn't here!' It's truly a wonderful moment that the young man is unlikely to ever forget and rounds off a convincing win.

Rothwell is still being congratulated at the final whistle as Barnoldswick Town trudge off the field and the Millers are given an increasingly common guard of honour by their fans.

'Coming off last again, Ryan?' shouts Sue as Hopper slowly makes his way up the steps and acknowledges the dozens of fans who've stayed to cheer the lads off the field.

'Me dad's here! I was just saying hello!' laughs Hopper.

'Always milking it,' teases Sue.

'What can I say?' retorts the former Millers captain. 'Fan's favourite, aren't I?'

As the lads come out of the dressing room jubilant, I manage to grab two of Church Lane's favourite sons again for a quick summary of the match.

'It was very pleasing today, from a personal point of view and a team one,' begins Hopper. 'It's been a very difficult season. The lads worked their socks off, worked really hard. The gaffer was pleased, the lads were pleased and it was a great feeling at the end but we just need to carry it on now for that final three games. Nothing is done yet, we want to stay in this division but that today is a stepping stone for where we wanna go.'

Ollie Martin nods his head in agreement. 'Yeah definitely agree with Hopper. We've got half a chance but at least it is a chance. You've gotta win the games to stay in the league but I think a 3-0 and a really dominant performance has been coming for ages and it shows again at home that we've been solid under Cal.'

Hopper continues: 'We've changed this into a really difficult place to come as well. At the start of the season, teams were coming here and rolling us over weren't they? At the back end of the season since Cal's come in we've made it a very difficult place to come.'

'Well, we've had a few more leaders come in,' suggests Ollie Martin.

'Yeah, definitely. We've got that winning mentality,' continues Hopper. 'And once we got that first win we just wanted to carry it on. There has been a big buzz around the place with the young lads (The Amber Army or New Mills Ultras) coming in and making a load of racket singing 'We've Got Hopper' and 'One Ollie Martin',' he continues, before they catch each other's eye and both laugh out of slight embarrassment at being fan's favourites.

'They are making it an atmosphere and, don't get me wrong, I know they are only young lads, but it's nice creating an atmosphere. When we played Abbey Hey it made the game and, to be honest, it helped a few lads through! We even said in the changing room at the end – they helped us through then, 'cos that was a difficult game, we were under a lot of pressure in the second half and we rode it out.'

'It motivates you, doesn't it?' agrees Ollie Martin.

Hopper nods. 'It makes it quite an interesting last few games I think, especially the mentality after today. The gaffer had the table up on the board before the game showing the points and the fixtures that they've got left and we've got left. He's instilling that mentality to show us that it's not over yet. You do what you need to do and maybe the people around you don't with a little bit of luck.

'The one thing that I'm a little disappointed in is that I wanted it to be in our hands, and if we win ours then we are up rather than relying on other people. But it is what it is, the results have happened how they've happened and you can't give up. Me and him and the lads will never give up, we will wear the shirt with pride and we will work hard and hopefully get the results. We are more than good enough. We've shown today by winning 3-0 against them - they are safe, they are comfortable, they are no mugs. They played like that at the start of the season and beat us.'

With that, the pair head off for the clubhouse to sample the unfamiliar taste of Ray's cooking. Meanwhile, Calum is in predictably high spirits on leaving the dressing room, greeting Sue and a small gathering of familiar Church Lane faces who've hung around to celebrate.

'Lobbers!' he says, greeting the generally quiet and mild-mannered photographer James. 'You've finally got pictures of a game I've won! I was beginning to think you were an unlucky charm. You've got pictures of games I've drawn and lost but we've finally got a win!

'Is that a smile I see there, Derek?' continues Calum, working the crowd as his usually sullen faced Fixture Secretary appears from the portacabin following the completion of his post-match duties. 'I'm sure it is! Maybe it's just a bit of wind?'

'Cammell Laird have won at Irlam!' announces Crossy as he leaves the dressing room beaming.

'You're joking?' replies Calum, with a glint in his eye. 'How've they done that?' Suddenly, Saturday's point doesn't look quite so bad – but, more significantly, it makes the upcoming must-win visit to North Manchester a little less imposing.

'That's the biggest shift I've ever seen them put in,' observes James. 'They never stopped running.'

'Might it change your mind then? Are you gonna stay?' asks Jon Warrior, in reference to James' revelation that this will be his final season volunteering. James smiles and shakes his head. He's resolute in his decision to commit more fully to university life next year, regardless of which division New Mills find themselves in.

One of the first out of the clubhouse is Warren Gaskin. Barely mobile after 270 minutes of football in the space of 72 hours, he appears with dressing room joker Sam Scott. Having put in another heroic shift at the back, Gaskin now barely looks capable of reaching the car park.

'You off now, Woz?' shouts Sam for everyone to hear as the Millers captain walks past Sue. 'You said you're not sticking around for any more of that watered-down curry?' Gaskin adds a hop, step and a jump into his geriatric amble as Sue turns to swing for him.

'Ray made it!' shouts Sue in her defence. 'See? He can still move, look!' laughs Sam.

The post-match cuisine might not be up to its usual standard. But as Ray and Sue prepare to fly out of the country, there's yet another fresh glimmer of hope that the Millers might still be a Premier League side on their return.

Winless: My Year with Football's Ultimate Underdogs

A first career goal for 17-year-old Joe Rothwell

The Millers faithful applaud their side off the Church Lane pitch. An all-too-rare occurrence in recent years.

LEAGUE TABLE

16	Congleton Town	40	-22	41
17	Barnton	39	-45	41
18	AFC Darwen	39	-51	38
19	Squires Gate	40	-27	36
20	New Mills	39	-37	29
21	Nelson *	39	-26	25
22	Cammell Laird (R)	40	-92	20

28

UNDERDOG DAY AFTERNOON

One logistical nightmare of combining a blossoming (well…) stand-up career with following the travails of a northern non-league team is the tendency for fixture clashes at opposite ends of the country each weekend.

As the final week of the North West Counties season loomed, New Mills had three games to close a six-point gap and preserve their Premier League status against the odds. With a potential relegation 'play-off' at Church Lane against Squires Gate on the final day looking like their best mathematical hope, there was just the small task of beating top-half mainstays Irlam and Padiham first.

While my own schedule mercifully didn't include any visits to Droylsden, I'd be spending the weekend on the East Coast, in part to make the most out of the Easter half-term holidays and also to take in gigs at Wetherby and Hornsea, a mere 225-mile round trip away from Irlam. It would actually have been much more convenient if I had been gigging in Droylsden, but the numbers didn't work. On what might yet prove to be a day of destiny in the history of New Mills AFC, I'd be spending another anxious afternoon on Twitter.

'Are you sure you don't just want to go and then maybe leave before the final whistle? You'll still get to your gig,' my wife enquired, observing my internal turmoil and attempting to be helpful as I distractedly walked down Filey beach on a warm and blustery Saturday afternoon. I pictured myself, tiptoeing out of the turnstiles in the final twenty minutes as survival hung in the balance. It wasn't as if I could catch the final moments via talkSPORT on the way home.

'I can't do that,' I replied as gently as I could, picturing just how late I'd be reaching the stage for hosting duties in Wetherby if New Mills extended hope to pull off the impossible and I'm at the bottom of a pile-on pitch invasion.

Adding to the afternoon's anxieties would be Tottenham's FA Cup semi-final against Chelsea as they attempted to reach English football's showpiece event for the first time since my sixth birthday. Even that, though, was beginning to feel less significant than the task at hand for the Millers. A win today in what the form table suggested was by far the most difficult of their three remaining fixtures would set up two very winnable ones at home in midweek. And with Squires Gate sinking fast and facing in-form Runcorn Linnets in their penultimate game this afternoon, it made them look ever more likely to become the sitting ducks for the Millers to leapfrog at the death and climb out of the relegation zone on the final day of the season for the first time since Bonfire Night.

As the minutes towards kick-off passed slowly, Calum's interview with High Peak Radio was one way to calm my nerves before an afternoon watching football via social media. His first answer was in response to the difference in form since his arrival.

'I don't think we've done too much differently,' he begins. 'I think the home form and the home support has been excellent. We've played six games at home since we came in, four wins. Of the three games left, two of those are at home as well. We've got to be positive. We've played Irlam and Padiham recently so we know the threats that they pose. We also know the weaknesses that they have as a team. If we can take the season to the final game against Squires Gate and be in with a fighting chance then we certainly feel confident we can do that.

'I think what people have seen, particularly at the home games, is that this team has got a lot of fight about them. If we felt we were down and it was done, as some people have suggested, you certainly wouldn't see the passion and the performance we put in on Monday to get the three points. That's a very good Barnoldswick side. So we'll stay confident, we'll stay optimistic and we'll stay as believers until it can no longer mathematically be done.

'I think we had to get the players to have more belief and more confidence that they could get results. If every time you go out there and play, you lose, then as soon as you start a game you can see it happening again. I think that's where the team probably was (when we arrived) in that they'd lost a lot of fixtures and the biggest thing for us was to turn that around. If you concede a goal, don't worry, it's part and parcel of the game and it's how you respond to conceding goals that makes you as a team.'

It's a familiar message of positivity and calmness from the gaffer and one that will be radiating through the dressing room as kick-off approaches. As I stare at the league table for the 23rd time and try and work out the machinations that would need to fall into place to keep the Millers up, it seems simple enough. Abacus at the ready? Then I'll begin.

With a six-point gap, a game in hand and considerably inferior goal difference, New Mills would need at least four points from today and midweek combined, and for Squires Gate to lose their final home game against Runcorn Linnets this afternoon to effectively set up a relegation play-off between the two sides on the final day, where it would be win or bust for the Millers.

Should Squires Gate pick up an unlikely point in their penultimate match, only six points - or four points and a very heavy home win on the final day to force a dramatic goal difference swing - would keep the Millers up at the expense of Squires Gate. If Darwen were to lose their three remaining fixtures, they too would still be within the reach of the Millers – but this would require New Mills to win all three matches in the week ahead.

A defeat for the Millers would automatically secure AFC Darwen's place in the division for another season and would leave Calum's men needing a cricket score in their two remaining fixtures. Equally, a win for Squires Gate and/or Darwen would also just about seal their fate regardless of what New Mills did at Irlam. You've probably got the general picture: it was a must-win match for the Millers.

'Is that going to be buzzing all afternoon?' asks my wife of my alert-ridden iPhone, as she attempts to relax by diving into a paperback about midwives in the 1950s that I'm almost certain she's brought on every holiday since Rhodes 2007 and still only appears to be 43 pages into. As the tweets gather pace at kick-off, I gaze out of our apartment window onto the Filey coastline and cross my fingers.

The first notable notification of the afternoon is the worst possible one. After hours of building myself up, culminating in a nervous walk of the dog down the promenade to convince myself that the Irlam lads will already have one eye on their metaphorical summer holidays, it happens after twelve minutes.

Irlam 1 – 0 New Mills.

I sink back into the chaise longue I've uncomfortably perched on due to its convenient location next to the power socket. I peer down at a man below our first-floor window as he gathers up the faecal deposits of his Alsatian on the lawn down below. I'm miserable.

Comparatively better news follows in the 27th minute as Squires Gate predictably fall behind at home to Runcorn Linnets. It's the kind of glimmer of hope New Mills will need at the break but it will count for nothing unless they can haul themselves back into their own game. AFC Darwen counter this positive news by taking fate into their own hands in the 40th minute through an unlikely lead at home to 1874 Northwich. Squires Gate equalise seconds later. As the half-time whistle blows, the Millers look very much relegated.

'Do you want a cup of tea?' my wife asks, putting her bookmark back in at around page 48.

'I need something stronger,' is my response. 'But go on then.'

Text messages from the Millers fans who made the trip suggest they've done everything but find the back of the net as news of the latest scores begin to filter around. I sip my tea and begin to wish I were there, however pointless or fruitless the journey might have been. There's a sort of survivor's guilt beginning to surface in me as the second half gets underway.

My intense staring at the screen in an attempt to will a goal from somewhere does little other than to see faint hope arrive when Northwich equalise against AFC Darwen on the hour mark. With each ping of my phone, however inane the update might be and from whichever tiny ground dotted around the north of England it comes from, there remains hope of a Millers leveller that will at least keep things mathematically possible for the time being. Until the 75th minute, at least, where things change very quickly.

First, there's a goal for 1874 Northwich that puts them into the lead for the first time at Darwen. It's of tiny consolation but is meaningless without a complete turnaround at Irlam. The second update is a complete surprise and an all the more fatal one for the Millers.

Squires Gate 2 – 1 Runcorn Linnets.

'That's it,' I announce dejectedly to no-one in particular. 'Squires Gate are winning. It's over.'

Another ping and 1874 extend their lead in the 77th minute. I think back to the freezing afternoon in Lancashire on Bonfire Night as the Millers failed to capitalise on their chances and fell into the bottom three for the first time after such a promising start to their league campaign. The small band of hardy fans who had drank beer in a sub-zero crosswind on the raised balcony over the pitch in Darwen that afternoon would probably be in party mood now, despite watching their side lose, as they scanned the latest scores on the North West Counties page.

In the 79th minute, the pendulum swings again, back towards New Mills this time, as parity and sanity is restored in front of the 175 fans at Squires Gate. With Runcorn Linnets now left with only local pride to chase in their battle with Runcorn Town to finish as the division's runners up, their equaliser again throws a crumb of hope out to the Millers – but not unless they can find an equaliser at the very least.

As each minute ticks by, even the surprise team news from Wembley that Kyle Walker has been benched doesn't really register. I'm completely focused on the battle at the bottom of the North West Counties Premier League.

As the 85th minute ticks past, the remaining hope dies. I've been there with Tottenham so many times but this felt different somehow. That eternal optimism becomes gallows humour when Squires Gate find a winner in the 89th minute to taste victory for the first time since a January 7th triumph against basement club Cammell Laird. It condemns Linnets to only their sixth defeat of the season but, more pressingly for the Millers, means that even an injury time equaliser would no longer be enough. It didn't really matter anyway. It finishes 1-0 at Irlam.

There were tears at full-time. Hopper and Ollie openly showed their emotions being clapped from the field. The two players who'd carried the most expectation and burden on their shoulders from the previous season had given everything to prevent the same fate from being repeated. In the end, it hadn't been enough.

'The support from the Millers fans today was superb. Large amount of today's crowd. Keep getting behind the club' tweets the main account. *'Not a good day for New Mills AFC today,'* tweets Nick Dowse of the management team. *'Relegation hurts especially for those who've battled so hard to keep us up but we will bounce back!'*

I trudge out to my gig feeling less than capable of raising laughter. After months of hope and expectation, there was a cruel inevitability that this book's ultimate conclusion should fall on the same day Tottenham lose an FA Cup semi-final to extend their increasingly unwelcome record at Wembley and, by extension, the wait for a first FA Cup final in my living memory.

I think back to the optimism of that opening day win and the trouncing of Barnton the following weekend that genuinely suggested a promotion challenge might be on the cards. I remember the momentum of that early season form dissipating and my own personal disappointment when Garry Brown decided to leave his post. I think back to the rot truly setting in as Paul Williams battled to turn around a disastrous run of form that culminated in the 1-0 home defeat to Darwen that would do so much damage. And then Calum's time, where a complete overhaul of the Millers squad improved the course but not the direction of the Millers' ultimate fate.

As I take to the stage later that evening and go through the motions to entertain the good people of Wetherby, one burning truth sits at the back of my mind. In the moments I'm not thinking about how quiet the table of six geriatrics in the audience are, who appear to have stumbled into the wrong gig at a time when I'm trying not to visualise a man in a high-vis vest falling asleep on the front row of every gig I attend until the ghost of Droylsden is truly banished like some bad gig post-traumatic stress syndrome – whenever those thoughts aren't in my mind, there's one niggling thought that keeps rising to the top. It's not even Tottenham, as even I might expect myself.

One nagging truth feels as disappointing as any moment of the repeated heartbreak Spurs have dished up over the years. New Mills AFC have been relegated.

Defeat at Irlam – and with it, a second consecutive relegation

29

THE FUTURE'S BRIGHT. IT'S AMBER AND BLACK.

The Wednesday after the Saturday before was always going to be a strange one. In more than twenty years watching football, I've never actually experienced 'my' side be relegated. I've seen teams I'm fond of go down, or sides I have a loose affiliation with experience it; but never the visceral pain of the team I invest all of my emotions into plunging down a division.

As I joined the other 88 fans at a subdued Church Lane, it could be argued I had no right to claim these emotions for myself about New Mills. I hadn't paid my dues season after season or rode the rollercoaster of the last few years as the big dipper kept on dipping, out of sight into a seemingly never-ending spiral.

New Mills were officially back in the tenth tier. Back where they had once been before all of the excitement took hold. Ground zero, in relation to their once ambitious plans to climb the non-league pyramid. Tonight would mark the beginning of their two-game farewell tour of the North West Counties Premier Division and I would be responsible for broadcasting it to the world or, at the very least, 6,000 or so people on Twitter.

'If you could, that'd be marvellous,' Sue had said when I offered to run the social media channels for the final two home games on behalf of the outgoing media manager James who'd smashed his phone screen. I couldn't help but wonder if his search for a replacement phone might have proved more fruitful had there been more than just pride riding on this evening's outcome.

Nevertheless, I was keen to take my duties seriously. Having been on the other end of this communication stream keeping an eye on the latest score on more than a few occasions, I was adamant the service provided would be up to the usual standards, starting with an image of the teams greeting each other on the field as the sun set behind the hills at the far end of Church Lane.

'I think I've brought the wrong coat,' I observe early on as Roy and I watch the game from the entrance to the portacabin. His wife, who has kindly stepped in to provide this evening's catering in Sue's absence, busies herself nervously to ensure the buffet is up to scratch. My light jacket, a stylish entry in the Spring collection of the catalogue, had looked a fairly safe bet on leaving the house this morning. Now, in intermittently wintry conditions and single figure temperatures, it's beginning to look less than suitable for a late April evening in the High Peak.

The Millers look solid tonight as a starting XI that's as close to full strength as they've been in recent weeks matches a decent Padiham side. The bench looks somewhat bare however as, with relegation confirmed, just a couple of players not selected for the starting line-up have made the effort to turn up. It looks like the dedication might be slipping for one or two with only pride to play for.

In the 33rd minute, and with little happening on the pitch to warrant it, the youngsters behind the goal break into rapturous applause. I make a mental note of it and ask Jon Warrior for the reason at half-time.

'It was in memory of my scooter,' he replies, of the mobility vehicle that so recently came to blows with a bollard and didn't live to tell the tale. '33 was its registration number.'

Padiham take the lead in the 42nd minute. A powerful header from the visiting team's striker is well saved by Ollie Martin on the stretch. The spin on the ball sees it cruelly roll over the line to leave the Millers undeservedly behind at the break.

'Are you on Twitter or whatever it's called tonight?' asks Derek, a little dismissively.

'I certainly am, Derek,' I reply cheerfully. 'Painting pictures with words. And sometimes painting pictures with pictures as well,' I add. I'm not 100% certain he's convinced.

The half-time treats are no worse off for Roy's wife stepping in. Sandwiches are plentiful and there's even a fine selection of cake, handmade this afternoon by another volunteer. At this rate, Sue might be delegating more often.

The introduction of Callum Collinson for the second half adds pace down the right-hand side as he fills in at right full back and bombs on with determination. The Millers are back on level terms in the 58th minute through a powerful Jake Pollard effort from outside the box before almost taking the lead in the 61st minute through a Sam Marshall set piece. As New Mills continue to pepper the Padiham goal throughout the second half, they leave the door open for Padiham to break a high line camped out in the opposition half and expose Ollie Martin to a one-on-one which is sharply despatched.

#Millers lose possession deep in the opposition half. Quick counter attack and composed finish from Padiham 9. Against run of play but 1-2 is my assessment on Twitter. Told you. Pictures with words.

The Millers are level again in the 82nd minute. This time, Collinson's marauding run and cross is met with perfection by the head of Callum Scott who finds the back of the net. Minutes later, Scott hits the inside of the bar to almost give the Millers a deserved lead. Step forward, Jake Pollard, who lines up another shot from outside the box in the 86th minute and finds the top corner.

The full-time whistle seals a 16th point from 21 available at Church Lane since Calum took over. The Millers' home form alone would usually be enough to seal a comfortable midtable finish over the course of a season. It's hard not to linger over what might have been, were he given a few more games to chase down the pack above the dotted line back in December.

'Sounded like a lot more than that,' is one Twitter reply from a generous Glossop fan in response to the attendance figures. He happened to be playing bowls down the road from North End's bitter rivals and offers the back-handed compliment. It was indeed another great atmosphere, driven by the young Ultras, and not withstanding a particularly poignant moment for Jon's scooter. May it roam in peace.

'*Great result tonight,*' texts Sue later in the evening. '*Thanks for the updates on Twitter. So proud of the lads and pleased for Calum. Damn football is cruel. I feel another gin and bitter lemon coming on* OR *a cocktail. Decisions, decisions…*'

****

I had big plans for the final day of the season. Had the Squires Gate relegation play-off transpired, it would have been the biggest game in the Millers' recent history, right up there with the narrow play-off misses for promotion into the Evo-Stik Prem just a few short years ago.

It would have offered the chance to bring back the bumper crowds of the glory days and regroup the lapsed supporters of old who'd long grown tired of defeat after defeat and wandered off to seek recreation elsewhere on a Saturday afternoon. They weren't the dedicated hardcore, of course, but their voice would have been handy in this hypothetical cup final of a fixture.

Along with the banners on the crossroads near the Co-op or up on the roundabout at the top of town, I'd have tried to get my old friends at Chalkers Snooker Club along. I'd have made a creative video for social media with the players and manager asking for the support of the local community to help lift the Millers out of trouble and begin the rebuild from the foundations up.

Instead, the afternoon of Saturday 29th April 2017 would play out somewhat differently. It would be the solemn duty of tweeting the latest from Church Lane for the final game of 2016/17 with the reverence of a funeral wake. The family had been expecting it for a while. Maybe they were in a better place now. No more suffering.

Few could have been as relieved that the above didn't come to pass than Squires Gate themselves. On wretched form for the best part of five months, their surprise win over Runcorn had not only defied logic – it had also given them the vital cushion they'd needed to extinguish the hopes of a resurgent Millers team and end any talk of a 'do or die' fixture this afternoon.

Despite the team sheet telling a somewhat different story, Gate appear to have arrived at Church Lane more than a man short. Much like the Millers bench a few days earlier, it looked like the manager had been let down by a significant chunk of his matchday squad for the long journey south now that safety was sealed. For once, the ultimate fan's dream that they might actually have a chance of a game if they'd only brought their boots has arisen – although, predictably, there aren't too many of those from the Fylde coast this afternoon either.

'Looking forward to this today,' says Calum as he looks calm and relaxed. He's with James Lobley, the young media manager who will be outgoing after today's match. 'I've told him he's an unlucky charm!' laughs the manager, who confirms his ambition to go out on a high this afternoon. For the sake of pride, the objective is a win to close the gap to within five points of safety before the final league tables are printed.

There's a heartwarming moment to begin proceedings today. A young lad of around four or five dressed in a Real Madrid shirt leads the team out as mascot. His massive smile during an on-pitch photo opportunity with Ollie Martin suggests at least one mini-Miller has had a day to remember.

'They've only got ten men,' is the hushed whisper that begins to grow as the game gets underway. Sure enough, a head count confirms that, alongside an empty subs' bench, Squires Gate are also a man down on the field of play. With New Mills camped out in the opposition half, things are already looking promising. Sam Marshall, often quickly identified as a danger man and double marked accordingly, looks the most dangerous as ever with the shackles off and space to attack.

It takes the Millers the opening quarter of the game to find the breakthrough with Abreu's shot spilled by the 'keeper and Neequaye there to finish from close range. It's a lead they're unable to extend before the break.

'Only 1-0 against ten men?' is the assessment of the fans next to me as the whistle blows. 'Let's hope the other lad isn't just stuck in traffic.'

'I'm off on my holidays after this,' announces Jon Warrior as we devour a cheese cob together for possibly the final time. 'I'm going to visit the island of Balamory,' he says, in reference to the long-running children's TV show. 'I've always wanted to go since I was a kid.' As island retreats go, it's not one you see in the window of Thomas Cook too often.

The second half begins in the worst possible way. A defensive mix-up in the Millers' half is pounced upon for an equaliser less than a minute after the restart. There's barely been enough time to actually double-check if Squires Gate's 11th man has arrived. He hasn't. It's the 100th league goal the Millers have conceded this season; an unwelcome landmark and footnote for the record books.

A quick response from a Samms cross sees several players rise to meet the ball in the box, which cannons off the crossbar and over the line via the back of the Gate 'keeper. Sam Marshall's attempt that bounces out via the underside of the crossbar in the 59th minute suggests the Millers have finally found their rhythm but it's not until the 78th minute that a great finish from Nathan Neequaye makes it 3-1 and seemingly puts the result beyond any doubt. But where there is New Mills, there's always a little doubt…

The final twelve minutes of the season might have been ludicrous had it not been for the nine months that preceded them as New Mills AFC gave up the points from a seemingly unassailable position.

The first goal to peg them back was probably the finest of the afternoon as Gate's number 9 broke free of the back line and finished clinically beyond Ollie Martin. With eight minutes to go, the Millers still just needed to remain organised and ensure they capitalised on their numerical advantage to see the game out, which they almost did; until the final minute, that is.

As Squires Gate's depleted line-up wheeled away to mob the scorer of a scrappy equaliser following a goalmouth scramble, heads are in hands throughout the amber and black shirted players. It's a real low to finish what had been a largely encouraging final third of the season and the players know it. Instead of the warm applause they've begun to get accustomed to upon leaving the Church Lane pitch, it's the ignominy of a lonely walk into the dressing room as most of the fans have already headed for the bar.

'They spent the first ten minutes looking around, counting how many players they've got, telling us on the bench (they're a man down). I know. I can count!' complains a deflated joint assistant Gareth Cross at full time. 'I think they thought it was over when we scored, but no, make it two, three or four like you should have done in that first half. Then you can shoot 40 yards because you've put it to bed.

'You can search around all you like and find the seven points we needed to close that gap,' he continues. 'A really disappointing way to end.'

'Are you getting one in for everyone, lads?' asks one of the familiar faces from the clubhouse as the players emerge and begin offering each other drinks. 'I think we deserve one after watching that,' he continues.

'Squires Gate killed it for us by bringing ten men. I think we thought "we'll play as shit as you, then"' says a downbeat Calum. 'The analogy I've just used with them is that if you're playing FIFA on your Xbox against a 10-year-old, you're gonna do all sorts of crazy shit and stupid tricks because you think you're still gonna beat them. And that was the mentality today. So I've bollocked them.

'They're telling me they were passing the ball about and keeping possession. Why? We weren't pulling them out of shape, we didn't have any purpose. They were just screening us and sitting back so we played into their hands, really. Statistically, it will say I only lost one game at home since I came in. And I'm pleased overall because we've won more points than we inherited and in fewer games as well, so there's been an improvement. But it's a hard one to take.

'They've (Squires Gate) been let down massively,' continues Calum of this afternoon's opponents. 'Six players not turning up. That's your six that aren't coming pre-season because they've got plans to be elsewhere.'

It's a day of unusual and remarkable results as the final day often is. Runcorn Linnets end their season on a high with an 8-0 victory over Darwen in front of an impressive crowd of 553. It seems that, despite Blackburn's relegation to League One, the 'Welcome to Darwen' sign will remain unchanged for at least another season.

Runcorn Town spoil the champions' party with two goals in the final three minutes to beat promoted Atherton Collieries 2-1 at the death. It's unlikely the 329 present would have been too concerned as Michael Clegg's men headed into the eighth tier for the first time in over 100 years. Exciting times ahead for Atherton, perhaps – but take heed this cautionary tale from the High Peak.

Back at Church Lane, Ollie Martin and Ryan Hopper remain two of the star attractions in the clubhouse for the loyal fans. Even on an afternoon like today, when the disappointment of the season has been compounded by the performance on the field, the regular faces who mock-shun each player as they enter the clubhouse soften quickest to Hopper and Martin. Alongside Sam Marshall, it's hard to imagine there won't be numerous suitors for their signatures at a higher level than the tenth tier once the day is out.

As well as likely farewells on the pitch, there are one or two off the field as well.

'See you again,' says Jon Warrior. He's already heading for the turnstiles as he shouts back. There's no time for sentiment, sadly, as he leaves Church Lane for the final time this season.

'I'm off now,' he continues to bellow in my general direction as he ambles away. 'I've got to catch the night bus later to go and visit the island of Balamory. Has anyone seen my care worker?'

And with that, he's gone. His drum has beaten its final note of 2016/17. The PA system is switched off for another season. When it's switched back on, the Millers will be back in the tenth tier. There are no more chants to be sung and no raffle tickets to be called. No teamsheets to announce or ABBA classics to play out. For now, at least, it's good night from him. On a night bus to Balamory.

Fans reflect on another difficult season on the final day

Ollie Martin leads out the team, including the happiest mascot ever seen, against Squires Gate

30

TIME TO SAY GOODBYE

If I look at it objectively, I'm probably a sentimental fool. I often linger at the door of a hotel room one last time before closing it on a brilliant holiday. I hoard football magazines and programmes from meaningless matches that I'll probably never read again. There's a car dealership just outside Buxton that I always smile at when passing because 10-year-old me stopped there for a wee up the wall on the way back from watching Tottenham at Burnden Park in 95/96. I'm sure we've all got a similar story, haven't we? Haven't we, though? Oh. Just me then.

It's of little surprise, to me at least, that I feel somewhat misty eyed about making the trip to Church Lane one last time - for this season, anyway. It's the afternoon of the New Mills Player of the Season Awards and I've the honour of hosting proceedings.

'We had the young lads pencilled in for playing football at 2pm but they've cancelled,' Sue tells me down the phone. 'The itinerary is beginning to look a little bare. Can you do something at the top?'

'No problem,' I reply. 'I could maybe do a bit of a recap on the season and why I've been hanging around all year if you like?' I enquire.

'Sounds perfect. Can you do about 45 minutes?'

After almost dropping the phone, Sue and I agree that a shorter speech before the presentation might be more appropriate. I've played some tough gigs in my time (Droylsden, anyone?) but a tricky mix of an entire football team and their supporters in a clubhouse on the subject of their relegation season for the equivalent of an Edinburgh Fringe solo show? It's probably not going to end well.

It's not my only football engagement of the day. A comedy gig at Chesterfield FC means I'll be heading straight to another clubhouse from New Mills, albeit a slightly grander one. It also offers an unlikely mini-tour of Derbyshire's relegated football teams. You might say I'm something of a lucky charm.

I sneak a bunch of flowers and a bottle of whisky to the front of the room in readiness to present to Sue and Ray, as the sound engineer battles screeching feedback through the speakers. Crossy and the rest of Calum's management team are already on the beers and, for the first time in the few short months I've known them, are all dressed casually rather than in their Millers training gear. The gaffer himself, of course, is suited and booted and somehow looks even smarter than in his regular match day attire.

As I scribble notes and James laughs at my obvious nerves, the clubhouse begins to fill with the familiar faces of the past ten months or so. There's no Garry Brown or Paul Williams here, sadly, and with more than a few players having passed each other in the revolving doors, there are quite a few fresh faces squeezed into skinny jeans and shirts with one eye on the array of awards on offer and the other on a taxi to Manchester later for a rare squad night out.

'We're waiting for Calum,' says Ray as we stand at the front of the room, microphone in hand and tension notching up to unbearable. 'He must be preparing the team talk for next year I think!'

The whole squad are seated down the left side of the room with the fans and families down the right. As the fans sit and wait patiently, the lads are like an over-excited school trip, with Sam Scott a generous ringleader and host as he continues to keep the drinks topped up. I take the opportunity to calm my nerves by having one last recap on the season with the Chairman.

'It was a disappointing start because we had a lot of expectation with Garry taking over,' says Ray thoughtfully. 'Garry had always asked for a pre-season and we weren't doing that badly but he walked away from it which was a shame. And then Paul took over – and he was a great lad – but realistically, I think we were too loyal. We let it go on too long. The first few games we did really well and then we had a spell where we couldn't win a game. It's just as easy to get used to winning as it is to losing and a lot of it is about confidence in this game. There were plenty of matches where we probably should have got something.

'You could see we were getting better when Calum came in but it was just too late. Even though we kept saying we could still do it, hand on heart, it was always a massive ask. It's been a strange season and it's ended up pretty good really. Our home form since Christmas has been outstanding. We've only lost one game at home. If we'd have done that from August, we'd be halfway up the league and job done.'

Alongside the changes of personnel, as Ray looks around a full clubhouse and perhaps reminisces back to the good old days, there've been the frustrations around the new ground and the ability to keep up with other teams while remaining on an even footing. As with any good Chairman, the financial stability of the club is always foremost in his mind.

'We tried to compete with the big clubs in the Evo-Stik and we couldn't do it – and a lot of clubs can't do it,' he reflects. 'Look at the big clubs like Ilkeston (*financially dissolved for a second time in June 2017 after reforming from Ilkeston Town's demise in 2010*) where Shaun Goater is at. Northwich have felt it, it looks like they're getting relegated two divisions. There are murmurings that a few clubs are struggling financially.'

Before we can go any further, Calum arrives with the sharply dressed Rueben Abreu who is greeted with a massive cheer from his teammates. And, with that, we get the nod to begin. My own introduction is something of a blur as I attempt to bat off the odd gentle heckling of the squad before getting my first big laugh - a cheap one in response to Warren Gaskin vigorously wafting his own t-shirt to cool down in the baking clubhouse which looks like something much more suspicious from my vantage point. It's the release of energy, so to speak, that the lads needed to calm down and begin to listen.

On recounting Ollie Martin's early season observation, mid-match, that I should come to every game as I'm now a lucky mascot, his teammates shout off a chorus of Inbetweeners-inspired jibes at his supposed faux pas in making 'friends' with the fans mid-game. The big 'keeper blushes and looks his youthful age for the first time since meeting him 10 months ago. I scald myself for giving such easy ammunition to the dressing room as the more mature half of the gathered fans begin to grow impatient with the juvenile antics of the team.

On presenting flowers and whisky to Ray and Sue, commenting on how they hardly miss a game, another heckle rises from the back that "they didn't make it along the day we were relegated though" in a somewhat confident shout from a squad member who sinks back into his chair on receiving a mock-glare from Sue.

In a nice touch, the New Mills Juniors manager brings his picks for adolescent players of the year out of the crowd before it's finally the turn of Calum Sykes.

'Everyone has given their all since we came in,' he begins as he scans the table of awards. 'I'm gonna start with the Manager's Player of the Year which was a very difficult pick to be honest. Out of the eighteen games that we've had, we've had players who've given their all to keep us up. One of the things we needed was a player to score us goals and win us games. For a man, at 35 years old, to move up to the Premier Division again and score 11 goals in 15 games is nothing short of sensational. Join me in a round of applause for Nathan Neequaye!'

The lads give the 'old man' of the squad the required treatment but there's warm applause for a player who has undoubtedly been a talisman for the turnaround in form.

'Players' Player was really close,' continues Calum, 'and it came down to two players with only one or two votes in it. The player that has gone on to win it has just been phenomenal. I know he was phenomenal before I arrived. He does everything he can and he thoroughly deserves this. A massive round of applause for a player who's been fantastic for me…Ollie Martin!'

'Look at the size of that shirt! He's tensing! Is that shirt XXXS?' shouts Sam Scott as Ollie steps up to collect his award.

'The next award is for the Golden Boot,' continues Calum.

'Fuckin' 'ell, it's not Warren Gaskin!' quips Sam Scott once again.

'Goal of the Season but not top scorer,' corrects Calum as he again brings Neequaye up to add to his haul.

'The next award is for Young Player of the Year…' Calum continues.

'At least it's not Nathan Neequaye,' comes the shout from the gallery as the squad erupt in laughter again. Calum expresses his disappointment that Callum Collinson isn't present to collect his gong having worked so hard to win over the manager despite them apparently working together previously and their relationship being less fruitful. It's a nice touch for a player who has played a bit-part in the second half of the season but has impressed from the bench in important results against Runcorn and Squires Gate.

The honour of crowning the Supporters' Player of the Year falls to me – the responsibility is sprung upon me mid-presentation – and as I shuffle the papers to reveal the joint runners-up as Ollie Martin and Sam Marshall, I don't need to glance again to confirm exactly who the winner is.

I do though, of course, just in case. I'm a consummate professional taking my duty seriously. You don't want to *not* glance at the name and announce something, just in case it descends into the Hallmark Security League's version of Moonlight/La Land at The Oscars. I don't need to, though. That's the point I'm trying to make.

Written in front of me are the words 'Ryan Hopper'. I subconsciously glance in his direction before reading it (told you I'm a pro…) and he looks eager. As the words leave my lips, a big cheer goes up in the clubhouse. Ryan makes his way to the front looking proud – he jokingly wears the title of fan's favourite but I've seen enough to know just how much the support means to him. He smiles like a seven-year-old on his birthday as he poses for photos with Calum and Ray.

As the Chairman takes the microphone, the squad do calm down, showing the requisite respect to the most experienced man in the room who has observed almost every minute at Church Lane this season and many more before it, hiring and firing on the back of what he's witnessed.

'I'd like to thank Calum, Crossy and the rest of the management team,' he begins, as even Sam Scott begins to shush his teammates and Sue backs him up. 'It was always a no-win situation, so difficult. We probably should have given them more time, but we didn't. We have to live with that a little bit. But I'd like to thank everybody involved with trying to turn the club around. It's been a fantastic end to the season, we've had a lot of support off the pitch.

'Les the Groundsman has had a terrible time with his health, he's been in our thoughts. It's been a real struggle getting the pitch ready for matches without him but I'd like to thank everyone who has stepped in. People don't realise what it takes to do this. It's difficult at any level but especially at this level. I'd like to thank you all.

'We shouldn't be where we are, we know we shouldn't. Calum's brought some good players in, you've all done a great job. I just want to thank you all, everyone who is involved in the club, everyone behind the scenes and all the volunteers. The people who come and watch us every week, you should give yourselves a massive round of applause. Thank you so much.'

There's the tiniest flicker of emotion in his voice as the clubhouse erupts but he clears his throat and it's instantly gone.

'MILLERS!' he shouts down the microphone, raising the roof one last time before bringing proceedings to a close. It's hardly the atmosphere you might expect from a team relegated once again but there's no mutiny here. Just a love for the club, whatever division they find themselves in.

I make my way around the clubhouse, saying my goodbyes

across a platter of Sue's buffet spread out over the pool table. There's Joe Rothwell, too young for a celebratory beer, but enjoying being in the surrounds of a proper football club. His parents look on as their talented young son continues to mature into a promising footballer.

There's Derek, crunching the numbers on Ryan Hopper's contribution to the club over the years in readiness for the presentation of a small award to mark more than 150 games surpassed.

'I can find out who he made his debut against if you like?' he offers helpfully.

There's Hopper himself, surrounded by a group of the young Millers fans who've sung his name so often this season. There's something about the way he separates himself from the squad for a while to spend time with them that reaffirms my hunch that he might have kicked his final ball in a Millers shirt, for now at least.

And, of course, there's Mr and Mrs New Mills themselves. I save them, almost, for last.

'You won't be a stranger, will you?' asks Sue as she gives me a hug and a kiss.

'I've got New Mills in the blood now,' I confess.

'Thank you for all you've done,' says Ray as he shakes my hand. 'It's been nice having you here. It's just a shame we couldn't win the League for you.'

There's a tug of my heart strings as I wish them farewell. Nobody could care more for this football club than the two of them. I hope the glory days return and give them another taste of the high life before they consider handing over the reins. That could be a while, yet. Plenty of time.

'Make sure you let us know when the book is ready, won't you?' requests one fan as I shake hands with several of the Church Lane stalwarts. 'Can we have a launch? We normally have our annual relegation party in March – will it be ready by then?' they joke.

'We'll be ok next season,' contests another. 'Pushing for the play-offs.'

'We'll be in bloody trouble if we are relegated again,' comes the reply. 'Chuffin' hell,' he adds as he stares into the middle distance at the mere prospect of it.

'Let's not worry about next season too early, eh? But keeping Calum in place is the start,' replies his pal.

As the beer begins to flow, they exchange mock suggestions on how to improve the existing squad, one of which involves getting them to kick a ball against a wall for the next three months. The gallows humour is never far away at New Mills AFC.

'It doesn't really matter what level we're at. It's not about winning,' one fan continues as I'm about to head for the door and bid farewell to Church Lane. 'We're a small town. We don't need to win everything. We just don't want years of getting beat and being in the national press. All we want is a team we can be proud of so we can come here, have a pint and a laugh and enjoy the football. That's it. Maybe next season will provide that.'

'I think next season will be a good one,' I say reassuringly.

'We've been saying that for about three years!' he laughs. 'This time next year Rodney, we'll be millionaires.'

There's no such thing as 'the worst team in England'. It's an inflammatory headline created to belittle and demean. It was invented to poke fun and kick New Mills AFC while they were down. Even if there was such a title, it couldn't possibly be the Millers. This vibrant community club has undergone a tough few years; nobody can deny that. There may yet be a few more tough ones to come.

But so long as Sue's laughter continues to echo from the turnstiles to the clubhouse. As long as Derek lets out a knowing chuckle at every goal conceded or Roy grumbles at being landed with more than his fair share of the match day duties while, perhaps, secretly enjoying every minute.

While ever there are balls flying into the coach yard to be discovered – and hopefully returned – each Monday morning. While there are still committed lads with hopes and dreams pulling on the amber and black for petrol money and giving everything for the badge, the fans, the dugout and even the intermittently scathing and encouraging voice of their Chairman.

For as long as those things remain and beyond, you won't find the worst team in England in this neck of the woods. You'll only find New Mills Football Club – Pride of The Community. If you're ever passing through, you should call in some time.

NORTH WEST COUNTIES PREMIER DIVISION FINAL LEAGUE TABLE 2016/17

Pos	Team	Pld	W	D	L	GF	GA	GD	Pts
1	Atherton Collieries (C, P)	42	32	4	6	103	39	+64	100
2	Bootle	42	30	2	10	134	57	+77	92
3	Runcorn Town	42	29	5	8	112	52	+60	92
4	Runcorn Linnets	42	27	9	6	105	45	+60	90
5	1874 Northwich	42	25	7	10	81	50	+31	82
6	West Didsbury & Chorlton	42	21	7	14	106	83	+23	70
7	Padiham	42	21	6	15	85	71	+14	69
8	Irlam	42	19	9	14	65	70	−5	66
9	Ashton Athletic	42	17	9	16	83	74	+9	60
10	Hanley Town	42	15	12	15	83	73	+10	57
11	Barnoldswick Town	42	16	8	18	78	75	+3	56
12	AFC Liverpool	42	16	9	17	79	84	−5	54[a]
13	Winsford United	42	15	7	20	76	85	−9	52
14	Abbey Hey	42	15	7	20	63	76	−13	52
15	Maine Road	42	13	10	19	67	72	−5	49
16	Congleton Town	42	12	11	19	75	89	−14	47
17	Barnton	42	13	6	23	50	95	−45	45
18	AFC Darwen	42	10	11	21	50	110	−60	41
19	Squires Gate	42	10	10	22	80	106	−26	40
20	New Mills (R)	42	8	9	25	65	102	−37	33
21	Nelson (R)	42	5	11	26	55	87	−32	25[b]
22	Cammell Laird 1907 (R)	42	3	11	28	40	140	−100	20

FOUR YEARS LATER

It's a Thursday morning just before Easter. It would usually be a time for an exciting end-of-season run-in, with an upturn in the weather offering a chance to work through a heavy backlog of fixtures fallen victim to the long High Peak winter. Instead, the shutters on the newly renovated Millers Bar are down and Church Lane is locked away as another season comes to a premature end.

I've booked a chat in with Mr and Mrs New Mills themselves and we're meeting up on Zoom. Unheard of as a communication channel during my time following the team for a season, it's now all the rage. 'You're on mute!', I begin, as the sight of Sue in her kitchen appears on my screen. How very 2021.

It's been over a year since I last saw Sue and Ray in the flesh; it's been over a year since I saw most people in the flesh, come to think of it. It had been while attending an encouraging display in early 2019 – a change of management offering the requisite bounce away from the dropzone following a typically difficult start to the 2019/20 season - before football across the globe came to a grinding halt.

The North West Counties First Division South would eventually record New Mills as finishing 14th of 20 teams in a tightly packed bottom half, but only for prosperity, with the season declared null and void. With 112 goals flying in across their 28 games, it meant you were likely to see an average of precisely four goals whenever the men in amber and black were in action, more than any other side in the division. Ever the entertainers.

A brief respite in the pandemic led to a return of football at this level but it wouldn't last long. More's the pity for the

Millers, as the stability instilled by management duo Dave Birch and Mike Norton in the latter half of the previous season was added to further, bringing steel and dynamism to see New Mills collect eleven points from their opening six games. Genuine optimism of a promotion push at the fourth time of asking following the relegation recorded within these pages began to build but, in the end, that early promise would remain unfulfilled for at least one more season.

'We've managed to adopt a French Bulldog,' Sue begins as Ray tears himself away from their four-legged new signing to take a seat beside her. 'Ray always said he'd never have a dog and look at us now!'

It's the first time I've ever seen them in the surrounds of their actual home rather than their spiritual one, but it could have been from a very different location. An appearance on Channel 4's *A Place in the Sun* recorded before COVID struck only enhanced their local celebrity status.

'It were good, that!' says Ray, lighting up at the mention of his all-expenses paid trip to their favourite away day of the Canary Isles. 'He'll go on for hours now,' Sue chuckles as Ray recounts the week of filming, a few inside secrets and the friendship they struck up with the owners of Union Deportiva Lanzarote, as arranged by production staff.

Sue heads off to bring back a replica shirt to show me as Ray explains how Brexit complications spooked them from committing to a holiday home, meaning the lure of watching football in slightly warmer climes is off the cards indefinitely, even if it has led to an exponential rise in being approached on the weekly food shop from locals who saw them on the telly.

Is a pre-season tour to the Spanish islands in the budget when leisure flights return, though? 'If you had the money, that's what you'd do!' says Ray. 'I'm not sure they'd get much football done.'

'We'd just put them in Glossop tracksuits in case they got in trouble,' adds Sue. 'It'd most likely be the managers.'

About these managers. With a fine reputation at this level,

having made their names as club legends at FC United of Manchester, it's another ambitious appointment from the Millers. Calum's spell in charge came to an end during the season following relegation and Crossy stepped up to the plate, leading a variety of coaching teams before the current incumbents took up the hotseat.

Since then, an influx of young players have come through the doors and made a difference, both in terms of results and on the gate, as attendances climbed regularly into three figures once again.

'We've got a really good team spirit and they've just pulled together,' says Sue as Ray nods in agreement. 'They made us a promise that they'll gain us promotion,' he adds, a firm soft spot for his very own Cloughie and Taylor becoming more apparent as he speaks. 'They're learning and so are the players, and it's a great place to learn. Take that step back, enjoy your football, then build back up.

'They're a good side - best team we've had in a while. The progression we've made under the two in charge, they've brought in good young lads and they just want to play football. They're allowed to train in small groups from the end of this month so that will help.'

And when football does eventually get underway, is promotion still the aim?

'Oh yeah, definitely,' says Ray. 'They wouldn't be here otherwise if they didn't have the same ambition. Their non-league playing CV is next to none, they've been at FC United and Curzon Ashton when they were in the third round of the FA Cup. They've not long stopped playing so they have that respect and those connections with players they've played with.

'We know we've got a side that would be in the push for promotion but that's in the lap of the Gods now, as will they stay loyal to us?'

'I think they will,' Sue interjects, as Ray's question hangs in the air. 'You've still got players who'll go for an extra fiver or an extra tenner at this level, but I think a lot of these lads are different. We've got to make it a community club, we've got great connections with the Juniors and there's a U21s team now to try and get some local lads in, and they're doing really well too.'

Off the field, things have been going remarkably well considering there has been so little income on the football side for over 12 months now. With belts tightened and attendances lowered since the glory days, New Mills have always had to diversify what little income is available to them. For starters, they've changed from AFC to FC and became a limited company by guarantor, to help ensure their long-term security.

'It's always been about protecting the club,' Ray assures me. And it's a similar story regarding plans to develop the existing ground after ambitions to relocate were quashed. With a local consortium keen to be involved and Football Foundation funding secured, COVID has put much of that on ice for the time being.

Ray continues: 'During the first lockdown, we got a grant to get a solicitor in and change the name over, then we spent money getting the clubhouse ready. We knew we'd got a good outdoor space and so we did it up and relaunched it as Miller's Bar. We launched Foodie Fridays, and last summer they were doing 70 covers a week, on which we take a donation and the bar. So that's been great. We've had street food: West Indian, Portuguese – they've been taking orders just for takeaway.'

The numbers are as impressive as the photographic evidence that popped up on my social media feeds last summer, as the dated clubhouse that had looked so modern when Brian McClair dropped in to cut the ribbon almost a quarter of a century earlier was now once more a sought-after hospitality venue on edges of Greater Manchester.

'People are wanting to do weddings now,' he says, with a touch of incredulity evident in his own voice at the prospect. 'So when we reopen, I think we'll get an influx. And now we're not embarrassed to have people in as it's so nice! There's a lot of businesses who won't survive all of this and I'm sure there will be a lot of football clubs who will suffer too; but now we've opened the clubhouse, it's vital to do more stuff like that,' he adds, referring to the more stringent measures in place at the time of our chat that has enforced their closure. 'We're desperate to do that, really.'

The feeling of abandonment by football's governing bodies is another regular topic. With schools returning through the use of lateral testing for the virus, it's not an option that's been put forward for football at this level. In the much-vaunted roadmap out of lockdown, they'll soon be able to open as a bar serving takeaways and drinks but remain unable to host spectators spread out in the Derbyshire breeze watching actual football.

'How does that work?' asks Sue. 'When the rules came in, they said we could have 350 in. We said we'll take them, when are they coming?'

Despite the lack of upcoming fixtures in their diaries, they're still as busy as ever with Sue even volunteering at her local school to help with COVID-testing.

'It's no different for me, I spend a lot of time pottering at the club and messing about,' says Ray.

'I'm ruining his retirement because I've been furloughed since December,' she smiles. 'He's put lights and seats in there, CCTV. In a sense, it's been good because he's been able to do it in his own time. There's still tonnes of stuff to do around the club but nobody to do it. I can potter at home all day though, do a bit of gardening. I'll be honest with you, I haven't missed the football! He has!'

'Well, let's be honest, there's only so much Premier League football you can stomach, isn't there?' Ray adds dryly. 'I do miss the banter on a Saturday, especially with these two muppets who are managers.'

'They've got Ray's sense of humour,' adds Sue, with a little trepidation.

Fans aside, there aren't many familiar faces to be found when the live action does return. Photographer James has moved on, the playing contingent continues to churn and change with each new managerial team and even Jon Warrior has found new pastures after a falling out.

'Ollie Martin still comes to watch us,' says Ray of the former fans' favourite. 'He got badly injured but he's been at FC United, Mossley, all at a higher level. I feel a bit sorry for him because he's struggled with this injury and I think he's between clubs. He still keeps in touch. And Tunde's done brilliant,' he continues, of Owolabi, the quiet and shy attacker with blistering pace.

Despite being overlooked by former manager Calum, he went on to score 29 goals in 35 games for FC United before securing a professional contract with Hamilton Academical in the Scottish Premiership. At the time of writing, he'd crossed the Irish Sea to join Finn Harps. 'Best of luck to him,' says Ray. 'We're still very proud whenever they go on to a higher level.'

As time has passed, the consistency with which the chairman speaks of Garry Brown hasn't faltered either. 'We get in touch with Garry a couple of times a year. He was a great lad for that level, he did us a great job and we're eternally grateful for the work he did. I don't believe there's another manager who could have finished the season. Any criticism, I take on the chin and I back Garry to the hilt.'

'Total respect,' adds Sue. 'I spoke to Calum a couple of times during COVID as well. One or two of the younger players did the same, asking if me and Ray were alright. I didn't think we were that old!' she laughs.

Half a decade on, there's a little more distance now for reflection on what must have been the most tumultuous period of this proud club's history in that unimaginably difficult 2015/16 campaign.

'I look back on it and football was changing,' Ray begins. 'It was going more money-orientated at that lower level. Teams were coming in with budgets and the split now is massive. Football is tougher now because there are a lot more decent players about at this level. The haves and have-nots is massive. But we've improved off the field; we've definitely improved on the field as we couldn't have got much worse, let's be fair. It's going to be a lot more difficult to get promotion in the future.

'No matter what anyone says, the best teams have the money. It doesn't always work, but 99.9% of the time it does. If they can afford it, good luck to them! I don't have any problem with it, we'd be doing it if we had the money. I don't think there'll be that many Salfords or Fyldes in the next few years.'

Sue nods in agreement. 'There are that many clubs at higher levels that are struggling, if anybody has got any money then it's going to be easier to take a club there than bother with a team at our level.'

And finally, with the past half a decade reflected upon, what might the five years to come bring on and off the field to this corner of Derbyshire? Sue takes the reins on that one.

'I'd like a 3G pitch at Church Lane, I'd like the Miller's Bar to be a big success, I'd like to be promoted twice back into the EvoStik and for me and Ray to be sitting back and enjoying it, having nothing to do with football,' she smiles, drifting off slightly at the thought. 'But will that ever happen? No.'

And with that, her trademark laughter momentarily startles the snoozing dog on her lap. She might do well not to predict the future with such confidence.

Half a decade ago, New Mills couldn't buy a win. Now there's talk of a promotion push, a waiting list for weddings and West Indian cuisine on a Friday night in what must be one of the very best beer gardens in the north of England, just around the time al fresco dining in sub-zero temperatures is all the rage.

It's never boring at Church Lane. It's unlikely to be for some time to come. When a football is eventually kicked again and the freedoms we once took for granted return in some form or another, you really *should* drop-in and experience it for yourself.

Make sure you say hello to Sue and Ray while you're there: Mr and Mrs New Mills FC.

ACKNOWLEDGEMENTS

A huge thank you to everyone at New Mills FC for allowing me such access to your wonderful football club. From the moment I walked through the gates, I was made to feel part of the family, and still do to this day.

Special thanks to Sue and Ray for overriding their initial hesitancy to let a comedian tag along for the ride after such a tumultuous year. Also huge thanks to Garry, Paul and Calum for giving their time so generously and talking to me when, at times, there were probably few things they'd have rather not done.

To the players, especially Ollie and Hopper, who mostly wore the shirt with pride and dedication even through the most difficult of times to provide some truly special memories, and to the small band of fans and volunteers who were ever-present whatever the weather to enjoy them.

Thanks to James Lobley for guiding me through and so generously allowing me to use his fantastic photos – he managed to avoid being in any by always being behind the camera - and to Jared Shooter for another cracking cover design.

Thanks to the Hanley Town FC squad* for not suing after I almost killed them with a gate and to every volunteer on the various away days who kindly poured me a complimentary hot drink in a foam cup and offered a slightly stale egg sandwich, sometimes in the dark, despite not knowing who I was.

Thanks to you for reading this far and supporting an independent author. Do leave a review and seek out more of my work if you've enjoyed it or just quietly take it down to your local charity shop if you didn't.

*except for the player who had to squeeze by so desperately. He can f**k off.

ABOUT THE AUTHOR

Carl Jones is a comedian and writer from Derbyshire. He lives with his wife, two children and a dog called Indiana.

When he's not on a stage or at a football match, he can usually be found enjoying a curry, on a long, muddy walk in the Peak District or putting off writing by enjoying just one more episode of a boxset.

You can see when he's next gigging near you via a tardily updated gigs list at carljonescomedy.co.uk or by finding him on social media.

Enjoyed this book? Share the love by leaving a review on Amazon or let Carl know on social media. Didn't enjoy it? Sssshhhhh….

OTHER BOOKS BY THIS AUTHOR

BE IN THAT NUMBER

Pochettino's final season through the voices of
Tottenham Hotspur Supporters' Clubs around the world

By Carl Jones

Be In That Number is the account of Tottenham Hotspur's 2018/19 season, told through the eyes and voices of their supporters' clubs around the world, as a growing global fanbase share their own devotion to a football club hundreds or even thousands of miles away.

2018/19 was supposed to mark Tottenham's long-awaited return home to N17 and the dawn of a bright new era under one of football's most coveted managers. What followed was an extended stay at Wembley, a wholly unexpected run to the Champions League Final and - eventually - the departure of the man many expected to remain at the helm for years to come.

Derbyshire-born comedian and author Carl Jones recounts his own experience as a matchgoing Tottenham fan of 25 years as he meets the chairman of LA Spurs who would catch up on Spurs results by waiting for a newspaper to hit the stands in the early hours of the morning, the Lebanese student who smashes plates to deal with his emotions while watching matches and the Icelandic fan who plans to walk down the aisle to When The Spurs Go Marching In.

He speaks to a Malaysian fan who met his best friend in a public bathroom after spotting a Tottenham pin badge on his lapel, the Chairman of OzSpurs who moved 'down under' for love and finally felt at home when meeting Tottenham fans in his adopted nation and the founder of Punjabi Spurs who formed his supporters' club to bring unity through football – despite being brought up in a houseful of Manchester United fans!

On the pitch, Tottenham thrill and disappoint in equal measure as they eventually return home, before an incredible night at the Etihad, an unforgettable comeback in Amsterdam and a bittersweet night in Madrid cap off an unforgettable season and the beginning of the end for Pochettino.

Critical praise for Be In That Number

"Carl Jones reveals the huge extended Spurs family around the world and shows us what's it like to support the famous Lilywhites. Informative, hilarious and moving it's a rip-roaring page turner for all Spurs fans." - **Mike Leigh, The Spurs Show**

Printed in Great Britain
by Amazon